PENGUIN BOOKS

# SHOOT TO KILL

'This book is not for the delicate, though the delicate should read it. Despite its military obscenities, the subject is a sensitive, rather lost young man who forced himself to brutal extremes, partly as a romantic search for self, partly because of an urge to belong. His book reads like an expurgation ... Asher's predicament is more common than many will think and he conveys it uncommonly well' – Alan Judd in the *Independent on Sunday*

'Not the usual boastful squaddie, but a man who writes with some feeling and understanding of the motives of a system which is designed to prepare a human being to kill in cold blood' – Allan Tudor in the *Herald Express*

'A marvellously evocative account of life on those dangerous streets, and of the fear, danger and hatreds that run through them like sewage' – Christopher Dobson in the *Evening Standard*

'A voyage into the murky shadows of human nature. Here are stories of barrack-room brutality, ignorance, prejudice and hatred. There are nerve-shattering patrols under the eyes of snipers and bar-room brawls in Aldershot. On the other hand, these violent young men are also extremely good at the job we pay them to do. Asher shatters a few illusions about the real nature of their trade' – Richard Williamson in the *Sunday Mercury*

Michael Asher has been called 'one of the two greatest living British desert explorers – the other being Wilfred Thesiger'. He is one of the few to travel consistently on foot and by traditional transport in preference to motor vehicles.

His early life was dominated by a quest for adventure which led him, at the age of eighteen, into the Parachute Regiment, and later into an SAS squadron. Later still, he served in the elite Special Patrol Group of the RUC.

His books include *In Search of the Forty Days Road* (1984), *A Desert Dies* (1986) and *Impossible Journey* (1988), an account of a 4500-mile trek on foot and by camel made with his wife, photographer Mariantonietta Peru. This journey, the first west–east crossing of the Sahara by such means, was lauded by the Royal Geographical Society as 'the most remarkable of recent explorations'.

# SHOOT TO KILL

## A Soldier's Journey through Violence

## MICHAEL ASHER

PENGUIN BOOKS

PENGUIN BOOKS

Published by the Penguin Group
Penguin Books Ltd, 27 Wrights Lane, London W8 5TZ, England
Viking Penguin, a division of Penguin Books USA Inc.
375 Hudson Street, New York, New York 10014, USA
Penguin Books Australia Ltd, Ringwood, Victoria, Australia
Penguin Books Canada Ltd, 2801 John Street, Markham, Ontario, Canada L3R 1B4
Penguin Books (NZ) Ltd, 182–190 Wairau Road, Auckland 10, New Zealand

Penguin Books Ltd, Registered Offices: Harmondsworth, Middlesex, England

First published by Viking 1990
Published in Penguin Books 1991
1 3 5 7 9 10 8 6 4 2

The moral right of the author has been asserted

Printed in England by Clays Ltd, St Ives plc

*Utrinque Paratus* ('Ready For Anything')

Motto of the Parachute Regiment


*Who Dares Wins*

Motto of the Special Air Service Regiment


*For Peace We Serve*

Motto of the Special Patrol Group, RUC

'Never snatch the trigger. Always squeeze it gently, as if you're stroking a cat. Hold your breath, squeeze the trigger, shoot to kill'

*Gurkha weapons instructor*

# *Contents*

## Author's Note

The characters portrayed in this book are real and the events described all took place, but fictional names and descriptive detail have been used in places where I felt this would protect privacy.

MA

# PART ONE

*The Paras*

# 1

## The Maroon Machine

On my first morning in the Parachute Regiment Depot at Aldershot, I met a sour-faced corporal. 'Excuse me, mate,' I said, 'but where's the Personnel Selection Office?'

The corporal was a barn-door of a man, an inch shorter than me. He sniffed suspiciously. 'You a recruit?' he inquired.

'Yes,' I said.

'Then I'm not your fucking mate! See these tapes?' He pointed to the two snow-white chevrons stitched on his heavy-duty pullover. 'I'm a corporal, and from now on you call me *corporal*! Got it? You'd better get it quick, or you'll be out on your arse before your feet touch the ground!' That was my welcome to the Parachute Regiment.

I followed his directions in something of a daze. Was he supposed to talk to me like that? I wasn't really in the army yet. I came from a school where colonels and generals were ten-a-penny in the Old Boys' Club. A corporal seemed very small fry.

I introduced myself to the clerk at the reception-desk. He was a corporal too. He was taciturn and morose with a moustache like a barbed-wire entanglement and sad brown eyes. 'Name and number?' he snapped.

I told him my name. 'I haven't got a number,' I said.

'Everybody's got a number!' he replied. 'Oh yes, here we are, Asher, private fourth class, 24246810, Asher, M. J. That number is yours till you die. Don't ever forget it!' Then, when I had put my suitcase down, he handed me a sweeping-brush and gave me my first order. 'Get sweeping!' he said.

The Personnel Selection Officer was a crusty captain who had risen through the ranks. 'Why did you volunteer for the Parachute Regiment?' he asked me.

'Well, sir,' I said, 'I wanted to jump out of the sky.'

'Perhaps you should have tried growing a pair of wings, then!' he suggested drily. He studied the file on his desk. 'I see you enlisted under an "S-type" engagement, as a potential officer,' he commented.

'Yes, sir. I failed the Regular Commissions Board, so I joined the ranks.'

'Well, at least you haven't given up. That's one thing in your favour. But it's not easy being an officer in this regiment. This regiment is the best there is. You've got to be the best. We'll be watching you, private. Now go and see the clerk. He'll assign you a billet.'

The clerk with the moustache told me to wait outside the store. A floppy latex mattress came sailing out and almost knocked me over. 'Get on the ball!' the clerk said, grinning. Then he fixed me with a piercing stare. 'Do you piss the bed?' he demanded.

'No!' I answered, surprised and indignant.

'If you stain the mattress, you pay for it!' he said. 'Now get that bugger up to your billet, last room on the left.'

The room was on the second floor of a four-storey block of granite and glass: 'the most up-to-date barracks in the country', the recruitment literature had claimed. Modern it was, but its newness only emphasized the atmosphere of bleak austerity. Each room held four bunks of a scarred battleship grey. With each bunk came a wooden bedside locker and a large equipment locker. As I squeezed my mattress in through the door, the lockers creaked open ominously. Their innards were turbid with fluff and sprinkled liberally with fag-ends and empty contraceptive packets. A formica-topped table, much chipped and besmeared with boot-polish, had been pushed into a corner. Four stand-up chairs were piled against a plate-glass window. I dropped my mattress on the bare springs of a bed near the window. Then I went back to collect my bedding.

Staggering in for a second time under a pile of sheets and blankets, I found someone else in the room. He was a young man of my own age, and he was fuming as he tried to insert his wobbly mattress into its canvas cover. 'Bleedin' thing!' he cursed in a northern accent. 'Give us a hand, will tha!' I clutched the mattress in a vice-like grip, while he drew the tight-fitting cover over it, grunting and sweating. 'You'd think they'd make 'em right size!' he said when it was done. Then he grinned at me and stuck out a calloused hand. 'Walker,' he said. 'Dave Walker. How's tha do?'

He offered me a Park Drive cigarette, and we stood smoking by the window. Directly below us a turtle of men in camouflaged smocks and helmets were tramping around the square. There were incomprehensible commands like cries of pain. The men moved in perfect unison, and the crash of their boots on the asphalt came up to us like thunder. 'That'll be us soon!' Walker said. I could hear the awe in his voice. We looked down on those strange animals in wondering silence. We were eighteen years old. That window was the shore of the rest of our lives.

'I wonder who else we'll get in this room,' Walker said. 'I hope it's not a coupla wankers as will get us back-squadded!'

'What's back-squadded?'

'Weren't tha at the Recruit Selection Centre? Don't tha know how they do it?'

'I came here straight from the Army Careers Office.'

'They give us twelve weeks basic training. At the end of that they assess thee. If tha's a dud, tha gets back-squadded to another platoon. That means tha's to do it all over again. Most of them as is back-squadded leave.'

A tingle of fear ran down my spine. What if I failed? I'd failed the Regular Commissions Board, and now I could never go home to my family and say I couldn't even make it as a ranker. They had advised me strongly against joining the ranks. No, I told myself, I *had* to pass now I was here.

Our faces dropped when we met our third room-mate. He was

a tall bumbling man called Chapman who ambled about the room with an expression of complete imbecility. He kept on insisting that he came from somewhere called the 'Dingle'. I wondered if he was quite right in the head. He had with him a moth-eaten cardboard suitcase held together by a leather belt. When he opened it, Walker and I saw a gigantic carving-knife lying on top of his clothes. Walker raised his eyes to heaven as if to say, 'We've got a right one here!'

Little Jock McGowan was the next to arrive. He had an apple-fresh face with an impudent look, and his hair had been honed to a fine stubble. His bomber jacket and baseball shoes reminded me of the local yobs I used to see hanging round Lambretta scooters in my home town. But McGowan had a genial manner. 'Here!' he said at once, when he saw me struggling with my mattress cover. 'Lemme show ye how it's done! I'm an old navy man. Four years in the merch, that's me!' He fitted the mattress with perfect alignment.

Our room was divided from the one next door by a thin partition. The two rooms were connected with the corridor by a common entrance. Soon that room filled up with recruits. There was a lanky, emaciated youth from Oldham named Clark. He had a long, lascivious face and looked like the worst kind of street-corner layabout. He announced that he would be known as the 'Oldham Stud'. There was a blond, rugby-playing Londoner called Smart. His father kept a tailor's shop in Soho, he said. There was a seventeen-year-old Welshman, inevitably called Williams, who was bandy-legged and came from Merthyr Tydfil. Finally, there was a solemn farm-boy from Gloucestershire called Smith. His black hair was cut Elvis Presley style with a long fringe which he kept flicking out of his eyes. He wore a crinkled leather jacket with the words SATAN'S SLAVES stencilled on the back.

I had just brushed out my locker and arranged my shirts and books on its shelves, when a voice screamed, 'STAND BY YOUR BEDS!' I turned to see the same squat corporal who had shouted at me on the way to the PSO. He advanced into the room menacingly. 'STAND STILL!' he yelled. We swayed by

our beds with uncertain rigidity. He stood there for a long
moment, hands on hips, regarding us with obvious contempt.
He wore polished boots, puttees and immaculately pressed
denims. His olive-green pullover was neatly punctuated by a
maroon stable-belt. An inch and a half of starched khaki collar
showed at his neck. His maroon-red beret with its silver parachute badge was tilted very slightly forward to accentuate the
contemptuous look. His face was broad and dark and full of
shadows. This was what a paratrooper looked like, I thought to
myself. I wondered if any of us here would ever look like that.

He sauntered forward, inspecting our faces and glancing at
our lockers. He stopped in front of me, so near that I could see
the red veins in his eyes. A nasty smile wavered on his lips.
'Well,' he said. 'If it isn't my *mate*! What's your name, *mate*?'

'Asher,' I said.

'Asher WHAT?'

'Er, just Asher.'

'ASHER, CORPORAL, you fucking TUBE!' His eyes seemed
to burn red with anger. He glanced at my locker again. 'Who
told you to put all this gunge in your locker?'

'No one, corporal, I just assumed –'

'DON'T FUCKING ASSUME ANYTHING! This locker is for
military equipment only! I'll teach you to put gash in it without
orders!' With a furious motion he swept my pathetic personal
belongings out of the locker. They included a framed photograph
of my fifteen-year-old girlfriend. She had given it to me the
previous evening as a parting gesture. It crashed to the floor,
and the glass shattered. 'Oh *dear*!' he said with heavy irony.
'What a *pity*!' He picked up the broken photo and examined it
nosily. 'All my love, darling Mick!' he read. 'How touching! You
might break her heart, Asher, but you won't break mine!
That'll be twenty press-ups for filling your locker without orders.
Come on, get pressing!'

I fell on to my arms and began heaving myself upwards. The
corporal rested a heavy boot on my back. 'Two-three-four-five!'
he counted. The other recruits stood to attention, petrified
'Eight-nine-ten-eleven!' My arms were already weakening.

There was a burning sensation in my shoulders. 'Thirteen-fourteen-fifteen.' My arms were trembling now. I tried not to groan in pain. 'Sixteen-seventeen . . . you're going, Asher!' the corporal jeered. Then I collapsed in a heap. 'Pathetic!' he said. 'My *darling* Mick! You should have sent her instead! She'd have made a better Para than you!'

I picked myself up, feeling shaky. He took a step closer, so that I could feel foul breath against my cheek. 'You think you're clever, don't you, Asher?' he said. 'I've seen 'em all. I can tell by looking: you think you're a clever sod. Well, let me tell you, there's only one clever sod in this room, and that's me!' He moved back to the door. 'I'm Corporal Jekyll, your section commander,' he said. 'You are very lucky you've got me. I am the best instructor in the Depot. I am not your mate. I am your god. Do as I say and we'll get on dandy. Do so much as a fart out of place and I shall *personally* shit on you from a great height!'

Thus spake Zarathustra, I thought.

The army was chock-full of colonels, colonels-commandant, colonels-in-chief, major-generals, lieutenant-generals, full generals, field marshals and Supreme Allied Commanders Europe. But so low was I that a corporal was as far above me as God.

The rest of the day was taken up with assemblies and disassemblies. Each time the order 'GET FELL IN!' rang along the corridor, we would line up outside. There were dozens of rooms along the corridor, and the line of recruits soon extended its full length. There were young men of all shapes and sizes, and from every corner of Great Britain and Northern Ireland. 'FROM THE RIGHT, NUMBER OFF!' the order would come. The first man would shout 'ONE!', the next man 'TWO!', and so on down the line, until the number reached the hundreds. It passed down the chain with such swiftness that it was difficult not to anticipate it and get your number wrong. If that happened, the nearest NCO would 'shit on you from a great height', and you'd do press-ups. Everyone would wait for you to finish, and then the entire process would begin again. We usually numbered off five or six times until we got it right. One or other of the corporals assigned to our platoon would bellow out some trivial orders and then dismiss us.

Jekyll had us strip down our bunks, mattress covers and all, and remake them 'the army way'. He said the mattress covers had to fit 'like French letters'. 'You will notice,' he told us, 'that sheets and blankets have three stripes down the centre. This does *not* mean that they have the rank of sergeant . . .' He broke off for polite giggles. 'The stripes will be *exactly* in the centre of the bed, and not a fraction out!'

The sheets had to be turned down exactly twelve inches over the blankets. 'How can you be sure it's twelve inches, corporal?' Chapman asked.

'Use your fucking dick to measure it, Chapman!' Jekyll answered. The blankets had to be smoothed out, tucked in and folded at the ends with hatchet-sharp 'hospital corners'. 'I want to see them like that every time I inspect them,' Jekyll said. 'Any bunk not up to scratch will end up on the floor!' And to demonstrate how easily this could be arranged, he flicked my bed over with a deft twist of the hand. The iron frame separated easily into its three component parts, as it crashed to the floor in a mass of sheet and blanket. 'Practice makes perfect!' he said. 'And it better *be* perfect when I get back. I want to see this room dug out and the floor gleaming like a mirror!'

Five times Jekyll inspected the room that day and five times he found it wanting. Five times our bunks crashed over on to the floor or the blankets parachuted out of the window. Sweeping, bed-making and dusting ('*Underneath* the lockers, not just on top!') were interrupted by more assemblies, which seemed increasingly meaningless as fatigue crept up on us. The work was broken by trips over to the mess for meals. We queued up to collect egg and chips from bulky army cooks who wore silver chevrons on their white jackets. Even the cooks were corporals, it seemed. Huddled five to a table, we ate quickly. We kept our eyes downcast, lest we drew the attention of the recruits from senior squads who swanned about the mess like magical creatures. By ten o'clock that night I was dropping with exhaustion.

As the bugler sounded 'lights out', I clambered into my bunk. I slipped gratefully between the abrasively starched sheets.

'I hope tha doesn't snore!' chuckled Walker with a hint of intimacy both warm and repellent at once.

'What do you make of this chap Jekyll?' I asked him.

'A reet bloody bastard!' he replied.

I closed my eyes and pictured my parents' house, only a few hours' journey away in rural Lincolnshire. It seemed impossible that I had left it only that morning. I had been away before, on camps and holidays, but this was different. There was something final in today's journey, some final cutting of the umbilicus. My childhood and youth were gone for ever. I was in the army, sharing a room with three faintly menacing characters from places I had scarcely heard of. I was gripped by the same mixture of fear and excitement which had come and gone all day. I had become the hero of one of the adventure books I read so avidly. I was afraid, yet I had no wish to return to my dull town and its dull grammar school. I had finally broken out of the prison of my humdrum childhood. For better or for worse, I had taken my destiny in my own hands. What the army represented most to me at that moment was escape.

Walking home from school every day, I used to pass a Territorial Army drill-hall. For several years a glossy poster was displayed outside. It showed a close-up of a handsome soldier in combat uniform. He had gleaming white teeth, and a black beret was perked rakishly on his head. Behind him a troop of armoured personnel carriers was poised for action. Several more soldiers emerged from their battle-hatches, wearing peaked combat-caps and toting sub-machine-guns. Above the picture in large red letters was written JOIN THE PROFESSIONALS and along the bottom IT'S A MAN'S LIFE IN THE MODERN ARMY.

As a teenager, the men on those posters seemed to represent everything I wanted to be. The romantic side of me had always been attracted to the idea of soldiers and armies since I had first heard my grandfather's stories of Kitchener's army and the Dardanelles.

'It was just after we advanced from the beach-head,' he would begin, 'when I got it in the leg. We got the order to fix bayonets. The Turks were dug in across the fields with machine-guns. Some fool gave us the order to charge. You were so carried away with the noise and the screaming that you hardly knew what was happening. Next thing I knew I went down like a skittle. I'd copped two rounds in the leg. There was blood and bodies all over the shop down there. I saw one bloke, I remember clear as daylight, trying to get up and shouting, "Mum, help me!" with half his head shot away. Then they were all retreating. What a cock-up it was! I tried to crawl back towards the beach. "Leave your rifle, mate!" somebody shouted. "Never!" I said. "They've set the goss on fire!" they said. "You'll get roasted!" You could smell the smoke on the wind. I kept on crawling till I fell into a shell-hole. Then I went out like a light. When I came round, I had another wound in the back. The Turks must have advanced and stuck a bayonet in me to finish me off. No one thought much of the Turks, you see. That was the big mistake. They were tough as old leather. Anyway, they didn't finish Tommy Kew. The stretcher-men arrived and carried me off to the beach. They winched me aboard the hospital-ship. Then the doctors said I had gas gangrene, and the leg would have to come off. I was only eighteen years old. I've been a cripple ever since.'

My grandfather remained disabled all his life, but to me he was a hero. I was enthralled by his stories. I can recall the exact words he used, the smell of his tobacco lingering in the room, which in itself seemed to evoke the reek of fear and cordite and burning gorse. I remember the polished brass cartridge-cases he kept on his mantelpiece. I imagined they were the very bullets cut out of his leg in that hospital-ship off the Golden Horn. It seems curious to me now that it was not the fact of his being crippled that struck me so forcibly. It was not the fact that the war had left him scarcely employable, a forgotten, half-helpless peg-leg of a man whose life was constant pain. I hardly thought about the incompetent surgeons who had sawed off his leg. I never wondered why he hadn't won a medal for his bravery, when all the decorations had gone to those upper-class idiots who had ordered the attack. Or gone to those aristocratic generals whose imperial arrogance had dismissed the Turkish army as ineffective, when it was plain that the Turks were amongst the finest soldiers in the world. No, it was the glory, the thrill, the romance of it all that remained with me long after my grandfather was gone.

But then, most boys think like that. If they didn't, they would be less willing to offer themselves for the testing-ground of war, year after year, generation after generation. The same must have been true of my father. Tom Kew's tales did nothing to prevent him from volunteering for the army when the war broke out again in 1939. As a trainee-surveyor, it was natural that he should be posted to the Royal Engineers. It was a Territorial unit, which shows that he was a volunteer, not a conscript. He could have gained a commission in the infantry, but he remained a sergeant in the Sappers. He fought his way through the North African campaign and the invasion of Italy, and returned with a 'Mention in Dispatches'. That citation hung on our lavatory wall through my childhood. My eyes would linger over it proudly as I sat there, awfully impressed by 'His Majesty's High Appreciation'. Dad wore his old battle-dress blouse for gardening until it finally disintegrated.

My father's war, like my grandfather's, was a patriotic duty which involved the entire nation. Things had changed since then. In the early sixties the army had become a professional organization again. Without an empire to hold up, it had become slimmer and more streamlined. The excess baggage of the upper-class twits had been shorn off. In a world which seemed to be getting smaller, more uniform and drearier every day, the army seemed the last bastion of adventure. At sixteen I was attracted to the idea of becoming a journalist. Opportunities were few and at the time it seemed to offer no more than a lifetime of drudgery on the local paper. And drudgery was what I wanted most to avoid. I had only one life to live, and I had no intention, even then, of living it in an office or a factory. I was a romantic. The army seemed to be my avenue of escape.

My parents were adamant that I should join the army as an officer. Otherwise it would be a waste of my education, my father said. At school, a class-mate called Geoffrey Deacon applied for a commission and passed. He described his experiences at the Regular Commissions Board in detail, and I listened avidly. He was already the man in the JOIN THE PROFESSIONALS poster. He was the same tall, athletic type, with the same gleaming white teeth. He was a school prefect, a rugby player and the winner of the coveted victor ludorum shield for athletics. He was also senior cadet in the school corps, while I was a lowly sergeant. Deacon persuaded me to take the RCB. 'If you fail, you'll know it's not for you!' he told me.

My reputation at school was saved only by my relatively enthusiastic performance in the corps and by my success as captain of the school fencing-team. Otherwise I was an incorrigible hooligan who dodged lessons, ignored prefects and behaved as though the school were Colditz and I the 'escape king'. I had my own escape routes and emergency procedures. Once, I was caught climbing out of a first-floor library window during a study period by a prefect whom I particularly disliked. I made my feelings clear with a crisp expletive idiom, of which the last part was 'off'. My reaction was duly reported to both my housemaster and the headmaster. I was very soon waiting nervously outside the headmaster's study. I should have realized it was serious when I saw them there together. 'Do you expect me to underwrite you for Sandhurst when you behave like this?' the headmaster asked me. I suppose I did. I was bitterly disappointed when I took the RCB and failed.

I had come to the inevitable fork in the road at which I should perhaps have taken the path of least resistance. I should have admitted that the army wasn't for me, and that I was never cut out to be a soldier. But this rejection got my hackles up. I dug my heels in and refused to admit defeat. If the army wouldn't take me as an officer, then I would show them anyway. I would join the ranks of the hardest, toughest, most elite unit open to me: the Parachute Regiment.

Of course, my parents were disappointed that I hadn't made

Sandhurst. They advised me to give it up as a bad job. 'And do what?' was a question they couldn't answer. I took a temporary job as a labourer on a vast arable farm belonging to my girlfriend's family. During the mornings I picked daffodil bulbs. I shuffled after the harrow with the other labourers, scooping the golden bulbs into a basket until my back ached. In the long afternoons there would be hay-making. We collected the great bales with pitch-forks and built them up into a vast monolith on the back of a wagon. At weekends she chose a mount for me from the eleven horses in her stable, and we cantered for miles through the wheat-field stubble. Evenings found me in the local pub, the Bull, listening to tales of wagons and horses and sipping my first pints of bitter with the old hands. I remember how they sat on the wooden plank-benches, transfixed by the last piercing beams of sunlight. Their carven granite faces under their flat caps seemed a thousand years old.

The army schools liaison officer was a retired colonel. He visited me one afternoon to tell me that if I wanted to join the ranks, there was a special arrangement called an 'S-type' engagement. 'You serve as a potential officer until you feel it's time to have another bash at RCB,' he told me. I agreed, but only on the condition that I could serve in the Parachute Regiment. 'The Paras is very demanding,' the colonel said. 'They accept only one in four applicants. You'll have to take your chances with no special treatment. If you fail the Paras' selection course, it would end your chances of becoming an officer.' He suggested the Royal Green Jackets instead. 'It's very fashionable now,' he said. 'They have a special potential officers' wing, in which you'd be specially prepared for RCB. In the Paras you'd be just another recruit.'

'That suits me,' I told him.

He said he would make inquiries and returned a week later. 'It's fixed up,' he told me. 'You can bypass the Other Ranks Selection Centre. You can swear the loyal oath and leave for Aldershot.'

The regimental sergeant-major was wearing his best parade uniform. He was a chunky Royal Signals man, evidently pleased with his sinecure job in the Army Careers Office.

'Are you sure you want to join the Paras?' he asked me dubiously.

'Yes,' I said.

'I want to be sure,' he said, 'because I don't want you coming back here in a month and complaining it's too tough.'

'I won't be back,' I said.

'Do your parents agree with you?' he asked me.

'Yes, they do,' I lied.

He wrote 'Parachute Regiment' on the form, and I signed on the bottom line. Then I held my hand up and swore an oath to protect the Queen and all her ministers. I had my doubts about the ministers. The RSM presented me with a cheap little Bible with my name and the date inscribed inside. 'Good luck,' he said. 'Let us know how you get on!' I dashed for the bus and arrived home in time for dinner. 'I've joined the army!' I announced. My parents were furious, but there was nothing they could do. I was over eighteen and I had signed upon the dotted line.


My second day at the Depot was taken up with kit issue, haircuts and mental tests. We were shuffled about from morning till night, juggling with piles of clothing and webbing, mint-new and smelling of the stores. I inspected the kit list with interest, noting how everything seemed to follow rules of English syntax different from the ones I knew. Our denim trousers were 'Trousers, Olive-green', our boots 'Boots, Dunlop-moulded Soles', our jackets 'Smocks, Dennison, Airborne', and our pullovers 'Jerseys, Heavy-duty'. There were 'Shirts, Khaki, Field', 'Puttees, Khaki' and 'Helmets, Steel, Airborne'. The most prized items of all were the two maroon-red berets with their silver-winged parachute badges. They were issued to us on approval. They had to be laid ceremoniously in our lockers until we had won the right to wear them.

The camp barber was a bored-looking man, completely bald except for grey tufts over his ears. You couldn't blame him being bored that morning, with dozens of regulation haircuts to perform. There was little chance to display the subtler skills of his art. I watched in horror as he applied the electric razor to head after head, leaving only a spiky stubble a quarter of an inch long. As each victim stood up, the barber divested him of 7s. 6d. for his trouble. It was like paying the executioner, I thought. My turn came. The electric razor buzzed across the back of my head and started on top.

'That's enough!' I told him, catching sight of myself in the mirror.

'What!' the bald man gasped. 'You'll have a regulation haircut like all the rest!'

'Not if I'm paying for it, I won't!' I said. 'I'll have it like I want!'

He stared at me in amazement. 'I'll make sure your platoon sergeant knows about this!' he said.

'You do what you like,' I told him. 'But I have no intention of looking like a convict!' I swept the white sheet aside and lurched towards the door. The other recruits looked on in horror. At that moment the door swung open and Corporal Jekyll walked in.

'What's going on?' he demanded.

'This recruit thinks he's something special,' the barber whined. 'Says he doesn't want to look like everybody else!'

'I see,' said Jekyll, grimly. 'Come outside, Asher.'

Outside he suddenly pushed me up against the wall with a force which knocked the wind out of me. 'Down on your haunches!' he snapped. 'Bend your knees!' He forced me to bend my legs until my thighs were parallel with the ground. My back was pressed straight against the wall, and my hands were behind my head. A fiery stream of pain whirled through my thighs. It was agony. I tried to keep still, but my knees began to quake. 'This is Torture Position Number One,' Jekyll said proudly. 'This is what we use for clever nancy-boys like you.' I fought to retain some dignity by staying upright, but my body slowly sank. He kicked savagely at my heels. 'Don't fucking move till I tell you!' he grunted. 'I've been looking at your file, Asher. Seems you're a potential officer, Asher. Potential shit!

I've seen more potential in the Girl Guides! You're not going to make it, Asher, because I'm going to break you. Got it?' I tried to nod, but instead I collapsed in a jelly-like heap, 'STAND UP!' he roared. 'You think you're tough, Asher, but you're just a nancy-boy. Get in there and finish your haircut before I put you on orders!'

When I looked in the mirror later, I could scarcely recognize myself. I looked as much a yobbo as any of my mates. In fact, with our uniforms on you could hardly tell us apart.

We took turns for medicals and mental tests. Meanwhile, Jekyll showed us how to use a steam-iron to press our denims sharp as knives and our shirt-collars like cardboard. 'You lot are used to having mum look after you!' he jeered. 'Load of mamby-pambies. You might break your mother's heart, but you won't break mine! I want to see these denims so sharp you can cut your finger on them!' He demonstrated how to bull boots. You could burn the rough leather down using a hot spoon, then you spread Kiwi polish over the toe-caps and heels. You polished with water and the corner of a duster in ever decreasing circles until your index-finger went white. The toe-caps and heels had to shine like glass.

I was called forward for mental tests. The supervising clerk was the same morose corporal who had met me at the PSO. 'The idea is to spot patterns in these squiggles of ink,' he informed me. Why did the squiggles keep forming into Jekyll's face? Then there were aptitude tests: simple physics, maths and vocabulary. 'Send Chapman next,' he told me. As the big-boned Scouse ambled out of the billet, I slotted myself into his place at the table for boot-bulling.

'I could save them the trouble of doin' mental tests on Chapman!' Walker commented darkly.

'Why?' I asked.

'Becos tha's only got to look at that greet big carvin' knife he keeps under his pillow to know he's bleedin' mental!'

That afternoon we stood on the drill-square for the first time. There were 120 of us in the new platoon. Some of them adapted naturally to wearing uniform. Others, like me, looked more like inmates of Stalag 14. We had dragged on our 'Trousers, Olive-green' so that the seams were twisted. Our 'Puttees, Khaki' were coiled on the wrong way, with their tapes hanging out. Our 'Boots, Dunlop-moulded Soles' were laced up incorrectly, and our 'Caps, Combat, Destructive Pattern Material' were clamped on our heads as if we were preparing for a typhoon.

Our platoon sergeant was called Tony Norris. He was a pint-sized man with a manner which suggested an aggressive Max Bygraves. He looked the squad up and down as if assessing a bowlful of maggots. 'A pack of rag-arsed bandits!' he said. 'I think they sent us a squad of mental deficients this time! LISTEN TO ME, YOU LOT! Just by being here you've proved nothing. Haven't got the cradle marks off your arse yet, most of you! You've got twenty-two weeks of grind in the Depot, and that's the lucky ones who get through all in one go. We know some of you will buy out. We know some of you will go *craphat*: that's what we Paras call anyone who doesn't wear a red beret. For the handful of you left at the end of the course, you'll have earned your right to wear the maroon-red beret, the Maroon Machine. And you'll have earned a place in the best regiment in the British army. And that's the most worthwhile thing I know!'

Captain Briggs was the platoon commander. He was as tall as a guardsman, with a freckled face and blue eyes. 'I want to read you what a former colonel-in-chief of our regiment said,' he announced. He took out a piece of paper and cleared his throat. 'What manner of men are these that wear the maroon-red beret? They are firstly all volunteers, and are toughened by hard physical training. They have the infectious optimism and the offensive eagerness that comes from physical well-being. They have jumped from the sky and in so doing have conquered fear. Their duty lies in the van of battle: they are proud of this honour and have never failed in any task. They have the highest standards in all things, whether it be skill in battle or smartness in the execution of peace-time duties. They have shown themselves to be as tenacious and determined in defence as they are courageous in attack. They are, in fact, men apart. Every man an emperor!' He paused, and I didn't know whether to cheer or cry. 'That's all I wanted to say,' he told us. 'But it might interest you to know that those words were written by Field Marshal Viscount Montgomery of Alamein. If you pass the course, you will be in good company. Dismiss.'

We were sitting around the table that evening, not feeling much like emperors, when someone shouted, 'GET FELL IN, YOU FUCKERS!'

'Gawd!' Walker exclaimed. 'What's all this about?' The question was cut short when the door opened and a young sergeant appeared.

'Come on! Get moving!' he roared. All pandemonium broke loose. We were wearing only underpants or shorts and PT shoes, and we grabbed for our uniforms. 'Leave that!' the sergeant ordered. 'Go as you are!'

Out in the corridor a picket of NCOs were chasing half-naked recruits towards the stairwells. As I doubled past the washroom, a voice called, 'Hey, you! Get in here!' I stepped through into near darkness and was immediately grabbed by two soldiers. 'Make any noise and you're dead!' a gruff voice told me. A third soldier came up from behind and stripped off my PT shorts. I kicked out, and my PT shoe connected with something soft. 'Just for that you're going to get beasted!' the voice growled. 'Get the shower on!' One of the men turned it on, and there was a sizzle of water. The others frog-marched me, struggling, into it. The freezing blast of the water drained the fight out of me. What the hell was this about, I wondered. One of them waved a long-handled lavatory brush in front of my nose. 'Give it to him!' another said. I wriggled and kicked, but the two men held me in a vice-like grip, while the third dragged the brush all over my naked body. It had evidently been laced with something acid like lavatory-cleaner. It raised angry welts across my skin. Suddenly they pulled me out of the shower. 'Just remember,' the voice said, 'you are a *crow*. That's just like being a turd. A turd's better, in fact. You're nothing but a fucking crow, don't ever forget it! Now get fell in with the others!' I ran out, dripping and shivering and trying to pull my shorts back on. A size nine 'Boot, Dunlop-moulded Sole' caught me squarely on the rump.

I was just in time to meet the rest of my section ambling off the drill-square. Some of the recruits were dripping like me, and others had been plastered with what looked like boot-polish. The NCOs were nowhere to be seen. 'It's a bloody con!' Walker said. 'Those swine weren't NCOs at all! They were recruits from a senior squad. Bloody bastards! We've been had!'


We were puffing and panting heavily in step, with beefy PTIs built like rugby forwards swearing obscenely after us. Our heads were encased tight in chin-strapped helmets. The surreal structures of the Depot assault course towered over us: parallel poles, ramps and bars, scaling nets and rope-swings and trenches filled with filthy water. We marked time at the starting-point to the accompaniment of 'Get those fucking legs up!' Three of the instructors lined up and urinated conspicuously into one of the trenches.

'COME HERE, THAT MAN!' an NCO screamed. Bandy-legged Williams from Merthyr Tydfil had got himself noticed. He froze in the act of wiping his nose with a dirty handkerchief and took a bandy pace forward out of the sweating ranks. 'MARK TIME!' the instructor yelled. He was a sinewy PT Corps full-screw with a dotted line tattooed around his throat. The words CUT HERE and a miniature pair of scissors were tattooed underneath, like a coupon in a magazine.

Williams lifted his bandy legs. 'What's this, soldier?' the corporal demanded. He pointed with distaste to the snotty handkerchief.

'Snot rag, corporal!' Williams answered breathlessly.

The instructor's eyes opened wide in mock disbelief. 'A snot rag! In the Paras? I don't believe it! Are you some kind of pansy?' He snatched the piece of soiled cloth out of the soldier's hand and ground it into the mud with a heavy boot. Then he carefully sealed one of his nostrils with a thick finger and blew half an ounce of mucus into the ground. 'If you want to blow your nose, do it like a *Para*!' he said. Williams, still marking time but slowing visibly, was about to retreat into the safety of the ranks. The NCO caught him by the arm. 'Where do you think you're going?' he demanded. 'Twenty press-ups! There!' He pointed to the trench in which the three NCOs had just urinated. 'Get pressing!' he said.

'GO!' the PTI yelled, and we were off. Scrambling up wet, slippery posts, balancing precariously on beams, slipping off and gouging in slime which gave out an evil, sewage odour when disturbed. Grunting, we pulled ourselves up the scaling net and shimmied down the other side. We mounted the long frame of wooden steps and jumped down into the mire. As I came to the rope-swing, I saw Jekyll standing on the opposite side in his denims and sweat-shirt. 'GET MOVING, ASHER!' he bawled when he recognized me. As I ran up, I saw him urinating gleefully into the trench. My hands closed on the rope, and in a single movement I lurched into the air and slipped down with a plop into the mud. I stood there for a second, riveted, watching Jekyll laughing. Then I squelched out of the mud and ran on to the next obstacle.

Back at the billets, they gave us five minutes to change into spotless kit for drill. That meant scraping all the gunge off our boots and puttees. It meant washing, changing denims and donning shirts and HD pullovers. It couldn't be done in five minutes, and the NCOs knew it couldn't be done. But that didn't stop them doling out press-ups. 'Five minutes means five minutes!' Sergeant Norris lectured us. 'If you have to RV with the chopper at ten hundred it doesn't mean ten-oh-one. The chopper's gone and Ivan's got you. *Tuvska shitski*, as they say in Russia!' After a good half of the platoon had finished pressing, Norris inspected our boots. 'I don't call that clean, do you, Asher?' he asked me.

'Yes, sarn't,' I answered unwisely.

'Twenty press-ups for the boots,' he told me languidly, 'and thirty for disagreeing with your sergeant!'

We stood on the square, hardly daring to breathe. It was our first proper drill session. Jekyll stood at attention, his taut cat-fat face sweeping the ranks.

'SQUAD!' he began. 'BRACE UP THERE WHEN I SAY SQUAD! As you were, you bunch of morons! Get it right this time or you'll end up in Dixieland! Now listen to me. SQUAD! SQUAAAAAD SHUN!' A clatter of boots like a lazy machine-gun. 'STAND STILL! Look to your front! Don't fidget! STAND STILL, THAT MAN!' We stood like statues. 'Belly in, chest out,' he told us. 'Heads up. Try to LOOK like Paras! Are you with us, Chapman, *dear*? BRACE UP THERE! Eyes front, heads up, little fingers touching khakeee!'

We moved to the right in threes, moved to the left in threes, marched off by the right, turned about in threes and marched back, all to an unending stream of abuse from the corporal. Chapman didn't seem to know his left from his right. He turned constantly in the wrong direction. 'Two left feet!' Jekyll's voice clanged out. 'Oh Jesus Christ! You should be in the Brownies, not the Paras! Call out the time, all of you. You crows will call out the time until you're good enough to pass off the square and wear your red berets! Shout out after me, ONE-tup-three-ONE!'

'ONE-tup-three-ONE!' we all shouted. And shouted. And shouted. Move to the right in threes. Move to the left in threes. 'ONE-tup-three-ONE!'

'Get moving up that rope, Asher!' Jekyll yelled. I dragged my aching body a little further towards the roof of the gymnasium. It was afternoon and the gobbled lunch of sausage and chips was still swilling nauseatingly around inside ('Don't make a meal of it!' Sergeant Norris had said). We were undergoing fitness tests, a scaled-down, indoor version of that morning's assault course: up and down on benches, over the vaulting-horse, pull-ups and press-ups and burpees and dodging round medicine-balls, sprinting agonizingly from wall to wall. I touched the gym roof and paused for a triumphant second to get my breath back. Below me the corporal had turned his attention to overweight Chapman. He was hanging from the parallel beam with all the energy of a giant sloth. 'Get up there, you fat slug!' Jekyll was bawling at him. 'I want to see another five press-ups yet!'

'Can't, corporal!' Chapman winced.

'CAN'T' Jekyll roared. 'You bloody well can! Get up there!'

I slid down the rope and landed heavily, only to find Jekyll waiting for me. 'You used your feet to climb the last few yards, didn't you?' he demanded.

'Yes, corporal.'

'Then do twenty press-ups for cheating, and climb it again, hands only! You think you're clever, Asher! You think you can put one over on me! Potential, hah! I've seen more potential in the shit-house being flushed! Don't try it on with me, Asher, because I'm watching you!'

After PT there were five minutes to change before being marched to the Education Centre for our first lecture. The lecturer today was WO1 Nobby Arnold, the regimental sergeant-major of the Depot. He was a great lion of a man, with permanently narrowed eyes. He had a bulbous nose which stuck out on his face like a bunch of purplish grapes. It had been broken so many times that the bone must have been like plasticine.

'I want to tell you about my ideal man!' the RSM began. 'My ideal man is James Bond, double-O-seven. He's a tough man, but he doesn't mouth off. He drinks hard, but he never gets drunk. He gets plenty of crumpet, but he doesn't abuse women. That's the way to behave. You don't have to be an officer to be a gentleman. If you want to keep your nose clean here, be like him.'

He paused and scratched the fruity nose pensively. There was a titter of laughter from the class. The titter soon stopped when Nobby opened his eyes fully. It was like a predator coming awake. His hot gaze strafed us, and I understood suddenly why everyone in the Depot was afraid of him. Nobby had led the regiment's last bayonet charge. It had been up a hill in the Radfan, against a superior force of communist guerrillas. Nobby had been a sergeant then. The officer had been killed, and the platoon had run low on ammunition. He had ordered them to fix bayonets, and they had erupted forth from their position with this great dragon in their lead, screaming and throwing

cans of chicken curry. The ridge they captured was later named
Arnold's Ridge.

There was a story that Nobby had a certificate of sanity on
the wall of his office. If everything said about him was true, he
probably needed it. Once he had marched a bicycle into gaol for
leaning against a wall in an unsoldierly fashion. One private
from the Parachute Regiment had passed Nobby every morning
on his way from the married quarters. 'Morning, sir!' he would
say. One day Nobby stopped him. 'No need to keep calling
me "sir" when we see each other every day,' he told him. 'My
name's Nobby.' The following day the soldier passed the RSM
as usual. 'Morning, Nobby,' he said. 'You're under arrest for
insubordination!' said Mr Arnold.

'I don't want anyone here going into the 'Shot and causing
bother with the craphats,' he told us. 'Because if there's anything
left to be picked up, you will certainly be picked up by the
military police. There's some pretty tough craphats down there,
including a battalion of Gurkhas. My advice is to save your shit
for the assault course and keep your trap shut. I don't want to
hear of anyone stealing. Stealing is filth. The army feeds you,
puts a roof over your head, looks after your health and your
teeth, and even gives you a few bob a week to buy fags and
booze. There's no need to steal. I don't want to hear of anyone
going AWOL, absent without leave. That's the same as deser-
tion. Sooner or later the Redcaps will get you, and then you'll
wish you'd never been born. If the Paras isn't for you, you can
get a discharge. You can buy out, or even go craphat if you
want. We don't want any square pegs in round holes. We want
only the best.'

Nobby's place was taken by a mild Education Corps officer. It
was his task to explain to us the structure of the strange world
in which we found ourselves. The Depot consisted of a number
of training platoons, he said, which together formed Recruit
Company. There was also a Headquarters Company of cooks,
desk-wallahs and bottle-washers. The third component was 'Pre-
Parachute Company', known more commonly as 'P Company'.
Once we had finished our basic training and advanced infantry

training, we would pass through 'P Company'. No member of the Airborne Forces could attain his parachute wings without passing 'P Company'. It was the most physically demanding selection course in the British army. If we passed all our training, which was unlikely, we would be posted to one of the three regular battalions, 1, 2 or 3 Para. 'And that's where your real training begins,' he said.

Then he began to reel off the names of the brigadiers, colonels, majors and other big bananas in the Depot. By that time my body and brain had endured enough. I had the picture now. The Paras was tough. It was the elite unit of the British army. If you weren't up to scratch, you failed. That was the message. But it had been a hard day. I could no longer keep my eyes open. I fought hard to stop my lids closing, but they were like lead weights. I jerked them open with a physical effort, but a second later they were slits again. The officer's voice droned on, soporifically. My head began to loll slightly over the desk. The lecturer's voice was a sea sound far away. Then a new voice stung my eardrums: 'ARE YOU TIRED, SOLDIER!' I almost leapt out of my chair. The captain stopped speaking, and I looked up straight into the eyes of Corporal Jekyll. 'If you're tired, I can easily find a way to wake you up!' he said.

Later, after I had jogged twice round the square as a punishment, Jekyll called me over. We had to pose for a platoon photograph. 'This is the *before* photo,' Jekyll said. 'We all laugh about it afterwards. I always enjoy scratching out the faces of those that don't make it!'

Before dawn the following morning, I watched Walker dragging himself from his bunk with the stiff motion of a clockwork toy. Already there were bags under his bleary eyes. 'I feel like a bleedin' zombie!' he muttered.

'You look like one!' I told him. Then I tried to get up and groaned as hot needles shot through my thighs. It was Walker's turn to laugh. 'Don't worry,' he said. 'There's a three-mile run this morning. That'll warm thee up!'

And warm me up it did. Before it had long been light, we were doubling in step out of the barracks, with our boots

clumping on the asphalt. In a moment we were running
along the side of the canal which flowed past the Depot, scuffling
through fallen leaves. The pace was set by Williams's old friend,
the PTI with the dotted line tattooed around his throat.
'Airborne-easy, airborne-easy!' he began to chant. 'Come on
you crows, SING!' The chant was picked up shakily by the
first ranks. Slowly it spread through the whole platoon, in time
with the crunching boots, until the landscape seemed to rever-
berate with the cry 'AIRBORNE-EASY! AIRBORNE-EASY!
AIRBORNE-EASY!'

The instructors buzzed around the stragglers like bees round
honey. They swung pick-helves and shouted, 'Keep moving,
you fuckers! Get them legs up, you bunch of pooves!' The
platoon began to string out as we pulled into the country. The
pace increased. The PTI leading inched further into the distance.
A breathless gasp for air drowned the 'Airborne-easy' chant.
Suddenly I felt a tremendous whack on my backside. I jerked
round to see Jekyll running behind me with a pick-helve and
grinning like a maniac. 'Catch up there!' he yelled. 'If any of my
section are in the last twenty, they'll be on Dixieland!' I put on a
spurt. My lungs were bursting, and my breath was coming in
sickening gulps. I was just about to slow down again, when a
new shock made me jump. It was a deafening 'TATTOOO!
TATTOOO! TATTOOO!' I glanced round and saw one of the
other corporals running along, blowing into a military bugle.
For a moment I wondered if I'd come to a madhouse.

The barracks were miraculously back in sight. The last brown
fields went past, the last of the fading hedgerows, bronze elms
and beeches. We were running back along the canal, and the
pace was slowing to let the stragglers catch up. 'AIRBORNE-
EASY! AIRBORNE-EASY! AIRBORNE-EASY!' the chant
began again. I felt my body flagging. Only a quarter of a mile to
go. In front of me were the thick, muscular legs of blond-haired
Smart, working like pistons. 'Sprint the last 200 metres!' the
PTI ordered. I burst forward with the last of my energy. Smart
was a little slower. A second later I stumbled against him, as he
let out an 'OOOF!' and fell sprawling. I just managed to dodge

the concrete bollard which had sent him flying. 'Stupid bastard!' someone shouted. The platoon was already forming up in front of me. I tried to count the number of recruits home, hoping desperately that I wasn't in the last twenty. Walker was home and so was McGowan. As I closed with the rest, a powerful stitch spread across my stomach. I leaned forward to ease it. 'Stand up!' Jekyll bellowed, running up behind me. 'You're not dead yet! Looks like you're going to be on Dixie tonight!' I finished counting the recruits as they formed up behind me. I was just in the last twenty.

But I wasn't quite the last in our section. That honour belonged to Chapman. He came limping in with three instructors chasing him, each taking it in turns to whack him across the backside with their pick-helves. Jekyll almost exploded with rage. 'Had to be one of my section!' he growled. 'You and Asher are a pair of useless tubes!'

'Yes, corporal!' Chapman moaned.

'Both of you are on Dixie tonight!' he added.

A little later they carried Smart off in a stretcher. His leg was broken in two places. 'One down and seven to go!' was Jekyll's instant reaction.

We never saw Smart again.

Chapman and I were the first members of our section to get put on Dixieland. It was not simply a bind, it was a disgrace. 'Dixieland' meant fatigues in the Depot kitchens, where every evening the great 'Dixies', or cooking-pots, had to be scrubbed clean. My heart sank when an obese army cook pointed at the pile of grease-smeared pots and said, 'Get scrubbing!' The worst of it was being ordered about by these craphats who couldn't even run a hundred metres. Things weren't going so well, I reflected. At this rate, I thought, I'd be 'out on my arse before my feet touched the ground'.

Chapman was almost in tears after two hours with the Dixies. 'That's not what I joined the army for!' he said.

'Take nay notice!' McGowan, the old campaigner, advised him. 'They only do it to sicken ye. Better to crack now than on the battlefield, that's what they say! They want ye only if you're

determined. If ye answer back or lay into 'em, they've beaten
ye! I tell ye, they're all the same. I've spent my whole life in
institutions: orphanage, Borstal, the merch. They're all the same
in the end. It's you and them!'

'Aye,' Walker agreed. 'There's nowt for me to go back for but
pit. And I've seen what it did to me dad. I'm not going to give
in!' Then a small grin tickled his lips. 'Still,' he said, 'I wouldn't
mind half an hour alone with that bleedin' Corporal Jekyll!'

'Join the queue!' I said.

The week passed in a delirious haze. There was no time to
think. We were on the go from reveille to last light, when the
long round of fatigues began. Every morning we dragged our
aching bodies to the drill-square for another dose: 'ONE-tup-
three-ONE!', another inspection, more press-ups, more gruelling
PT, more 'Airborne-easy'. There seemed no end to the physical
torture and no end to the abuse the NCOs could dish out. I
avoided getting put on Dixie again, but I felt Jekyll's hawk eyes
watching my every move.

At the end of the week, I was called to the platoon office. I
stood uneasily at attention before Captain Briggs and Sergeant
Norris. 'Not a brilliant start for a potential officer, is it?' Briggs
asked me. 'Already on Dixie! Do you really want to be a Para?'

'Yes, sir,' I replied. For the first time I realized that it was
absolutely true.

'Then you've got to pull your finger out. You've got to *want*
to be a Para. I know it's not easy. I was in your position once.' I
looked at him incredulously, and he saw the disbelief in my
eyes. 'Yes,' he went on, 'I failed the RCB first time, and I joined
the ranks. I made it to lance-jack and then I passed the RCB
and went to Sandhurst. So you see, it can be done!'

That night Walker called me to the ablutions. He had cornered
a recruit from another platoon. 'Caught him using our bogs,'
Walker said. 'Now, does tha recognize him?' I looked hard. It
was the recruit from the senior platoon who had masqueraded
as a sergeant the day I'd been beasted. 'Let's beast the swine!'
Walker said. He grasped the man in his powerful hands.

'Hold on!' the recruit said. 'Don't waste your energy! The rest of my platoon will come looking for you, and you'll never get any peace. And by hell, you'll need some peace next week. The second week is the worst. You won't know if you're wiping your arse or having diarrhoea!'

Walker and I exchanged glances, grimly acknowledging that it was true.

And then we beasted him anyway.

# 2

## *Martial Arts*

———

'This is the best high-velocity rifle in the world!' Corporal Gurung said. He held up the self-loading rifle with both hands as if it were sacred. 'High velocity means stopping-power. If you hit a man with this, it'll blow his head clean off!' Gurung was a Gurkha on detachment from his brigade. His chiselled, oriental features lent a proper solemnity to the occasion of our first firearms session. He wore a green beret, not a maroon-red one, but no one would have dared to call him a craphat. Everyone could see the curved *kukri* which never left his belt. He was a career soldier, the third generation of his family to serve with the British army. He was particularly happy that week, because his wife had presented him with a third son. In the Gurkhas your pay increased with each son.

The awe with which he seemed to regard the SLR quickly rubbed off on us. Under his guidance the naming of parts and the repeating of safety precautions became a satisfying ritual. 'The rifle is a good friend,' he said. 'Handle it with care. It can save your life.' I could imagine the Gurungs of this world patting their weapons in battle and speaking to them endearingly like the Germans in Caesar's praetorian guard. Gurung told us to pick up the weapon, to feel the balance and the weight of the thing and to touch the smooth, slumbering surface of the gun-metal. He taught us to cock the mechanism, to peel the working parts back and feel them wheeling in perfect harmony – the superb precision of the killing machine.

For unheeded hours we repeated the motions of the ritual: safety-catch, magazine on, cock, safety-catch, magazine off, ease springs, strip and assemble, make safe. Each part of the communion was carried out with a loving precision, an attention to detail which was almost beautiful. Then we lay down in the firing position, legs up, chest-cavity raised, looking down the battle-sights and taking the first pressure. 'Never go for the limbs or head,' Gurung told us. 'Always go for the trunk, the big target. Never shoot to disarm or disable. Your enemy might get up again. Never snatch the trigger. Always squeeze it gently, as if you're stroking a cat. Hold your breath, squeeze the trigger, shoot to kill.'

Whang! Whang! Whang! The bullets zapped into the wood and paper frames of the targets a hundred metres away. It was our first day on the ranges, and we were letting rip at 'figure elevens': pictures of little yellow men who charged at you with gigantic bayonets and menacing snarls. Whang! Whang! Whang! The targets went down, and I snapped on the safety-catch. I counted the seconds off in my head and took the first pressure on the trigger. I held my breath in check and clicked off the safety-catch as the little yellow man appeared. I squeezed the trigger and felt the thrill of power crackle through my blood, as the rounds whizzed through the target and thumped across the sand-bank behind in ricochets. The fumes of cordite filled my nostrils. My heart beat furiously as more rounds blatted out. There was a caveman inside me bashing a leopard with a club, a warrior in armour slicing the throat of an infidel. 'Make safe!' Gurung ordered, and we doubled forward to check the targets. Six bullets smack through the target's midriff. 'You zapped him, soldier,' the corporal said.

From that day each of us had his personal weapon, his 'trusty bunduk' zeroed in to suit each man's eye. We handled the weapons for hours every day, repeating the rituals over and over again, until they became instinctive. The rifle became so much an extension of our arms that we felt naked without it. Familiarity was what our training was about. Handling your weapon had to become so instinctive that you could kill auto-

matically without any intervening moment of thought. Gurung
said that the measure of a real soldier was accuracy under fire.
Anyone could shoot at a target on the ranges on a sunny day,
but making your fire deadly when you were in someone else's
sights was much harder. In most ordinary units, especially
conscript units, half of the soldiers froze during a contact and
were unable to fire. Their negative instincts had taken over.
You had to conquer that fear, to lay down a solid wall of fire, to
sting like a cornered bee, to take out the enemy. An aggressive,
determined response was the only way to win the firefight.

One day, Gurung explained, we would sense a kind of fusion
between ourselves and the weapon, and on that day we would
become real soldiers. On the surface it seemed like oriental
mysticism, but later I sensed the truth beneath his words. The
army had learned over centuries how to harness the savage
horse of aggression in every man, to channel that wildly raging
river between its banks, to sharpen those savage impulses into
something useful, something really destructive, a finely shaped
cutting blade. Everyone is a killer to a greater or lesser extent.
The Paras just took that capability and articulated it. They
dressed it up in a maroon-red beret and gave it an identity.
They replaced its primitive bone-club with a high-velocity rifle,
so that it could reach out and kill its enemies from afar. You'd
spent eighteen years learning to be 'civilized', to contain the
violence which boiled in your brain, and now the Paras opened
the floodgates and told you to let rip. Only now they controlled
the floodgates.

At the end of our second week at Aldershot we had our first
taste of field soldiering on Hankley Common. We lived in two-
man bashas, mere shelters of rainproof poncho, strung eighteen
inches above the ground between the trees. Your basha had to
be well camouflaged with branches and leaves, and sited so that
you had an escape route and good cover from the air. You
unrolled your sleeping-bag inside and slept on a hair-trigger
with your boots on and your trusty bunduk as bedfellow. The

instructors had a habit of sneaking around the camp at night and stealing unguarded weapons. If you had to report your rifle missing, you'd be put on a charge for negligence.

At no time was your rifle to be more than arm's length away from you, even when relieving yourself. Especially when you were relieving yourself, Jekyll told us. 'There's been more squaddies shot having a shit in the *ulu* than anything else!' We had to learn the proper techniques for patrolling hostile country, how to cover each other while crossing obstacles like walls and streams, and how to move as silently as snakes in response to the strange new alphabet of field signals. We had to learn how to become invisible: camouflage and concealment. 'Everything has its own shape, colour, size and texture,' our instructor told us. 'That's how you recognize what it is. If you change the shape, size, colour or texture, then it becomes something else. You can't recognize it any more. Camouflage is the art of invisibility.' We learned how to streak our faces with the greenish oil they called 'cam-cream'. It came in plastic tubes with screw tops. 'Not too much, not too little' was the rule for application. The corporal demonstrated how a totally black face was as visible as a totally white one, even at night, when a black surface would shine. The idea was always to break up the pattern. We decorated our helmets, belts and boots with plumes of brushwood and leaves, and draped our camouflage veils over our packs and webbing. The vegetation had to be carefully changed when moving from one environment to another.

We learned basic field skills: how to judge distances by comparing the size of objects; how to give fire orders by describing reference points, how to view the landscape in arcs like the face of a giant clock. We learned the use of cover: never to use obvious gates or holes in the fence, never to hide behind the only bush in the field or at the prominent window of a house. We were taught to use dead ground and concave slopes to approach objectives, to leopard-crawl and monkey-walk. We learned to use our eyes and ears, to see without being seen. At night we were taught how to move in the folds of the darkness, to avoid cracking twigs and rustling leaves. Concealment at night required even more stringent discipline: no smoking, no talking, no eating: even the sound of a water-bottle being unscrewed could alert the enemy. We were drilled in the recognition of sounds in the darkness: the scuff of metal on metal, the crunch of a footfall, the soft murmur of voices, the whiff of woodsmoke or toothpaste. We were taught to listen, waiting motionlessly with our ears cocked and our mouths open. We learned to adjust to night-vision, to look only obliquely at sudden flares or headlights which might otherwise blind us for twenty minutes. We learned to read and orientate maps by night and to march on compass-bearings in the dark.

On a more prosaic level, we had to absorb the techniques of camp life. We ate from 24-hour ration-packs, each divided into bags labelled 'Snack', 'Breakfast' and 'Dinner'. The packs were designed to fit into our pouches and contained 'astronaut food' like tubes of jam and evaporated milk, packets of soya biscuits, tins of concentrated stew, sachets of instant tea, coffee and sugar, processed cheese ('cheese, possessed' as the NCOs called it), salt, toilet-paper, matches, a 'combat' tin-opener and, most prized of all, a ration of sweets and Mars Bars. 'Mars Bars are always to be kept in your top left-hand pocket,' Jekyll joked, 'so if you stop a bullet, your section commander will be able to find them quickly!' Cooking was an individual task, a ritual of grave importance. We cooked in small aluminium mess-tins, or Dixies, on a pocket-sized Hexamine stove with blocks of solid fuel. The Hexamine was designed to burn with intense heat, but it was difficult to light in windy conditions. Once it was going well, you packed your knapsack and belt, clearing the ground for a quick getaway if you happened to get 'bumped'.

We carried only one quart-sized water-bottle for this exercise, and with good reason, I discovered. I made the obvious mistake of drinking my two pints before sunset in the confident expectation of being given more. 'You want some more water, Asher?' Jekyll jeered. 'Just nip back to the Depot and get some. It's only ten miles away. Oh, can you get me some while you're about it!' That night on sentry-duty I was ravaged by thirst, and for the rest of the night I tossed and turned sleeplessly. I had to march the ten miles back to the Depot with the platoon, suffering from a mouth full of mucus and as dry as sandpaper. 'Perhaps you'll remember next time,' Jekyll said. 'A Para has only what he can carry!' It was a lesson I never forgot.

I soon got to know my room-mates with an intimacy possible only amongst those who live together. I no longer despised them. Wearing the same uniform, enduring the same petty humiliations, had reduced us all to a common denominator. The army had made us children again. Now the natural order was reasserting itself like new plants growing on a ploughed field. My grammar school education mattered not a jot here. What mattered was courage, strength, endurance and aggression – the warrior's qualities. Many of my companions possessed such qualities to a far greater degree than I.

Within a few weeks the ties that bound us to our backgrounds became less distinct. The new ties which bound us to each other – the common home, the common section, the common regiment – became increasingly important. Walker summed it up when he said, 'Tha's got to work as a team in this mob. Tha stands no chance alone.' That, I realized, wasn't just the army talking. It was three generations of Barnsley miners, Walker's forebears, struggling together in the darkness and the stink of the pit. The working-class qualities of friendship and mutual help, the sense of humour and the feeling that you were 'all in the same boat' were the raw material on which the army grafted its 'buddy-buddy' system. To be a loner, to show eccentricity, to separate yourself from the crowd, were taboo. The Paras talked about 'airborne initiative', but it was mostly just talk. 'Don't get yourself noticed' was the first rule of the recruit.

'I'm going to get them little blue wings if it kills me!' Walker would say. 'I'm not going back to Barnsley without them!' He looked forward to the day he could go home with his 'Number Twos', complete with red beret and wings. He dreamed of showing off to his fiancée, a bank manager's daughter. 'She's much posher than me,' he told us. In his spare moments he would write letters to her. He would hunch over the table with a biro, tongue protruding, emitting small groans

of concentration as if he were carving the letters into rock. I
noticed that he always wrote in hesitating capitals. 'Never bin
much cop at this writing lark!' he said appealingly. Thereafter I
wrote his letters, while he, rocking back lordly on the rear two
legs of his chair, dictated. The letters were half taken up by
greetings and inquiries after the family's health. They were full
of lame little jokes with the words 'Ha! Ha!' interjected after
them. Nevertheless, I admired his style: there was a quality of
solid resolution in it which was both virile and eminently
endearing. It obviously never struck him as undesirable that an
outsider should know what was in his letters.

Soon, however, the 'Oldham Stud' got in on the picture, and
asked me to write a letter for him. I had less respect for him
than for Walker. He affected the same northern 'hail-fellow-
well-met' warmth, but it sat less convincingly on his narrow
shoulders. He was forever coming out with snide little quips.
Once, for example, he asked me, 'Do you get out of the bath to
have a piss?'

'Of course I do!'

'That's my definition of a pansy!' he chortled. I soon regretted
having agreed to write his letter. It was full of blood and guts. It
related detailed, rambling and totally fictitious accounts of his
prowess in the gym and in brawls in local pubs, which none of
us had ever been able to visit. 'This letter's for a bird in
Oldham,' he explained. 'A little cracker she is! I've had me eye
on her for ages. As soon as I get me wings up, I'm going back to
flash them to her. She'll drop her knickers like greased lightning!'
A week later the letter came back marked 'Return to Sender'.
He never asked me to write another.

At first, little Jock McGowan was the star of the room. His life
in institutions had prepared him well for the army. His kit was
always perfectly clean and pressed, and his was always the last
word on how to bull boots or make beds. 'Just like this in
Borstal!' he would say. 'I mean, the way they treat ye. See, they
test ye to find out how hard you are. The hard nuts are called
"Daddies". They're like the corporals here. They take sweets
and smokes from the others: it's sort of like a protection racket. I

wasna bothered about sweets or smokes, but I like to look after me bedspace and me clothes. See, those clothes were bought for me by the orphanage, and they were all I had. When the Daddies took me clothes, I lost me rag. Threw one of them through a plate-glass window, I did! He ended up with fourteen stitches and a scar for life. They never messed with me after that!' Out of Borstal, Jock had trained as a seaman in the merchant navy. 'I got me able-seaman ticket,' he said. 'You had to learn a lot for that: all about navigation, sextant, knots, semaphore. You even had to jump off the deck of a tanker into the sea – no joke, I can tell ye! Och, it was great visiting all those ports, but there was a load of shit too. Most of the stewards were queers, and they used to pick on the young lads like me. They talked about nothing but sex. You should see what they used to do with a loaf of bread and a piece of raw liver! Disgusting!'

'Why didn't you just give them what you gave the Daddies?'

'Hah! They was a lot harder than the Daddies! Not all queers are like Danny La Rue, ye ken! A lot of them were body-builders, hard as old nails!'

For all his talk, I never worried about McGowan. It was Chapman I worried about. He walked around in a dream-like trance from which he seemed to emerge only at meal-times. The way he polished his carving-knife before retiring was disconcerting.

'Why does tha need that thing?' Walker asked him coaxingly. 'Is tha training to be a butcher or sommat?'

Chapman eyed him defensively. 'You never know when you might need protection!' he said.

His kit was never quite up to scratch, and he was the first in the room to get put on showclean. This meant carrying the offending item of kit, suitably improved, to the guardroom after working-hours for a special parade in front of the duty NCO. Not only was the dirty piece of equipment supposed to be immaculate, but the rest of your uniform was too. If anything was found below standard, there would be another showclean, and perhaps another and another as you got worn down with the extra effort. Once on showclean you might stay on it for ever.

When we started 'soldiering', I expected the emphasis on bull to diminish. Instead, it got more intense. Every week, it seemed, just when you had got abreast of the continual round of cleaning and pressing, some new refinement was added. When we were dismissed at night, hours of work still stretched before us. First we had to press and starch our denims, shirts and puttees for inspection the following morning. Then we spent at least an hour bulling and water-polishing our boots. When that was done, we had to begin work on the room. Every surface had to be dusted and polished: lockers inside and out, top and bottom, the table, the chairs, the beds. The window had to be cleaned and polished until it was spotless. The floor had to be brushed and mopped, then 'bumpered' with a heavy polisher. It was hard work after a full day's training.

When the room was ready, the corridor had to be 'bumpered'. The washroom and lavatories had to shine like hospital washrooms, scoured with cleaning powder and rubbed with disinfectant. Occasionally, Jekyll himself would be there to supervise. We never knew when he might appear. We suspected that he hovered around the billets, listening secretly to our conversations, ready to pounce on us just as we made a disparaging comment about him. Once I was detailed to clean the urinals and found one of them blocked and containing a pool of evil-smelling liquid. I was searching around for something to poke into the drain, when Jekyll appeared. 'Don't just stand there like a dummy, Asher!' he told me. 'Get your hand in!' Seeing that there was no escape, I began to poke gingerly at the nauseating fluid. Jekyll shoved me hard on the arm. 'Come on, soldier!' he roared. 'Up to the elbow!'

We soon devised a rota for cleaning the lavatories, but it was an almost impossible job. No sooner had you got them spotless than someone would dash in to use them. After a while we agreed that only one lavatory out of our four could be used in the evenings. If there was a queue, we would sneak into another section's latrines. Should they catch us, there would be trouble. Burning with righteous indignation, they would drag the interloper to the showers and black his testicles with boot-polish. This naturally led to retaliatory raids, which soon got out of hand. We would wait till the other section had retired, then sneak into their room and tip over their bunks. It was done easily with a practised flick of the hand. It was wonderful to see how quickly the bunk would come apart and how helplessly its occupant struggled as he was plunged nose-down on the immaculate floor, all in a matter of seconds. But it was a double-edged weapon. You never knew when your room might be raided. Just as you drifted blissfully off into sleep after an excruciatingly hard day, the door would crash open. You would feel the sudden jolt of your bunk being twisted before you ended up with the iron frame on top of you.

Another job that had to be done was cleaning the dustbin. Every section had one, and each evening it had to be polished with Silvo, inside and out, lid included. It was a long and finicky task. Since it occupied most of the evening, any rubbish accumulated from cleaning the billets and ablutions had to be carried all the way to the kitchen waste-disposal. Our dustbin was purely for show. When Chapman's turn came to clean it, he complained, 'I joined the army for a man's life! They didn't say nothing about dustbins!'

'It's a man's life in the modern dustbin!' Walker said, grinning.

We were always up well before the bugler sounded reveille. We padded along the corridors in our underwear, trying to shake the sleep out of our eyes. Every morning felt like waking up before an important examination. The billets would be full of the smell of warm winter bodies and the sweet scent of Gillette shaving-cream. Then, while Chapman hovered in the corner for the first cigarette of the day, McGowan, Walker and I would be sweeping out our bedspaces and adding the finishing touches to our locker-layouts.

These layouts were the most demanding job of all. Everything in the locker had to be arranged according to a detailed plan issued to each room. The plan showed exactly where each item was to be displayed. It had to be followed to the last fraction of an inch. All our suits – Dennison smocks, combat suits and

'Number Twos', our formal parade dress – had to hang on one side, brushed and facing the same way. The left side was taken up by shelves on which our shorts, shirts, pullovers and long johns were displayed. They had to be arranged in a certain order and folded a specified number of inches. At the back hung our webbing: pouches, poncho, sleeping-bag, bum-roll, packs and braces. Midway down was a small shelf on which our shaving-kit was spread out: shaving-brush, shaving-stick, soap and razor, immaculately clean and laid at six-inch intervals. Spare boots, scintillating with polish, were exhibited below the uniforms, together with black canvas PT shoes, also bulled with polish. On the top shelf was the crowning glory: a pile of shirts and PT vests, scarlet, white and khaki. They had to be folded exactly one inch by twelve and were flanked by spare puttees, neatly brushed, rolled and folded.

The locker had to be like this every morning. The NCOs even brought rulers with them to ensure that the dimensions were exact. At first I despaired of getting it right. How do you fold a shirt exactly one inch by twelve? It was the canny Scot McGowan who solved the problem. 'Put paper in 'em' was his advice. It worked. We cut sheets of crisp paper the right size and stuffed them inside the shirts before ironing. The results were amazing. We learned never to use our spare boots and puttees. We acquired extra shirts and PT vests and a complete set of shaving-equipment so as not to disturb the locker-layout. Like the dustbin, our lockers quickly became largely ceremonial. There was no room for anything personal in them anyway. All civilian clothes had to be stowed away in the stores.

The work didn't end with locker-layouts, though. At the end of the second week, Jekyll introduced us to blanket-boxes. These were made up of sheets and blankets, covers and pillow-cases. They had to be removed from the bed after we got up and folded into rectangles of perfectly matched size. They were arranged attractively: blanket-sheet-blanket-sheet-blanket, all to precisely the same length. A fourth blanket, folded a different way, was lapped around the outside. Pillow, pillow-cases and cover were balanced on top. Getting it right was like solving a Chinese puzzle. Since the blanket-box required at least an hour's work, it meant getting up an hour earlier every morning. I presume it was designed just to increase the pressure. Inventive as always, the recruits took to making up the box at night and sleeping in their sleeping-bags on the bare mattress of their bunks. The staff got wise to this, though. They started sneaking around the billets after lights-out, booking anyone who was in his sleeping-bag.

When everything was as spic and span as it could possibly be, we eased ourselves carefully into our working uniforms. To have spoiled the creases so painstakingly applied the previous evening would have been a disaster. Then we marched across to the mess for breakfast. It was fatal to try to make up time by missing it. Without solid food inside you, you were likely to faint on parade. Anyone who fainted and was found to have missed breakfast was put on a charge. We had to march everywhere in the camp, even if we were alone, swinging our arms to shoulder height. If there were two or more of us together, we had to march in step with someone calling out the time. It was only about a hundred yards from the block to the cookhouse, but all the way you were exposed to the view of instructors quartering the drill-square or lounging about the Naafi windows above the mess.

One morning I was half-way across the no-man's land, when a familiar voice crackled out like electricity. It was Jekyll. 'Get that bloody fag-end from behind your ear!' the corporal stormed. I raised a shaky hand and removed the stub of a Players' No. 6 I'd been saving for my two-minute after-breakfast treat. It wasn't that I'd forgotten it. I'd just imagined that no one would notice. 'Where the hell do you think you are?' he asked me. 'Butlins?'

There was an inspection every morning. Sometimes Jekyll did it, but more often it was done by the company commander or the commanding officer of the Depot. On one occasion we stood apprehensively by our beds, brushing the last specks of fluff from our shoulder-pads, when we heard the determined step of Jekyll's DMS boots along the corridor. Our faces dropped. Jekyll was the worst inspector of all. No matter how good we thought the turnout, he would always find something wrong. Then there would be hell to pay. Not only did he have showclean and Dixieland to play with, he had also devised a whole scheme of devilish little tortures of his own.

The boots paused for a few minutes as he inspected the ablutions. Then the steady tread resumed. A palpable tension spread over us. The shadow of his squat form, almost hunch-backed in the distorting light, fell over the doorframe. 'STAND BY YOUR BEDS!' came the dread order. Then, as he moved into our section of the room, 'ROOM, ROOOOOM 'SHUN!' A smart clap of boots on the polished floor. Out of the corner of my eye I saw Jekyll scowling at McGowan's immaculate turnout, his bedspace, locker and blanket-box. 'You can do better!' he commented. I tried to suppress a shiver. McGowan's kit was by far the best in the room. Jekyll dipped his hands into the Scotsman's locker and came out with an exquisitely cleaned and folded shirt. He crumpled it in his hand and dropped it on to the floor. Sighing, he scooped all the other shirts and shorts out of the same compartment, and for good measure kicked McGowan's gleaming spare boots across the room. He seized the bottom blanket of the blanket-box, moulded and smoothed with such dedicated craftsmanship, and destroyed it with a single flick of the hand. 'That's what you get until it's perfect!' he commented. 'Got it?' The Jock's cheeks were cherry red. He knew that his kit was as near perfect as could be. For a moment I thought he might really lay into the corporal. But instead he answered, 'Yes, corporal', and Jekyll moved happily on to me.

I tried to hold myself still as his gaze gutted my locker-layout. I saw him shake his head gloatingly. He knew he'd got me. 'Number Twos to the right,' he said quietly. 'Dennison smock to the right. But which way is your combat suit facing, Asher? TO THE FUCKING LEFT, YOU PISS-ARSE TUBE!' For a second I almost thought he would hit me. His breathing was heavy, his face red. He was really angry now, I thought. He spun round and dived at my locker like a raging bull. He scattered clothes, boots, puttees and shaving-gear behind him. He took out the heavy combat suit from where it hung and held it up by its wire coathanger. 'Open your mouth!' he ordered. I did so, and in one movement he looped the hook of the coathanger over my gum. I bit down on cold wire. The sharp end of the hook cut deep into my flesh. 'We'll see you don't forget!' Jekyll said. The weight of the thing pulled my head down automatically. 'STAND UP!' he roared.

There was an explosion of laughter from across the room. Walker, directly opposite me, could stand it no longer. His guffaw drew Jekyll's vulture-like stare at once. 'So you think it's funny, do you, Walker?' he asked.

'Yes, corporal.'

'Well, try this for a joke,' Jekyll said, dragging Walker's own combat suit out of his locker. In a second there were two of us, full grown men, with combat suits dangling from our jaws. If it hadn't been so painful, I might have laughed myself.

Jekyll was really enjoying himself now. He stepped over gaily to Chapman's bedspace. He took a long look at Chapman's locker and smiled. 'I don't know how you do it!' he said. 'This must be the worst locker-layout I've ever seen!' Then he launched all his weight against a corner of the locker so that it lurched violently forward. He gave it a playful extra shove. The whole heavy edifice tottered and crashed on to the floor with a resounding bang. Chapman was forced to leap out of the way to prevent himself being crushed. 'DID I SAY MOVE?' Jekyll demanded.

'No, corporal.'

'You're on showclean tonight, Chapman, for that entire bloody locker.'

'But corporal –'

'Shut up, else you'll be on a charge!'

We all knew what that meant. Poor old Chapman would have to trundle his entire locker over to the guardhouse for show-parade. After Jekyll had gone, we removed the wire coat-hangers from our gums and laughed ourselves silly.

Every time Jekyll inspected us, things went like this. Kit was strewn across the floor, lockers went over, boots went out of the window, entire blanket-boxes went out of the window. These antics were accompanied by wild paroxysms of rage which seemed entirely genuine. Once, twice, three times, Chapman had to borrow a hand-cart from the mess to wheel his locker over for showclean. Once, the entire room was put on show-clean, which meant an extra inspection after hours. On another occasion Jekyll discovered a small tin of aerosol shaving-foam in Walker's locker.

'What's this, Walker?' he demanded.

'Foamy, corporal.'

'What does it say on the layout diagram, Walker?'

'Shaving-stick, corporal.'

'Where is your shaving-stick, Walker?'

'Don't use one, corporal. Nobody does. It went out with the ark!'

Jekyll smiled his familiar, truculent smile. He took the can of foam from the locker and began to spray it on Walker's face. He sprayed left and right, up and down, until the can was empty and Walker resembled a melting, green-uniformed version of the Michelin Man. Then Jekyll ordered him to bunny-hop up and down the corridor, shouting, 'I must not put foamy in my locker!'

What amazed me about Jekyll was that he never offered us a crumb of encouragement. There wasn't even a begrudging 'Not bad!' It was as if he wanted to crush and batter any vestige of pride out of us. It was never good enough. Jekyll had joined the army at the age of fifteen. He had spent two years in the Junior Parachute Company, a sort of mixture of army and school, before entering the Depot. It was true that recruit company men gave ex-juniors a hard time. The recruits looked down on them, saying that they had had no experience of real life, and that they had come into the Paras by the 'back door'. Perhaps Jekyll was trying to get his own back on the recruits. He'd been in the army eleven years, all his adult life. The army was his world. He might have afforded a grudging respect to anyone above the rank of corporal who wore the Maroon Machine. Everyone else was a civvie, a craphat or a crow. Crows particularly were non-humans. They were there to waste the army's time and his.

Room inspection was the prelude to the day. Afterwards we would fall in outside for personal inspection, usually by Sergeant Norris or Captain Briggs. We stood in open order, while the inspecting officer assessed our turnout. Anything out of place would be a black mark against you: a slight scuff on the boot, fluff on the pullover, dirty nails or a spot of blood from a shaving-cut. Any such mark went down in a book and might result in showclean that evening. Haircuts were the biggest problem. Your hair had to be tapered smartly, so that it ended at least an inch above your collar. There was no give or take. Those who had overlooked it would get a mate to shave off the excess just before the parade. Unless the mate was an expert hairdresser, this was generally fatal. 'Who cut your hair, soldier?' the inspecting officer would ask.

'A friend, sir.'

'What did he do it with, a fucking clasp-knife?' If the 'friend' was discovered, both you and he might end up on a charge.

Often, when the morning roll was called, you noticed that there were men missing. Some decided that the army wasn't for them and asked to be discharged. Others opted for transfer to a craphat unit, where life might be easier for them. Once a man opted out, he was whisked away from the billets at once to prevent him 'tainting' the others. He was issued with a black beret and sent to work in Dixieland until his papers were completed. If you spotted him across the square or in the mess, you learned to avoid him. To go craphat was beneath contempt. Jekyll pricked the faces from the platoon photo with glee. Occasionally the whole recruit company would parade together, three or four platoons, of which ours was the most junior. It was embarrassing to have to get on parade still calling out 'ONE-tup-three-ONE!' in front of these senior recruits. Naturally, ours was the last platoon to be inspected. This meant a long and agonizing wait for the inspecting officer. The first time it happened, and the inspection had gone off well, Sergeant Norris gave the order, 'In close order, RIGHT DRESS!' Everyone in the front rank had to take a single pace backwards. 'ONE-tup-three-ONE!' the platoon bellowed. Only one person stayed where he

was, a muscular ex-miner called Butcher. As the rest of the
front rank dressed by the right, he keeled slowly over and
crashed headfirst on to the asphalt. He had missed breakfast
that morning.

After a few weeks, though, we were deemed proficient enough
at drill to 'pass off the square'. This meant that we could salute
officers and were smart enough to mount guard. The humili-
ating 'ONE-tup-three-ONE!' was dropped, and from then on we
were allowed to wear our red berets. This was something of a
let-down for me. I had expected the berets to be presented only
at the end of the full twenty-two weeks. Norris explained that
until we attained our wings, the berets were ours only on
approval. We treated our berets with the respect they deserved.
We shrunk them in the bath and wore them wet, moulding
them like clay into the desired shape. We had to wear them
with a white patch behind the badge to show we were still recruits.

After that we were no longer confined to barracks. Although
we had no time for anything but work during the week, at
weekends we could occasionally have an hour or two on the
town. Our elation at being let out soon evaporated when we got
to know Aldershot. 'The arsehole of England' the squaddies
called it, and with good reason. The spirit of aggression brooded
over it like a haunting demon. At night, squads of full-blown
paratroopers would prowl the dingy pubs, drinking themselves
berserk and inevitably getting into a fight. You could hardly sit
and enjoy a pint without someone hurling a beer-mug across
the room. The place would erupt. The floor would clear as if by
magic, revealing several thrashing bodies, flying boots and
flailing fists. We hardly ever knew who was fighting whom.
Often it would overflow into the street, and bodies might be
hurled through shop windows or spread-eagled over the bonnets
of cars. Then a Redcap patrol might arrive. The riotous squaddies would leave off fighting each other and attack the Redcaps.
Who would have been a military policeman in Aldershot? It
was the most violent place in Britain.

\*

The runs and battle marches got longer and tougher. The PT got more demanding, the staff more critical and more savage in their punishments. Twice round the assault course in the first week had seemed an almost superhuman task. Now we were doing it twelve times without a break. A three-mile run in helmets and denims had been exhausting. Now we were 'bashing' ten miles in full equipment with rifles and ammunition. We were working from six in the morning till ten at night and we went to sleep shattered. Yet lights-out wasn't always the end of the day.

Once, I was woken from a deep, dark sleep by a shout of 'STAND BY YOUR BEDS, YOU FUCKERS!' I clawed myself desperately awake. What had gone wrong? Why hadn't we woken up for breakfast? Then I noticed my watch. It was only two a.m. Jekyll pounded into the room in full working uniform. 'GET UP!' he screamed. 'WHAT THE HELL ARE YOU DOING IN BED AT THIS TIME? STAND BY YOUR BEDS!' We dragged ourselves sheepishly from the warm sheets. The floor was icy cold, I remember. Walker's movements were as slow as a diver's, and his eyes were still half closed. McGowan's cheeks were bright red, a sure sign that he was fuming inside. Chapman clambered out with a look of total bewilderment. 'STAND STILL!' the corporal ordered. Then he marched out and left us there. I was dying to get back into the inviting warmth of my bunk, but I dared not move. Walker's broad face twisted and expanded into a rubbery yawn. I felt my own facial muscles contracting of their own accord. Soon we were all yawning. Five minutes passed. Then ten. We were too terrified to move or speak. Soon we had been standing for twenty minutes. Was this some special test no one had told us about? We were on the verge of collapse, when we heard the crunch of boots along the corridor. A second later Jekyll's face peered at us from the doorway. 'WHAT THE HELL ARE YOU DOING OUT OF BED AT THIS TIME?' he raged incredulously. 'IT'S TWO THIRTY IN THE MORNING! GET BACK INTO YOUR BEDS, YOU MORONS!' Nobody argued. We climbed back in wearily and instantly fell asleep.

That morning Jekyll inspected us as usual, and Chapman received his fourth showclean. 'Not putting enough hours in, Chapman!' Jekyll commented wryly. The brawny Scouse went off sadly that evening to borrow the kitchen hand-cart. It was Friday, and we had a 48-hour pass. My old school chum Geoffrey Deacon had invited me to visit him a few miles away at Sandhurst. He showed me into his spacious room in Old College. His immaculate blue Number Ones hung in plastic in his locker, with his polished sword and peaked cap. He told me that a servant made his bed and bulled his boots in the evening. Cadets were sworn at only on the drill-square, and then the instructors had to call them 'sir'. He and his colleagues seemed preoccupied with clothes. They had to possess two Saville Row suits, and weren't allowed out unless they were wearing one of them. They were not allowed to use public transport or to hitch-hike. They were forbidden to carry anything heavier than a rolled umbrella and a briefcase. All these rules seemed ludicrous to me, but they held a certain fascination. Naturally, I was envious of Deacon's status, although not jealous. I had always admired him, and knew he deserved to be there. I ate with him in the cadets' mess that evening. You had to collect your food from the bar, but thereafter servants came round with the vegetables.

'How's it going?' Deacon asked me.

'Fucking awful,' I said. 'There's this bastard of an instructor who's got it in for me!' I paused suddenly and realized that Deacon was looking around in embarrassment. Several cadets had stopped eating and were staring my way.

'Er, one doesn't usually swear in the mess,' Deacon explained.

Later, in the pub, I told one of the cadets that I hoped to be coming to Sandhurst the following year. 'As an instructor?' he asked me.

'No, as an officer-cadet!' I said, incensed. He regarded me with evident disbelief.

'You've become just like a squaddie,' Deacon told me before I left.

'I *am* a squaddie,' I replied.

Actually, from what I'd seen of these officer-cadets, my companions in the Depot were tougher, more aggressive and more mature. After all, we were an elite. They might have been officers, but they were still craphats.

On Monday, Chapman was missing. His bed hadn't been slept in, and his clothes and suitcase were gone out of the store. Even his carving-knife was missing. 'He said he was going home to the Dingle for the weekend,' Walker said. 'I bet he met his mates and decided not to come back!'

'It's an AWOL job,' Jekyll commented brightly. 'We'll set the Redcaps on him. Who's going to be next? You, Asher?'

'Not me, corporal!'

'We'll see about that!' he said. He seemed quite pleased with himself.

It was a sharp morning in November. There was ice on the parade-ground when we turned out in full kit with helmets and PT vests. We had to stand for what seemed like hours in the biting wind. We slowly turned blue as the cold penetrated to the bone. Jekyll inspected our kit with deliberate slowness. He checked the weight of my water-bottle and a thoughtful expression came over his face. He took the canteen from its pouch and unscrewed the top.

'Your orders are to fill your water-bottle, Asher!' he said.

'But corporal,' I protested, 'it's full!'

He held the neck of the canteen down so that I could see it. It was filled to within half a centimetre of the rim. The rest had probably run out while I was screwing the cap on, I thought. 'That's not full!' Jekyll sneered. 'Full means to the top!' He held the bottle up for everyone to see, like a priest blessing the chalice. Then he tipped it with measured care down my neck. The water was literally freezing. It touched my already chilled skin like a tongue of cold flame. I shivered involuntarily and caught my breath. I knew better than to move. The corporal emptied the bottle and thrust it into my quaking hand. 'Go and fill it!' he ordered me. 'Full, this time!' No sooner had I filled it and rushed back to the ranks, than Sergeant Norris came thundering out of the billets like a madman. He picked up a

fistful of gravel from the ground and hurled it ferociously at the
front rank. We ducked and dodged out of the way, but an egg-
shaped nodule of quartz slapped me squarely on the cheek.
'STAND STILL!' Norris shouted. 'WHO TOLD YOU TO MOVE?'
Everyone who had moved got twenty press-ups. But we were so
cold that we considered ourselves lucky.

That morning there was a ten-mile 'bash'. It was the most
dreaded thing on our programme, a cross between a march and
a run in full equipment, with rifles. The ten miles had to be
completed in under ninety minutes, which was an incredible
speed for a man carrying more than fifty pounds. Moreover, we
were supposed to keep together in ranks of three, so that in
theory we would all arrive at the battle at the same time. You
marched uphill at a buzzing pace and doubled downhill or on
the flat. The instructors ran behind us with their pick-helves,
beasting and cursing anyone who fell out until they caught up.
Sometimes I wondered if this was why they called it a 'bash'.

I kept going well for the first five miles. Then I fell a little
behind. The moment I was out of the ranks, Jekyll caught me
and jumped on my back. He hung there like an evil incubus,
prodding me with his pick-helve and shouting, 'Come on, you
useless git! You're not good enough for Sandhurst, and you're
not good enough for the Paras! I said I'd break you and I will!'
He clung to my back, kicking and prodding, until I caught
up with the squad. On and on we went, as the landscape
of Hampshire passed by, chanting, 'AIRBORNE-EASY!
AIRBORNE-EASY!', until it seemed impossible to go on. The
pain in my legs and lungs and back seemed to press down on
me. There came a point when my body felt like it was about to
burst. Then the will came into play. You had to force yourself
beyond the barrier of pain and into your second wind. The pain
was still there, but it was numb and distant, your body carrying
on robot-like on its own. You no longer noticed the swinging
pick-helves or the raging voices of the instructors. It was all a
joke, it was all a dream, it was all a breeze blowing across the
unfathomed world. 'AIRBORNE-EASY! AIRBORNE-EASY!'
The words lost their shape and meaning and became something

else, a sound heard in a waking trance. It filled your mind, and you could imagine nothing else but this constant pace. There was no beginning to it and no end. You had to plunge through that pain barrier: you had to reach a point where natural fitness and strength counted for nothing. It was the realm of pure will, the realm of pure determination. And that was what made a Para.

My performance began to improve steadily. Little Jock McGowan's declined. He got further behind in the 'bashes' and runs, and even his turnout began to suffer. Once, when Jekyll was feeling even more zealous than usual, he opened McGowan's army-issue suitcase. It was supposed to stand empty on top of the locker. Inside he found two civilian shirts. 'What's this?' he demanded. 'Isn't this suitcase supposed to be empty?' He screwed the shirts up like paper and drop-kicked them across the billet. 'Civvies in the store, McGowan, REMEMBER?' he said.

I closed my eyes for a second, tempted to warn Jekyll how close he was to being thrown through a plate-glass window. McGowan clenched his small fists tight and said nothing.

A few days later we were running across the 'tank tracks'. It was a wide area of scrubland punctuated with stinking marshes and deep ruts made by tanks, which quickly filled with oily ooze. We reached the half-way point, a plateau where we generally waited for stragglers to catch up. One of the stragglers was McGowan. I saw him panting up on his short legs with Jekyll hot-foot after him. He whacked the Scotsman across the rump. Normally, Jock would have spurted towards the ranks. This time, I saw him stop dead in his tracks. I saw the look of astonishment on Jekyll's face.

'Fuck off!' McGowan spat at him.

Jekyll halted as if he'd been punched. '*What* did you say?' he demanded.

'Fuckin' bastard!' McGowan said slowly. In one incredibly fast movement he flung himself on Jekyll's neck. 'I'LL KILL YE! I'LL KILL YE!' he screamed. So unthinkable was it that a recruit should attack an instructor that none of us moved. Then Sergeant Norris sprinted up from the front with two big PTIs. They pulled Jock off, still wriggling and shouting. His face was as red as a cherry.

In a second, Jekyll was his old truculent self again. 'That's you finished in this regiment, McGowan!' he said. 'You've cracked!'

McGowan was marched back to the Depot in the custody of two PTIs. By the time we got back, his bedspace had been cleared. We never saw him again.

We were down to five now. A new look of triumph seemed to dominate Jekyll's features. He increased the pressure deliberately as the end of basic training approached. He challenged us to crack. Any torture his twisted mind could devise was 'all part of the training'. It was all part of the training to beast us with pick-helves on the battle marches. It was all part of the training to pour freezing water down our necks. It was all part of the training to pelt us with stones while we tried to stand at attention. It was all part of the training to turf us out of bed in the middle of the night. The staff swore, prodded and goaded us into defying them. But the moment you defied them you were finished. One morning we were on the drill-square as usual, ordering arms, shouldering arms and marching left and right. My mind was in neutral. I disliked drill. It seemed a boring waste of time.

'SQUAAAAD, HALT!' came Jekyll's order. It took me by surprise and I overbalanced, piling into the recruit in front of me. I heard the corporal's quick footsteps approaching from behind. They stopped suddenly. Without warning, he gave me a powerful, smashing blow in my kidneys. I tried to stop myself doubling up in pain.

'STAND UP!' Jekyll roared. 'If you EVER do that again, you'll end up in the pokey! Do you understand, Asher?'

I didn't answer. I was fed up with this bullying. No one had the right to hit me from behind, I thought. My fists bunched automatically. My muscles tensed. HIT HIM! something was telling me. BASH HIM!

Jekyll noticed my silence. He stepped around to face me, his furious eyes burning with challenge, threatening, dominating. I

looked at his eyes and saw a trap there waiting to shut. I
imagined for a second his flickering smile. 'That's you finished
in this regiment, Asher.' I fought back the anger and indignation. I forced my muscles to relax and unclenched my fists.
Willpower, the control of the instincts: that was what this
training was about.

'Do you UNDERSTAND?' Jekyll repeated.

'Yes, corporal,' I said.

The soldiers near me sighed audibly as the tension eased. I
hadn't lost the battle, I told myself. I had won.

The last week of basic training took place at the Parachute
Regiment battle school at Brecon in South Wales. It was an old-
style army camp of Nissen huts and red brick buildings. We
slept in double bunks in several communal rooms with pot-
bellied stoves. There were no locker-layouts or blanket-boxes at
Brecon. Instead, we lived under battle discipline. We no longer
marched from place to place, we ran. Our punishments were
field punishments: bunny-hopping around the square with a
machine-gun held on our shoulders; jogging twenty times round
the camp in full kit; leaning against the wall in Jekyll's 'Torture
Position Number One'; singing 'Ba Ba Blacksheep' as we crawled
a hundred yards through snow or nettles; advancing in review
order over a cliff and into a freezing lake.

At Brecon we learned to operate in harsh conditions; to hike
for miles over the hills in blizzards; to sleep out in snow and
slush; to navigate in fog and mist. We learned to lay ambushes
and to execute section attacks; to lay on the freezing ground all
night to attack an enemy patrol; to skirmish forward using the
'buddy-buddy system' to cover each other in pairs until the
objectives were achieved.

At the end of the long week at the battle school, every
surviving member of the platoon was to be assessed. Some
would be kicked out, others back-squadded. Those who achieved
a grade C or above would go on to advanced training. Assessment was our first big obstacle. During the last couple of days,
the instructors walked about with smirks on their faces. Jekyll's
was as big as a Cheshire cat's.

'If you get back-squadded, you'll have to do it all again,' he told me.

Yes, I thought privately. But at least I won't have to do it with you! On the appointed day I waited outside the platoon office with the others. On the surface I remained calm, but underneath I was terrified. The thought of enduring those terrible weeks again was too much to bear. Of the original section of eight, only five of us remained: Walker, the Welshman Taffy Williams, Clark, the 'Oldham Stud', ex-farm labourer Smith and myself. Smart had been injured in the first week, Chapman had gone AWOL, and McGowan had cracked. In addition, Walker and myself had good reasons to be apprehensive about the result.

During our week at Brecon, many items of kit had gone missing. The effect snowballed, because if someone 'borrowed' your water-bottle, for example, you would be obliged to 'find' another before the next parade. To be 'diffy' in kit was a misdemeanor, punishable by a fine and a great deal of acrimony. One evening Walker was busy pressing his shirt, when a recruit from another section came in. He was a squat, powerful man called Geordie Harris.

'Hey, have any of you wankers nicked my PT shoes?' he demanded. 'I bet they're here somewhere.'

Walker looked up from his ironing and grinned. 'Tha daft apeth!' he commented. 'Who is there here that's got great clod 'oppin feet like thee?' Harris's feet were at least size eleven. There was no one in our section with feet larger than size nine.

But Geordie was spoiling for a fight. 'Watch your lip, son!' he said.

'Get lost!' Walker said.

This was too much for Harris. The mocking Yorkshire humour infuriated him. He marched upon Walker threateningly. He snatched the hot iron out of his hand. Before anyone could stop him, he punched it hard into Walker's bare chest. The Yorkshireman groaned and sat down heavily. A livid orange mark in the shape of an iron now decorated his chest. Harris retreated hastily as I ran over to Walker.

'Geordie bastard!' he moaned. 'Now what the hell am I going to do? It's assessment in two days!' The burn looked raw and painful.

'I'll take you to the medic,' I said.

'No!' he exclaimed. 'That'll be the end. If they think I'm injured, they'll back-squad me!'

Later, he sent me to get some cream from the Naafi shop. But by morning the wound was worse. When the time came for Walker to put on his pack, Jekyll noticed him wincing. 'What's up with you, Walker?' he inquired.

Reluctantly Walker showed him the wound, now smouldering bright orange between his pectoral muscles.

'That looks to me like a self-inflicted wound,' Jekyll said. 'Some people will do anything to get out of a battle march! It's a serious charge, Walker!'

The Yorkshireman had been *hors de combat* for two days, and awaited assessment results with trepidation.

My own nervousness equalled Walker's. The previous night we had been allowed into Brecon for a platoon 'knees-up' at a local pub called the Cwm Inn. We had all got happily drunk, cavorted around the dance-floor and propositioned every girl in sight. I had arrived back at the guardhouse to find my ID card missing. The guard corporal had been sympathetic. 'But it's got to be reported,' he said. It was a grave offence, and if Captain Briggs found out about it, I would certainly be in trouble.


We waited nervously outside the office. The results were not announced in alphabetical order, so no one knew exactly when he would be called. The 'Oldham Stud' went in with a wink. 'B plus at least for me!' he said. He came out five minutes later with a scowl. They had given him a D. Williams marched in next and emerged with a C. Then it was Smith's turn. The mask of misery on his face as he stepped out told its own story. 'They back-squadded me,' he complained. 'They said my effort wasn't good enough!' I shivered inside. God only knew what would happen if they had found out about the ID card! Walker straightened his beret and sallied forth, ready for the worst. 'If they back-squad me, I'll not give up,' he declared. A minute passed. A murmur of voices filtered through the door. I heard Walker saying, 'No, sir. No, sir.' More time ticked by. It seemed that he'd been in there for an age. Suddenly the door flew open, and Walker marched out, beaming. 'They said I was a good soldier,' he reported. 'I got a B! Asher next!'

I marched into the little office. There was nothing inside but a desk. Behind it sat Captain Briggs, Sergeant Norris and Corporal Jekyll. I halted smartly and saluted. The captain returned my salute.

'You're a potential officer, Asher,' he said. I saw Jekyll sneer. 'The standard we expect of you is high. You made rather a poor beginning. Fitness, discipline, schoolwork, all bad!' My heart almost skipped a beat. They were going to throw me out. They knew about the missing ID card. 'There are some people who don't think you'll make it,' he said. 'But looking at your performance, there's been a marked improvement from the first week. We know it takes some people a little time to settle in. But there is one big black mark against you.'

Now he would bring up the ID card.

'Turnout,' he said. 'You look like a sack of shit tied in the middle. Buck up your ideas, soldier!'

'Very good, sir,' I said.

I saluted, and was about to march out, when Briggs called me back. 'Don't you want to know what grade you got?' he asked. 'C plus. That's average.'

'Thank you, sir,' I said. As I marched out smiling, I heard Jekyll say, 'There's still Advanced Brecon and P Company to go.'

I was marching back to my own billet, when a young corporal called me. It was the guard corporal from the previous night. 'Aren't you Asher?' he inquired.

'Yes, corporal.'

He thrust a small oblong of plastic into my palm. It was my ID card. The corporal tapped his nose with a long forefinger.

'You're in luck,' he said. 'The landlord of the Cwm Inn handed it back before I made the report. You won't be so lucky next time!'

# 3

## *First Blood*

———

We had been lying on the freezing ground all night, it seemed, and the cold had stabbed like a blade into every part of my body. I had never been so cold. The cold was an affliction, a paralysing sickness from which I would never recover. My feet were burning with cold, and the gloveless hands which clamped my rifle were numb with pain. I was lying under a pile of leaves and branches, invisible from almost every angle. I had been there for hours and I prayed that any minute the enemy would come into view and allow me to move. It was almost dawn. The first gold swell of the sun was spreading over the hills and through the valley. It gilded the ferns and the broom and filled our killing zone with the scent of caramel.

I sensed a movement to my left. A patrol was approaching: four men in camouflage smocks. The lead scout carried a double-barrelled shotgun for snap-shooting. He was moving cautiously, looking left and right and listening. I hardly dared breathe. The man was in my sights now. My finger was already taking the first pressure. He was inside the killing zone. His foot brushed the trip-wire. 'SHOOOOOSH!' went the flare. The dim yellow light was thickened suddenly by scarlet. The machine-gun on my right opened up with crisp double-taps. At the same moment I shot the lead scout. The man dropped into the gorse. 'Whang! Whang! Whang!' The bundles of camouflage around me came alive with fire and smoke. The rest of the enemy patrol was hit. Another flare went up, an orange one. 'CEASE FIRE!' Jekyll's voice rang out.

The corporal appeared inside the killing zone with his fat-cat face and his mirthless grin. He looked warm and rested. He didn't look as if he'd been lying on cold earth most of the night. He called us forward to inspect the 'bodies' of the demo platoon, still playing possum in the gorse. As I got up, my joints cracked like balsa-wood. The movement sent a new current of blood through my veins. Suddenly my teeth began to chatter. Jekyll watched as I clumsily dragged the supine body out of the undergrowth with hands too numb for sensation. He ran up beside me.

'Not that way!' he said. 'Like this!' And he lay down on the hard ground parallel with the 'corpse'. He rolled it over on top of him with a single arm. 'Bodies have booby-traps under them,' he said. 'And you've just had your balls blown off!'

We were back at the battle school in Brecon for our advanced infantry training. We hardly ever slept in the billets. Mostly we pitched our bashas in a foot of snow and shivered half the night on stag. It was so cold that the gun-metal burned your skin. We had climbed Pen-y-fan and Fan Fawr, navigating in cotton-wool fog and gale-force winds which tried to lash us off the mountain ledges. We moved in patrol formation for miles through the hills, ready to strike and run and merge back into the red, green, grey landscape like wild creatures. And always the cold was there, the accursed, heart-stopping, blood-chilling, hypothermic cold which seeped like poison into every basha, every trench, every sleeping-bag. The Brecon Beacons had been chosen especially for their savage climate.

The Beacons were particularly freezing that January. We were ordered once to dig shell-scrapes in ground that was frozen as solid as rock. The task seemed impossible, yet we had to stick at it. We scraped the frozen soil back for hours with pick and shovel in the glacial wind. We were never allowed to wear gloves or extra clothing, and our hands and feet turned blue and numb. We were not allowed to light fires or even brew tea on our Hexy stoves until the shell-scrape was dug. The time passed, the trench got a little deeper. Jekyll appeared wearing a heavy-duty parka with mittens, but still he looked pinched with cold. He shuffled about, stamping his feet and jumping up and down to keep warm. 'Come on!' he stormed. 'Get on with it! Imagine there's a nuke on the way! You've got three minutes to get your head under. ZAP! *Tuvska shitski!*'

The cold gave you a burning, nauseous feeling. It dulled your brain, so that no matter how frantically you worked to keep warm, the effort was ineffectual. Jekyll got fed up and wandered off to find a cup of tea. We worked on with desultory enthusiasm. I felt light-headed and occasionally chuckled to myself. Suddenly Taff Williams hurled his pick-axe down, narrowly missing my feet.

'It's a lot of shit!' he gasped. 'This is all a lot of shit!' His face was bluish white and drawn with cold.

'Aye, tha's reet!' Walker agreed grimly. 'But tha' knows what they say: "It's all part of the training!" '

Williams didn't appear to be listening. He mumbled incoherently to himself and staggered away across the bald hillside, grumbling.

'Hey! Where's tha off to?' Walker called after him. As we watched, he began to lurch unsteadily from side to side, muttering and guffawing like a drunk.

'God!' said Walker suddenly. 'He's got exposure!'

Williams sat down heavily on the ground, still burbling. Walker, Carson and I ran to pick him up. He waved us away with a furious gesture. 'Fuck off!' he slurred. 'Fuck off, you wankers! I'm all right. Jus' need a li'l sleep, that's all!'

I remembered our lecture on exposure: 'Victim may display physical resistance to succour and use violent language.' This was exposure all right.

'Get him in his sleeping-bag!' said Walker. Williams's face was now ghastly white, and his skin was as cold as marble. 'Get a brew on as well!' Walker said.

'That's against orders!' Carson objected.

'Bugger orders!' Walker insisted. 'This bloke is dying of exposure!'

I took the Hexy stove out and built a shelter of boulders around it to keep off the cutting wind. Carson and Walker unrolled a sleeping-bag and fed Williams into it slowly. Soon the tart, chemical smoke of Hexamine wafted across the hill. The other two dragged Williams's inert form into the shelter of some rocks. Within a few moments Jekyll appeared in his thick parka.

'I smell Hexy!' he said. 'Did anyone tell you to light a stove, Asher?'

I pointed at the others. 'Williams has gone down with exposure, corporal,' I explained.

Jekyll sniffed incredulously. He mooched calmly up to the others and examined Williams's face. Then he felt his pulse. 'Anything to get out of digging a shell-scrape, eh, Williams!' he said. But you could tell that he knew it was serious. 'We'll call an ambulance,' he said. 'And then I'll deal with you, Asher, for lighting a stove against orders.'

Williams was still rambling incoherently when we hoisted him into the back of the Land Rover ambulance. They carried him back to the battle school, where they dunked him in a hot bath and gave him a hearty meal. Within two days he was back on his feet again. Williams's attack was good for our morale, though, because Jekyll decided to go off with the ambulance. As soon as it disappeared, we sat down and shared a brew of hot tea.

But Jekyll had not forgotten my punishment. After a withering night in the trenches, eventually blasted open with explosives, we stood-to at dawn. Half an hour later we filled in the shell-scrapes that had caused us so much anguish and moved out. We moved down the track in open formation, packs on and rifles at the ready. During the morning Jekyll halted us by a stream. It flowed down from the high peaks through a deep cleft in the valley. The water was fast-moving, crystal-clear melt-water, with a thin crust of ice like a rind in places on top. We had stopped for a brew, but before I could get my stove going, Jekyll called me over.

'Now Asher is going to demonstrate how to crawl through a mountain stream, aren't you, Asher?'

'Am I, corporal?'

'Yes. Now get into that water. I want to see you crawl upstream, and I *mean* crawl!'

I saw that there was no escape. I removed my head-gear and smock and felt the icy claws of the wind grip my body. I walked down to the edge of the stream and stood there looking at the clear, icy water like a high-diver.

'Get in, or I'll get you in!' Jekyll threatened.

It took all the nerve and willpower I'd developed in four months to get into that water. I forced my legs forward and jumped. There was a sudden, numbing shock, a sledge-hammer blow of cold. After that there was nothing. I tensed my muscles and reached down to the cold stream-bed, grappling myself along with an insect-like grip. After a moment I thought I would faint. Then something inside me said, that bastard won't finish me, and I dragged myself on, inch by inch, yard by freezing yard. I had crawled ten yards before the corporal called me back. I clambered out, and as the wind's tentacles touched me I began to feel *really* cold. I shivered uncontrollably and my teeth chattered. Without being asked, Walker brought me a towel and a steaming mug of tea.

I felt the effects of my immersion in the afternoon. We were moving out of the hills into sub-zero winds. I felt light-headed and dizzy. There were twitching cramps in my muscles. I no longer seemed to be able to march straight. My hands and feet were throbbing with cold. I began to mutter to myself and then to giggle, as pictures of me crawling through the stream arranged themselves stodgily in my brain. I staggered on further and my light-headedness turned to misery. 'All I wanted to be was a Para!' I kept saying, in a fit of self-pity.

'What's up with you?' asked a recruit called Bradley, a new addition to the section. He saw me staggering and grasped my arm. 'Keep going!' he told me. 'There's only one more klick to go!' He generously fed me his Mars Bar and goaded me along for that last long kilometre. I tottered along muttering, 'Airborne-easy! Airborne-easy!' until we came to the disused cottage we were supposed to occupy. Once we had moved inside, I climbed into my sleeping-bag, and Walker gave me tea.

'You're lucky!' Bradley told me. 'This is only a mild dose!' Ten men had been casevac'd with hypothermia, and six were already in the medical centre with frostbite. It was the worst weather for years in the Beacons. With unprecedented indulgence the authorities pulled the whole platoon back to base. Jekyll wasn't pleased about it. 'They should be kept out in all conditions!' he was heard to say. Still, he didn't look too miserable when the four-tonne trucks came to pick us up. I felt weak and exhausted when I got back to camp, but I knew that the sudden change of plan had saved me. I refused to report to the medical centre, knowing that to miss some of this vital training might mean back-squadding. But my real motivation was deeper and more primitive. I simply was not going to let Jekyll beat me.

Bradley was a hefty man with a chubby face. You could tell at once that he didn't belong with the rest of us. He had appeared on parade mysteriously one day, wearing a beige-coloured beret and a blue stable-belt. The beret bore a winged-dagger badge with the words WHO DARES WINS embroidered beneath.

'Which battalion of the SAS do you belong to?' Captain Briggs had asked him.

'22,' Bradley answered.

The captain's face dropped in surprise. 'The regular battalion! What are you doing here, then?'

'You tell me, sir,' came the reply. To the rest of us it had sounded like a conversation between giants. Briggs was as high above us as the sun, but this upstart private with the dirt-coloured beret spoke to him as an equal.

Bradley was posted to my section. He was obliged to change his beige beret for a maroon-red one, which, much to my surprise, he seemed reluctant to do. I wondered what it could be, this mysterious and aloof SAS unit, that its privates could talk like officers and could scoff at the Maroon Machine. Bradley told me that SAS meant the Special Air Service Regiment. It was a unit trained in clandestine guerrilla operations and counter-insurgency. Normally you had to serve for three years in another army unit before being accepted for the selection course. This was 1972. It wasn't until eight years later that the whole world saw the SAS storming the Iranian Embassy in London,

and the regiment rose to instant stardom. In 1972 few people
outside the army had ever heard of them.

Bradley was an unusual recruit even for the SAS. He had a
degree from a red brick university. While an undergraduate he
had not only been a rugby blue, but had also served in one of
the little-publicized regional SAS reserve units, 23 SAS. Serving
with one of these Territorial SAS units was the only direct route
into the regular SAS from civvy-street. All SAS men had to
have a parent unit in the regular army. Having come in from
the TA, Bradley didn't have one. He was 'given' the Paras, and
sent to train with a recruit platoon to sharpen up his infantry
skills. 'The SAS is a different army,' he told me. 'It's all self-
discipline. No shouting, no bull. No one pulls rank, and everyone
in the regiment is expected to express his opinion. If you don't
like what an officer has to say, you tell him so.' I understood
why Bradley resented having to serve with us Paras. His was a
lofty, elevated world which I felt I could never aspire to. At that
moment I was going all out just to become a Para. I had never
guessed that there was a regiment as far above us as we
thought ourselves above the craphats.

Bradley was careful to preserve the mystique and the reputation of his regiment. Occasionally the ends he went to were
ludicrous, I thought. Once, he and I were in an observation-post
in the hills with the general-purpose machine-gun. After a
couple of hours, Bradley developed severe stomach cramps. He
was reluctant to leave his post on the gun to relieve himself.
'It's OK,' I told him. 'I'll man the OP, while you go for a crap!'
He considered it for a moment, then resolutely dropped his
trousers in front of me. 'An SAS soldier never leaves his post!'
he said.

The first solid date I remember from my military career is 30
January 1972. On that day the mists of time suddenly clear and
I find myself on a trajectory bound for the mainstream of
history. In the evening we sat around Walker's transistor radio
and listened to the news. The main item concerned events in

Ulster. The first battalion of our regiment had been drafted into Londonderry to help contain an illegal demonstration. The crowd's advance had been blocked by troops. The peaceful demonstrators had retreated, leaving a hard-core of stone-throwers and hooligans. What happened next is a matter of dispute. 'I know in my heart of hearts that we were fired on first,' one corporal said. Whatever the case, the Paras fired with gusto. At the end of half an hour thirteen civilians lay dead and sixteen had been wounded. None of the dead or wounded was found to be a member of the IRA, and none of them was armed.

The Paras had been chosen for the job because of their toughness and aggression. It was this reputation that mattered to us. We were proud of them. Morale was high as a kite. Few of us knew anything about the situation in Ulster. It never even occurred to us that there was a moral issue. It occurred to us still less that opening fire was bad tactics. We had had no preparation for the propaganda. We did not know or care that this action would bring about the downfall of the Stormont Parliament and turn world opinion staunchly against the British. We didn't know that it gave the advantage to the IRA. We were not trained or schooled in subtlety. The Paras had taken out the enemy. They had won the firefight. If there were no weapons found on the dead, they must have been removed. If there were no known IRA men amongst the dead and injured, then the bodies must have been removed. None of us identified with the suffering of the victims or their families. *They* were different. *They* deserved it. They were like the cardboard figure elevens we shot at on the ranges. Like most of my colleagues, I felt no animosity towards the Catholics of Northern Ireland. What was significant was that the victims of Bloody Sunday were against us. They were but one guise of the enemy that wore a thousand faces. When the news of Bloody Sunday came through, I am ashamed to say we cheered.

There was one member of my section who didn't share our aloofness. He was Carson, a back-squad from a senior platoon. Carson was a skinny, eager man from a place called Sandy Row in Belfast. He had been one of the notorious B-specials until their disbandment in 1970. The 'Bs' were police reservists, staunchly Protestant, well armed and intensely conservative. Their main function was to smother Republican activity. They had done this on more than one occasion by standing back and letting armed Orange thugs beat seven bells out of the Catholics. Their partisan nature had led to their downfall. Later they had been replaced by the supposedly less sectarian Ulster Defence Regiment, the UDR. 'They should never have got rid of the Spashuls,' Carson said. 'If there was anyone that knew the Taigs, it was them. The Taigs were shit scared of the Spashuls. The only good Taig is a scared one, so it is!'

Carson had joined the Paras because of the regiment's tough reputation. He was pleased as punch about Bloody Sunday. He hoped we would soon be sent over there to shoot some more. 'I wanted to serve with a hard unit,' he said. 'So I'd get the chance to give the Taigs what they deserve.'

'Do you think they'll send us to Northern Ireland?'

'You can bet on it, boy. There's trouble brewing, so there is. The whole British army will be there before long!'

I disliked Carson for his hatred of the 'Taigs'. There were plenty of 'Taigs' in the platoon, and you couldn't find more friendly and pleasant people. It wasn't for us to take sides, I reasoned. Next we might be sent against the Protestants. We weren't political. We would kill people irrespective of race, colour or creed.


During the day we kept warm learning 'debussing' drills and anti-ambush, to paddle assault-boats and to launch attacks from helicopters. We learned signals procedure with radios and field-telephones. We were allowed not a moment's respite. At meal-times we fed in the field. The NCOs would devise interesting little diversions to liven up the lunch-hour. This might include not allowing us to eat till we had pushed our mess-tins with our noses for a hundred yards through nettles or till we had bunny-hopped through a freezing stream. They might make us roll in a snow-drift or climb a pine tree and pelt stones at us. More than once they urinated on us while we stood in trenches, trying to hold our rifles still with hands shivering with cold. Once, Jekyll sat us all in the snow and ordered us each to tell him a joke. Anyone whose joke failed to make him laugh had to crawl through a snow-drift. That was the real joke, he said.

An important part of advanced training was the 'live firing attack'. Before moving to Brecon for the second time, we had been through three weeks intensive firearms training at Folkestone. We had become expert in all platoon weapons: SLR, Sterling sub-machine-gun, pistol, GPMG, mortar, rocket-launchers and grenades. Here in Brecon we had to learn to use live bullets in action, rather than just on the ranges. To simulate a real battle, the staff would fire bullets over our heads and around our feet. It was a part of the training that everyone looked forward to with apprehension.

At eight a.m. we were ordered into the attack. Our objective was a cottage that lay on the floor of the valley. Bradley and I were the GPMG group and went left-flanking. We set up the machine-gun at the hoof of a blackthorn bush and laid down a good pulse of supporting fire.

The section moved down the gorse-covered hillside, yelling to each other as they skirmished forward. They worked in pairs, one giving covering fire while his 'buddy' danced and zigzagged. He dropped and rolled and crawled into position, so that he could cover his mate. Bullets whanged out and whizzed across the valley. The tracers from the GPMG cut an orange pattern across the crisp mountain air. I breathed in the cordite and the caramel scent of the gorse. As I loosed off a couple of rounds in support of the gun, I noticed the advancing men getting dangerously near to the arc of fire. 'Switch right!' I urged Bradley, and he moved the gun barrel a few degrees away from the advancing men. 'Boom! boom! boom!'

Then the whistle trilled.

The skirmishing section froze. The guns went silent. 'CEASE FIRE!' came the order from the rear. Already I could see Jekyll, Norris and Captain Briggs rushing headlong down the hillside. On the floor of the valley a camouflaged figure lay writhing in agony. With a shock I realized that it was Dave Walker.

I looked round in the confusion for some clue to what had happened. Dave Walker had been shot, that was obvious. But by whom? My first horrific thought was that my own rounds had hit him. I realized how near the advancing section had been to our arc of fire. We unloaded and moved into the valley. The medics had already arrived with the stretcher and were lifting Walker's body carefully on to it. With relief I noticed he was still talking. As the medics fought to move the stretcher up the treacherous concave slope, Jekyll ran forward to help them. 'You were supposed to be on guard-duty tonight, Walker!' he told the prostrate figure. 'Some people will do anything to get out of a guard-duty!' Just before the doors of the ambulance closed on Walker, Jekyll asked him, 'Who's going to do your guard-duty tonight?'

'Asher!' the Yorkshireman replied weakly. Then the two halves of the great red cross bisected by the crack in the doors came together with a crash.

In the battle school guard-house that night I huddled close to the pot-bellied stove, thinking about Walker. I remembered the grin and the big, calloused hand offered to me on the first day in the Depot, strangers in a strange land, the first friendly face I had seen. We had stood at that window, looking over the distant horizons of our young lives. 'I'm going to get them little blue wings if it kills me!' Walker had said. How bad could the wound be? Would it mean back-squadding? How would he cope with that? Staunchly as ever, I supposed. He was tough as old boots, Dave Walker. How bravely he'd borne the pain of the steam-iron. At least, I thought, he'd still been cheerful, kicking and conscious when they'd put him in the ambulance. The wound couldn't have been as bad as all that, could it? I thought of Gurung. I thought of those moon-shaped eyes. 'If you hit a man with this, it'll blow his head clean off!' Thirteen bodies on the streets of Derry. A chill went through me. The fire died and the stove lost its warmth. An icy wind lifted like a wave over the Beacons and pounded on the guardhouse door. Dawn came, and with it the stone-cold certainty that I would never see Dave Walker again.

'I'm very sorry to tell you that Private Walker died peacefully in the night,' Captain Briggs told us. His face was haggard but resigned. 'I'll get them little blue wings if it kills me!' clanged like a bell in my head. Dave Walker had been determined to get his wings if it killed him. And now it had.

We buried him in the coal-saturated earth of his native Barnsley. Six of us from the section carried his coffin with bare heads and black bands. The coffin was draped with the Union Jack and crowned with his maroon-red beret. The beret was still his 'on approval'. A tiny brass plate held his name, rank and number. In the church a nest of hardened miners' faces turned to look at us. There was hatred in them. We were a foreign race, bringing back their dead. Dave Walker had finally broken with the tradition of the pit. He had gone away and joined the army. And now the army had killed him.

At the battle school we found a team from the Special Investigation Branch, the army's detectives, in residence. They called us into an office one by one to make a statement. The man who interviewed me was calm and matter of fact. He had a grizzled face and long curly hair. It was difficult to believe that he was a soldier.

'Did you think at any time that the GPMG fire was too near the advancing section?' he asked me.

I hesitated, not knowing what Bradley had told them. 'Before it did, we switched right,' I said.

'Did any members of the section actually cross in front of your own sights while you were firing?'

'Definitely not.'

The man seemed only mildly interested, as if he knew how it had happened anyway. I signed the statement and left the office. I wondered if it could have been a chance ricochet from the GPMG which had cost Walker his life. Already the SIB had collected all the weapons we had used, and those used by the staff. They were even now being subjected to ballistics tests. The tests would almost certainly reveal which weapon had fired the round that had caused the terrible accident. Which had it been? It was impossible not to speculate. Whose erratic shots had hit my friend? Could it really have been super-trooper SAS man Bradley on the gun? Could it have been the ex-B-man Carson or the immature Taff Williams? Could it have been the truculent Jekyll firing from behind, or the uncompromising chauvinist Norris? Could it have been one of the others? Could it, after all, have been one of my own shots?

The attack on the cottage was an integral part of our training. We had to know what it was like to move and skirmish using live bullets, while someone was actually firing at us. With blanks you could never achieve that realism. To have gone into battle without that kind of training would have been like carrying a sharp sword after months of training with a blunt one. Later, I saw the fatal bullet. It was flattened and twisted out of shape. It had been a ricochet which had bounced off a rock at Walker's feet. It had flattened out into a deadly 'dum-dum' shape and smashed through his arm-pit and into his lung. But it was the shock which had killed him. A high-velocity bullet gathers momentum and mass, so that when it strikes it is with a massive sledge-hammer blow out of all proportion to its size. The result is a deadly shock to the nervous system.

During our skill-at-arms training at Folkestone a few weeks earlier, our instructor had demonstrated the power of our weapons. They had prepared a box containing wood, brick, earth and sand. Then one of them had fired at the box with an SLR from a hundred yards. When we looked at the box later, we saw that the round had sliced through the wood like butter, punched through the brick, ploughed through the earth and come to rest only in the sand. When they repeated the demonstration with the GPMG, a burst of sustained fire had cut the wood and brick to shreds in less than a second. 'Now imagine that's a human body!' the instructor said.

They took us back to the same range with a new man to replace Walker.

'So you were at the funeral!' Jekyll commented when I saw him. 'Why? Did he leave you his moped or something?' Was this callousness genuine or an act, I wondered? If it was an act, it was a very good one.

'It's not every day you lose a mate, corporal,' I said.

'No good getting dewy-eyed about it,' Jekyll said. 'It's all part of the training!'

# 4

## A Common Soldier

————

A few days after we arrived back in Aldershot, there was a terrific explosion in the middle of the barracks complex. We rushed out of our billets to find that the officers' mess of 16 Parachute Brigade had disappeared. In its place stood a smoking blitz site, where military policemen were already poking about in the rubble and vomiting vilely. They found the pieces of seven charred and dismembered bodies. The IRA had planted a car-bomb outside the mess, hoping to trap the brigade's officers. If the bomb had gone off during lunch, it might have slaughtered most of them. Instead it exploded a few minutes after, when they had all left punctually for work. The bodies belonged to five cleaning-ladies, a gardener and a Catholic chaplain. The incident made us hopping mad rather than afraid: it only sharpened our appetite for war.

The bomb sent the whole brigade scuttling about like ants. Previously the barracks had been open to all comers. Now we uncoiled vast bales of shiny barbed-wire, installed TV cameras, erected red and white striped barriers and doubled the guard. It was all a hopeless case of closing the stable door, but it made us feel good. We were now senior platoon and trusted to mount guard at night. We bristled with pride when they paraded us in parachute-smocks and issued us with pick-helves. We slept on camp-beds in the guardroom, taking turns, or 'stags', to prowl the perimeter-fence in pairs.

I remember being woken up late one evening by a stiff kick

on the leg from the guard commander, a corporal. 'The Redcaps are bringing a civvy in,' he said. 'You and your oppo go and collect him, and keep him here under guard.'

We took our pick-helves and went to collect the prisoner. He was a stringy, nervous man with long hair and a neat beard. We brought him into the guardroom and sat him down.

'You want tea?' I asked him.

'Thanks,' he said. But when I gave him the mug of tea, his hands were shaking so much that he couldn't drink it.

'What's up?' I asked. 'You're not IRA, are you?'

'No!' he almost choked. 'I'm an AWOL, that's what I am. I went AWOL when I was a crow here in the Depot. I thought they'd forgotten about it. I even set up an estate agent's business. Then I got picked up for speeding. That was only this morning. They checked up and found I was on the AWOL list. They handed me over to the Redcaps, and here I am.'

'What are you so nervous about?'

'The Redcaps said the Paras hate AWOLS worse than crap-hats. They said you'd beast seven bells out of me and throw me in the pokey!'

His helplessness made me feel so tough that I was tempted to threaten him a little more. Then I remembered: 'You're just a crow!' someone had said.

'Don't worry, mate,' I told him. 'There's only us here, and we're just crows. No one will touch you as long as you don't try to escape.'

He didn't look reassured, and I could sympathize with him. The prospect of military gaol after settling down in civvy-street must have been terrifying. An estate agent of a morning and a soldier again by evening: what a nightmare! My thoughts lingered on the whereabouts of Chapman and the others who had gone missing from our squad. The army never forgot. They would be sitting here one day soon, I thought.

'By the way,' I said. 'How long is it since you went over the wall?'

'Eight years,' he replied.

Soon Bradley donned his beige-coloured beret with a sigh of relief and packed his bergen.

Make sure you let me know which of us shot Walker!' he told me before he left.

I hadn't thought of Walker and the ballistics tests for some time. 'You're still a bloody craphat!' I said, as he grasped my hand powerfully. That night he marched off to join his SAS squadron in Hereford, to catch up with who knew what secret war.

We were too busy that week to think much about anything. We were in P Company now, for the last dreaded obstacle of our programme. The week of tests began with the 'milling' competition. You were matched against another recruit of the same size and weight, and had to slog it out in the boxing ring with him for exactly one minute. The idea was to test recruits for aggression, and you weren't expected to box. You were supposed to go in with fists swinging and keep on fighting till the bell dinged. A minute didn't sound very long, but they said it was the longest sixty seconds of your life.

When I saw who I had been matched with, I almost gagged. It was Geordie Harris, the recruit who had branded Walker with the steam-iron. I started shaking as soon as our names were called, though whether from fear or anger, I still don't know. We sat down together self-consciously on the gym bench like a couple of newlyweds. The entire platoon squashed around to watch. Half the desk-wallahs from the Depot were there too. The milling competition was rated as great sport. Two feather-weights were called forward. As soon as the bell went, their small fists starting buzzing like mechanical saws. The crowd burst into an excited frenzy as they battled with the vicious energy of wasps. One of them went down. The bell dinged. The PTI held up a red tape and a blue tape. A draw. Then two heavy-weights came on. They strode to meet each other like gladiators. The crowd whistled in anticipation of a good fight, but they were disappointed. The larger of the two pugilists stopped the other's advance with a massive, roundhouse blow. For a split-second the man stood there stunned. His eyes seemed to dim and cross exactly like the cat kayoed in a Tom and Jerry cartoon. He slumped down heavily and sprawled across the floor. The PTI held up a red tape. 'Asher–Harris!' he announced.

I felt an elastic band of fear tightening in my guts. Harris himself had gone pale. I hardly noticed as someone laced my gloves up. 'DING!' went the gong, and we both jumped. 'Kill the sod, Harris!' his section was shouting. 'Knock seven bells out of him!' my own section called. Two almighty wallops slopped greasily into my jaw, and I twisted sideways. I righted myself in time to receive another whacking blow which drove me to my knees. 'Get up, you fucking nancy!' someone snick-ered. It was Jekyll's voice. For an instant I glimpsed his fat face at the ringside. Then a tidal wave of anger burst inside me. Nancy-boy was I? I'd show that bastard! I launched myself at Harris, lashing out savagely. The Geordie's face dropped. He backed away as I charged at him, jabbing straight to his face. His stubby nose suddenly bent and ruptured like a blister, dribbling blood. The roar from the crowd was a hot current burning in my veins and baying in my throat. 'Kill him, Asher!' I heard. 'Splatter him!' High on my small victory, I didn't even see the next punch on its way. Something like a steam-train hissed into my teeth and knocked me down again. 'Get up! Get up!' the crowd yelped. I got up, and he promptly knocked me down once more. I dragged myself to my feet again and swung my fists hazily, thinking, this is one hell of a long minute. Just then the bell clanged. A deafening cheer went up.

'Good fight!' the PTI said, but he held up a red tape. I had lost. I looked at Harris's ugly, bloody face, and we grinned at each other whitely. The Walker affair no longer counted. I'd lost, but we had both passed our initiation. As I sat down and let the NCO unpeel my gloves, someone clapped me on the back. 'Well done, Asher!' a familiar voice said. I turned in astonishment, expecting to see Jekyll. Instead I saw Sergeant Norris, standing and leering at me. Still, it was the first compli-ment I'd ever received in the Depot. It was a moment in-comparably sweet.

*

There were PT tests that afternoon, and in the morning we paraded for the 'ammo resupply race'. Each man carried a pack-frame to which were lashed six mortar-bomb cylinders filled with sand. The idea was to carry the 'mortar bombs' to a certain map reference in the tank tracks within forty minutes. The RV was five miles away, which meant you had to run. The 'mortar bombs' weighed a hundred pounds, and the straps cut into your shoulders like blades. I remember clambering through deep marshes, their oily slop up to my calves, stomping uphill and panting with pain in my legs and back. I ran downhill and pushed through a thicket of thornbush at the bottom. The thorns ripped at my hands and face. Who should be waiting behind the thicket but Corporal Jekyll.

'Hold on, Asher!' he called. 'Your cylinder's leaking! That means you're underweight!' He picked up a heavy round boulder which just happened to be lying near by. He unscrewed one of my cylinders and thrust the boulder in. It must have weighed two or three pounds. To this day I don't know if my cylinder was actually leaking, or if I carried an extra weight most of the way for the sake of Corporal Jekyll.

I ran through the Long Valley, with the square-topped hill standing out sharp against the sky. On the hill I saw the inviting shape of a four-tonne truck waiting to take me home. I burst forward, squeezing the last juice out of my muscles as I struggled drunkenly against the slope. 'Come on, keep moving!' screamed Captain Briggs, hovering on the summit. At last I was there. Briggs was noting down my name and time. Just as I moved to fling off the heavy pack-frame, he turned to me and grinned knowingly. 'Don't bother!' he said. 'The trucks have broken down. You've got to run back to base!' I stared at him, speechless. He laughed as he saw the understanding cross my features. This was only half of the race. The hardest part was yet to come.

The following morning, still sore from the 'ammo resupply', we had to complete the assault course six times in full kit. In the afternoon there was a gruelling ten-mile bash to be completed in under an hour and a half. Still limping and blistered from the bash, we ran a five-mile steeple-chase. This was a cross-country course in PT kit, incorporating several ingenious variations on the theme of deep pits full of stinking mud. We arrived back from the steeple-chase spattered and encrusted, in time to be briefed for the Trainasium that afternoon.

We had all seen the high scaffolding of the Trainasium many times during our training and had often puzzled over its use. Now we discovered that it was a confidence test, designed as a final check that the recruit possessed the 'right stuff' for parachuting. The first part of the course was the 'shuffle-bars'. They were two parallel bars of iron placed about three feet apart. You had to shuffle along them, keeping your balance and stepping over staggered brackets on each side. There was nothing technically hard about this. The only drawback was that the bars were forty feet up. There was no safety-net, and a single wrong step meant plummeting forty feet to a sticky doom. It was no place for vertigo sufferers.

I watched O'Keefe as he stepped out on to the walk, forty feet above us. His arms were flung out horizontally for balance. He shuffled to the centre of the bars, and even from where I stood I could see his legs shaking.

'DON'T LOOK DOWN!' the supervising PTI shouted to him. 'Name, rank and number?'

O'Keefe, white as a sheet, did not respond. He was rooted to the spot, unable to move forward or back, and dropping his gaze fatally down towards the ground.

'DON'T FUCKING LOOK DOWN!' the PTI bellowed again. 'NAME, RANK AND NUMBER?'

For a split second I was sure O'Keefe would fall. Then he shook his head in limp defeat and shuffled back to safety. Five months of hardship and torture wasted, I thought.

Soon it was my turn. I scaled the scaffolding and squeezed in with the PTI on the platform.

'Don't look down!' he told me. 'Ready? GO!' I waddled forward, holding my arms out just as O'Keefe had done. 'Name, rank and number?' the PTI demanded.

'24246810, Private Asher, SIR!' I shouted back, trying desperately not to glance down at the anxious faces forty feet below.

'OK, step over the brackets!' the PTI ordered.

I lifted one DMS boot and placed it safely on the other side. I took another step, and was about to lift my foot over the second bracket, when my body trembled involuntarily. I wobbled dangerously, and for a moment I saw myself plunging down and slapping into the mud. Then I regained my balance.

'Take it steady!' the instructor called.

I stepped over the bracket and paced quickly and surely to the other platform.

'NEXT!' the PTI croaked.

While another victim hauled his body up to the shuffle-bars, I was sent off to the cat-walk. You had to sprint along a foot-wide plank and across a see-saw which threatened to throw you off balance. At the end of the plank you had to hurl yourself down to a tiny square platform ten feet below. If you missed the platform, there were still another ten feet to fall before you crumped into the earth. Then you had to swing between trees like Tarzan, always high above the ground, and finally to drop like a free-faller into a net. Each part of the test was done to the order 'GO!' and a momentary hesitation was enough to fail you. It was excellent preparation for military parachuting, when on the order 'GO!' you had to fling yourself into thin air, 1,000 feet up.

The final test of P Company was the log race. For this, the platoon was divided into teams of six. Each team had to carry a pine tree-trunk for several miles at a run. It was just possible for six strong men to carry it on toggle-ropes strung underneath. It was supposed to be the most exacting test of the week.

I was preparing myself for this last obstacle before parachute-training, when Sergeant Norris called me and said, 'Get your Number Twos on, Asher, you're not doing the log race!'

'Why not, Sergeant?' I asked in amazement, thinking I had somehow been failed.

'Officers' selection panel,' he said. 'In the HQ building in thirty minutes!'

'Wait a second!' Jekyll cut in, scowling. 'He's got to do the log race! It's part of the course. And it's the only thing left to do!'

For the first time, I agreed with Jekyll. I had been through all the other tests, and I had passed them. Now the final triumph was to be taken away from me.

'It's orders!' Sergeant Norris said.

The selection panel consisted of the second-in-command of the Depot and another major.

'Do you still want to be an officer?' one of them asked me.

'Well, sir, I think so,' I said vaguely, unable to concentrate. I could think of nothing but my mates struggling with that tree-trunk. I hadn't thought about being an officer for weeks, I realized. I had thought only about passing P Company and getting my wings. The interview had taken me by surprise.

'I don't think you're quite ready for RCB yet, do you?' the major asked me. Good God, I thought, didn't he know how tough the Depot course was? How could I think of more than that?

'Perhaps not, sir,' I said, still confused. I wanted to be out in the tank tracks with my section. I was a common soldier like them.

'Just one thing, sir,' I said. 'I hope that missing the log race won't mean failing P Company?'

The major looked startled. 'If you weren't up to the standard, you'd never have got this far,' he said. 'We have no doubts about you passing P Company. It's a commission and your career that's at stake here!'

'Thank you, sir,' I said. 'Only I really want to get my wings!'

He regarded me as though I were brain-washed. I suppose he was right.

'Dismiss,' he told me.

I marched back to the billets ruefully aware that I must be the only man ever to pass P Company without doing the log race. Far from exulting, I felt cheated. At that moment I just wanted to be a Para. A commission didn't seem to be of any more consequence than a tinker's cuss.

# 5

## *Airborne-easy*

———

Number One Parachute Training School, RAF Abingdon, was a place of smooth green lawns and flower-beds. It had several bars, a dance-hall and a cinema. There was every facility to encourage us to forget the strain of making our eight parachute jumps.

Operational parachuting takes place at 1,000 feet or less. Free-fall jumps of tens of thousands of feet sound more spectacular, but, in fact, are far less dangerous. At 1,000 feet you have only forty-five seconds to choose between life and death. At Abingdon, the training was designed to break us in slowly, by stages. My instructor, Sergeant Brown, was a dumpy man with a boyish, moon-like face. He was an RAF dispatcher and a one-time member of the Falcons, the famous RAF parachute display team. The first thing he did was to convince us that our parachute, the PX, was reliable. He even took us on a guided tour of the parachute packing-plant, where a bevy of nubile WRAF girls folded the silk canopies with extreme care. They added to them the minute knots which held everything in its place. The knots had to break during the descent to allow the canopy to deploy correctly.

'You see the PX has a skirt of mesh,' Brown told us. 'It doesn't look much, but it's a life-saver.' Apparently, the early Paras kept on getting 'blown peripheries' and piling in: the edge of the canopy got the wind under it and folded, reducing the amount of air inside. That led to a 'Roman candle': the canopy emptied of air, and the parachutist plummeted to his death. 'The skirt stops that,' Brown said. 'We've never had a blown periphery with a PX.'

We practised jumping out of the doors of mock-ups, and then graduated to the 'fan'. This was a sort of wind-machine with a steel hauser attached. It was sited on a platform up near the hangar roof. On the magic word 'GO!', you stepped off the platform and hurtled down to the hangar floor with the hauser tied round your middle. As the floor rushed up to meet you, the wind-blades of the fan slowed you down. It deposited you with the same force as a parachute would have: they reckoned it was the same as jumping off a six-foot wall.

After three or four goes on the fan, you moved on to the 'knacker-cracker' outside the hangar. This was a thirty-foot tower with a crane-like structure on top. The crane was actually a manoeuvrable parachute-harness. You were strapped into the harness, leaning disconcertingly against a steel gate, thirty feet up. The gate suddenly shot open, and you swung forward, hanging in the air like a fish on the end of a rod and line. The dispatcher took you through the various flight-drills, then dropped you unceremoniously to earth like a sack of spuds. Once you had learned to land and roll, you were ready for your first parachute jump.

The first two descents were made from a barrage-balloon at Weston-on-the-Green. The balloon was shaped like a miniature Zeppelin and carried an open box-car beneath it. The box-car was just large enough to take two parachutists and a dispatcher. Carson and I were crammed into the car with Sergeant Brown. The balloon began to rise menacingly. There was no wind, but the car swayed gently as it rose. You could feel the vibration of the winch through the metal.

Brown broke the silence by giggling. 'A free bottle of Scotch to anyone who gets an erection at the gate!' he said. 'I make the offer on every course, but no one's won it yet!' I wasn't surprised. 'Hey,' he went on, seeing our glum faces, 'this is nothing! Some of our boys ride bicycles out of these things at 800 feet! And they're not sooper-dooper paratroopers like you!'

The green plinth of Weston expanded below us. The buildings were miniatures on a child's train-set. Down there was the RAF pub they called the Drop Inn. It was the custom to celebrate your first jump there – if you were still in one piece. Suddenly the vibration of the winch ceased, and the balloon stopped rising. The car was still swinging hypnotically from side to side. Now came the moment of truth, I thought, after eighteen weeks' solid training. If I failed this one, there would be no second chance. There was no back-squadding for those who failed to jump. Anyone who refused to jump was discharged the same day or sent off to another unit. Failure to jump during an operation could risk everyone's life and abort the operation. That was one risk the army couldn't afford to take.

'NUMBER ONE READY!' Sergeant Brown yodelled. I realized with a jolt that I was Number One. I moved to the open gate. Something horrific lay beyond that gap, but I knew not what it was. I felt the weight of the PX on my back and the smaller reserve chute on my chest. If anything went wrong, there would be no time to use it. I was poised by the gate, staring straight ahead. My hands were locked either side.

'RED ON!' the dispatcher roared. I crossed my hands in front of me. Four seconds to wait ... three ... two ... one ... GOOOOO! The billion GOs I have heard in my training are crashing into my ears at once: assault course, bash, ammo-resupply, Trainasium: GO! GO! GO! into that freezing stream, across those shuffle-bars, into that milling ring with Geordie Harris. Jekyll's face snarling at me: Jekyll, Jekyll, Jekyll is chasing me into the air. I am plunging through cool air like a stone. My stomach is somewhere above me. Wow! Wow! Wow! What's happening? It's like being on a gigantic Ferris-wheel, 200 feet high. The horizon flashes giddily past. I push my head back as I've been taught. There is a slight clutching sensation on my shoulders. Everything goes deathly still. There is not a sound, not the faintest breath of wind. Above me a great ribbed flower has opened. I am floating down in gossamer, swaying erotically.

A disjointed metallic voice drifts up from below. 'OK, Number One! Assess your drift! That's it! Pull down on those lift-webs!' I am no longer alone. I am back in the world. But the green earth is still far below. 'Feet together!' the megaphone says with touching urgency. 'Feet and knees together for the landing!' I draw my feet together lazily. Without the least warning the earth comes up to meet me. There is a pleasant crump as I hit the ground: a smell of grass and wet soil. I roll over helter-skelter and come to a halt. The canopy drags me slightly. I turn on my back and press the release-catch. The harness springs open. I have made jump number one.

'Get yourself a pint in the Drop Inn,' the RAF officer says. They seem the most welcome words I've ever heard.

That afternoon there followed our second balloon-jump. Curiously, it seemed more terrifying. It was as if your body knew what to expect and was shying away from it. No one had refused to jump that morning, but in the afternoon three recruits failed to jump. Naturally, that was the last we saw or heard of them.

The remaining six of our qualifying descents had to be made from aircraft. This was doubly frightening for me, since I'd never flown before. We got an hour's flight in a Hercules C130 as 'familiarization'. The next time we entered an aircraft, the only way out was the fuselage door at 1,000 feet. To make it easier, the jump was from an Argosy, an outmoded plane used only for training. We were cushioned in seats of netting, silently contemplating the ordeal. Carson sat next to me, ruminating silently. Today there was no talk of Taigs and Provies. Our main chutes were already on our backs and our reserves lay on the deck, their tempting red handles uppermost. Suddenly the blue-overalled dispatcher got up and slid the door open. The slip-stream crashed in like a shot from a cannon. The breeze that washed through the cabin was laced strongly with sickening aviation-fuel fumes. The boom of the engines was louder. 'PORT STICK, STAND UP!' the dispatcher hollered. Like clockwork soldiers we leaned forward, picked up our reserves and clipped them into place. Next we had to hook up the static-line, a belt of

thick webbing, to the bar over our heads. 'CHECK EQUIP-
MENT!' the dispatcher told us. Then he took up his place by the
door.

The seconds ticked by with heavy agony. Nothing was visible
through the port-holes but the open sky. 'ACTION STATIONS!'
came the order. The first man in the 'stick' shuffled up to the
door. Everyone else struggled forward three or four paces. By
the door was a red light and a green light, operated from the
pilot's cockpit. When the red light came on, you had four
seconds to wait. 'RED ON!' the RAF man screamed. The blood
rushed out of my extremities. My heart pumped like bellows.
The world went hazy, except for that terrible door grinning at
the end of the stick like the jaws of hell. The green light flashed
on. 'GOOOOOO!' The man at the door was gone. The second
one followed him, eaten up by the sky. I was marching in-
exorably into that gnashing maw. Only Carson was before me. I
was going out. I was going out. Then the unexpected happens.
With the vision of a trembling lens-shutter I see Carson shying
away from the door. His face is bleach white. The RAF man
snatches Carson's rigid frame out of my way. I see his cold,
silent eyes and then someone shoves me out into the sky.

There was no sensation of falling this time. The slipstream
carried me down sideways, and within a second or two my
canopy had plopped open like a fresh fungus. There were more
white canopies below me, dry dandelion seeds wobbling in the
wind. I checked the air and looked back to see another parachutist hurtling straight at me like a kamikaze. I pulled down on
my back lift-webs in order to steer away from the inevitable
collision. For a second the raider hung there like an acrobat on
a trapeze. I saw in that instant the pale, drawn, exhilarated face
of Geordie Harris. 'YAAAAAAA!' he wailed as he sailed past
me, a foreign body spinning forward on its own secret trajectory.
It wasn't until he'd gone past that I noticed his rigging lines
were twisted.

When I hit the ground, the ambulance was already on its
way for Harris. They loaded him in, groaning on the stretcher.
Poor old Harris. He'd won the milling, but he'd lost the bigger

battle. Now he wouldn't be collecting his wings with the rest of us. His leg was shattered in three places.

Two young Parachute Regiment subalterns were celebrating in the Drop Inn when I arrived. They had just made their first jump with us, and were into their second Martini. They'd evidently seen Harris pile in. 'Five per cent casualties on every jump, that's what they say!' one of them recited. He was a thin blond man with a grammar school accent. SECOND LT HAIG was written on the name tag on his smock. The other was a taller dark-haired handsome man called Second Lieutenant Foster. He was very public school. 'I've got a feeling about you, Haig,' he was saying. 'I think you're going to be the next one to pile in. On tomorrow's jump, you'll come a cropper. I can just see it now!'

'Cut it out, Foster!' Haig told him, but you could see by his face that he half believed it.

In the mess that night there was a kerfuffle. A spindly RAF storeman pushed into the queue, and one of my platoon resented it. The recruit was Butcher, the ex-miner who had once fainted on parade. Butcher lashed out at the storeman as if he were milling. By the time we managed to separate them, the RAF man had a split lip and a black eye. 'Bleedin' Brylcreem Boys!' Butcher said.

Next morning we were queueing up to collect our parachutes from the stores, when I noticed that the storeman was he of the split lip and the black eye. I wondered if Butcher had noticed him too. Butcher's turn came. The storeman was about to hand over the chute, when a look of malicious humour came into his eye. 'No, not that one!' he said. He whisked the chute out of Butcher's grasp and replaced it in the rack. He walked down the entire length of the shelves to the far end of the store. He returned carrying an old and worn-looking parachute which he handed to Butcher without a word. In the fitting-room I found Second Lts Foster and Haig. They were still arguing. 'I tell you, you're going to pile in!' Foster taunted Haig. 'Strawberry jam for tea today!' Just before we filtered into the aircraft, I saw Butcher standing there, his face bloodless with fear. I had no doubt that the 'Brylcreem Boy' had already exacted his revenge.

We made the jump, and I landed safely on the green. I was about to pull in my canopy, when I heard a plaintive wail from above. I looked up to see a figure dangling oddly from his canopy and shouting lustily. One of his legs was in the required landing position, but the other had evidently got caught in his twisted rigging-lines. It was suspended almost at a right angle to the other. He was frantically and comically trying to do the impossible: to get both legs together for a safe landing, and screaming desperately for help that no one could give him. From where I stood, fascinated, he looked like a mechanical monkey on a stick. He hit the ground with an audible crack. 'MEDIC! MEDIC!' he screamed.

I was too far away to see who the unfortunate parachutist was, but the two most likely candidates in my mind were Butcher and Second Lieutenant Haig. When I got to the Drop Inn, though, Butcher was standing at the bar, cheerfully downing a pint. Not far away, blond-haired Haig was into his second Martini.

'Hey, Butch!' I said. 'Who was it that piled in?'

'That was Second Lieutenant Foster!' he smirked. 'Strawberry jam for tea today!'

'Twists' was the dreaded word at Abingdon. Twists in the rigging-lines – the strings of cord which connected the parachute-harness to the silk canopy – had done for Harris and Foster. They were caused by something called a 'rivet-inspection'. On my fourth jump I learned first-hand what that was. Instead of leaping out into the slipstream, I flopped out ineffectually. My parachute-pack caught on the step and tilted me head-first through the air. My nose-dive was brought to a sudden halt by my half-open parachute which was twisted like a corkscrew from my shoulders up to the canopy. I was falling quicker than I should have been, but luckily my legs weren't trapped. I kicked out frantically to unwind the twists, spinning round dizzily until they snapped out, only seconds before I hit the ground.

'That was a rivet-inspection,' Sergeant Brown told me. So now I knew.

The other big horror was 'Russian roulette'. This happened if you came out directly above another parachutist. His canopy 'captured' your air. Your chute would collapse, and you would plummet into position below him. Then the reverse happened. Your parachute inflated and 'stole' his air. His chute would collapse, and he would plump down beneath you. The process continued like this for the entire flight, until one of you hit the ground. You had a fifty-fifty chance of ending up as strawberry jam.

Our final training jump was done at night and with full kit. With your rifle, pack and webbing, main parachute and reserve, you were hefting about ninety pounds. The kit was strapped to your legs so that you could only just manage to stagger to the door. The equipment was wrapped in a canvas sheet and fixed to your harness by two metal hooks and a length of rope coiled on your hip. To have landed with all that weight on your legs would almost certainly have led to a snapped thigh-bone. Instead you jettisoned the container in flight by releasing the hooks. The kit swung beneath you on fifteen feet of rope and landed just before you did.

We left the aircraft just after sunset. Operational jumps were always made in darkness: a descending parachutist is a sitting-duck in daylight. My exit was perfect for once. My canopy developed right on cue. I drifted for a moment, watching the headlights of vehicles, like eyes on the hidden roads far below. Then I felt for my hooks. The right hook released at once: the left one didn't. I scrabbled frantically at the jammed hook, swearing. This was it. Strawberry jam. 'Five per cent casualties on every jump!' Haig had said. Just then a shadow fell across me and another canopy swanned past, silent as a bat. I forgot the hook and jerked excitedly on my lift-webs.

'Bugger off out of it!' a frightened voice yelled.

'You bugger off!' I yelled back, indignantly.

I grappled with the hook again, but the ground lights were getting worryingly near. I left it and tried to compose myself for the landing, whispering a silent but very fervent prayer. Ground rush came at ten feet, grey and indistinct like the wave of a dark sea. I slammed into the earth like a sack of wet manure and lay still. I sent my nerve-messengers around my body to assess the damage. Miraculously, everything seemed to be in place. I could hardly believe my luck. I had landed with my container, and I was still in one piece! A torch strobed out of the darkness.

'You all right?' a voice asked. It was the friendly, boyish voice of Sergeant Brown.

'Yes, sar'nt,' I answered.

'Well done, Para!' he said.

It was only then that I remembered: this was jump number eight. I had qualified. I was a Para.

The next evening we staggered home from a crawl around the Abingdon pubs, arm in arm and as drunk as lords. The only thing I remember clearly about that crazy march home is singing 'Flying Fortress' to the tune of 'John Brown's Body':

> Corporal Jekyll was the last to jump,
> The first to hit the ground,
> Corporal Jekyll was the last to jump,
> The first to hit the ground,
> Corporal Jekyll was the last to jump,
> The first to hit the ground,
> And he ain't gonna jump no more!
>
> They scraped him off the tarmac,
> Like a lump of strawberry jam,
> They scraped him off the tarmac,
> Like a lump of strawberry jam,
> They scraped him off the tarmac,
> Like a lump of strawberry jam,
> AND HE AIN'T GONNA JUMP NO MORE!

In the morning I woke with a splitting headache and a badly swollen lip. I felt as if I really had been scraped off the tarmac. 'What happened?' I asked my room-mates. 'Did we get into a scrap?'

Williams, the bandy-legged Welshman, looked at me guiltily. 'We didn't get into a scrap, Ash,' he said. 'But Corporal Stevens came in roaring drunk and ordered us to stand by our beds. You were so pissed, you just went on snoring. He got mad and tipped you out of bed. You hit your head on the edge of the locker, but you didn't even wake up. We thought you were dead. I've never seen anything like it!'

I could hardly credit it myself. After all the near-misses of those weeks at Abingdon, my worst injury came from being thrown out of bed by a drunken NCO!

And that was how, in time-honoured Para fashion, I came to get on parade for my wings ceremony with a split lip and the great grand-daddy of all hangovers.

'You are now members of the airborne brotherhood!' I remember the RAF commandant saying. 'You will find a special spirit amongst those who jump from the sky, not found amongst *penguins*. The penguin is a flightless bird, but you are the airborne!' Despite my hangover, I felt eleven feet tall. 'I wish you good luck in your careers,' he went on. 'But remember one thing: the day you are no longer afraid of parachuting is the day you should stop!'

He called us forward one by one to collect our wings. My name was called, and I marched proudly out of the ranks. The rest of the course cheered and clapped. I took the little cloth badge in my hand, blue wings embroidered on a white parachute-canopy: a flimsy, paper-thin thing. For this, I thought, I had endured pain and humiliation, terror and torture. For this reputations had been won and lost, careers had been made and broken, men had gone through injury, exposure, madness and agony. For this a man had died. In a sense it was nothing. It ensured neither a fabulous advance in pay nor better conditions. But for me it was a symbol of passing from childhood to manhood. It was a thing of real value in a world of transient materialism. Money could not buy this: no friends, connections or privileges of birth could attain it. It was mine through blood and sweat and tears. I had earned it. I never doubted for one minute that it had been worth every drop of sweat.

The cheers subsided. I saluted the RAF officer, and he returned the salute. Then I marched back to the ranks of my platoon: not an officer, not a superman, but simply Asher, M. J., 24246810, Private fourth class, the Parachute Regiment.

# 6

## *Valkyries*

———

On our first day back in Aldershot we all marched to the mess in our Number Twos to show off our wings to the new recruits. Several junior platoons had formed in our absence, and the crows looked on in envy and awe. We had made it. We were there.

Outside, I almost collided with a squat little corporal in working-dress. It was Corporal Jekyll, fresh from his leave. Why did he look so unimpressive now? Had I really been in fear of this man? He glanced at my wings, and he glanced at me. 'Don't tell me you *made* it, Asher!' he said incredulously. His voice carried the familiar mocking note, but today it didn't quite sound genuine. There was something new behind the dark eyes, or was it something old I had never noticed before? Was this Jekyll's way of saying 'well done'? After all, even in his terms I had done well. I hadn't shone, perhaps, but I was one of only two survivors of the original section. Perhaps, I thought, he was far more astute than I had imagined. Perhaps he had deliberately thrown out a challenge, knowing that I would take it up. Jekyll had seemed the nearest thing to the Devil incarnate for me, but now it was almost over I was brought face to face with stunning reality. It was Jekyll I had to thank for my success. Adversity, like love, makes you a person: it defines you and gives you an identity. Identity, not food or land, is what the fighting is really about. The enemy is what makes you yourself. Without the enemy you are nothing. Jekyll had been my enemy, yet he had brought out in me all that was best in courage, determination and grit.

Two weeks of airborne training lay ahead of us. After that, there would be the official passing out parade in front of family and friends. Meanwhile, it was business as usual at the Depot. One morning we were briefed for a night exercise. 'We'll be using a new night-sight on this ex.,' Captain Briggs explained. Darkness fell, and the platoon gathered near the weapon-training hangars.

'Before we go, each of you has to test the new sights,' Norris said. 'So I'll call you forward one at a time.'

My name was called, and I marched forward to the hangar door. Norris was there with a powerful torch in his hand. 'Is that you, Asher?' he demanded, squinting and shining his torch directly into my eyes. I was surprised by the move, which was certain to spoil my night-vision. I blinked and turned my head away, but Norris followed me with the torch-beam. 'It's me, sar'nt,' I told him.

'Go in!' he ordered, and I stepped into pitch-darkness. The door slammed shut behind me with frightening finality.

'Come forward, Asher!' Briggs's voice came softly out of the darkness. 'Move forward to the centre of the room!' I groped forward, still intent on seeing these new sights, when a thick arm like an octopus tentacle closed on my neck. 'I've been tricked!' was my immediate reaction, then, 'It's another test!' I lashed out with an instinct sharpened by fear and twenty weeks of training. My fists connected with flesh. There were more hands on me, hauling me down. I kicked out and struggled. Somebody kicked back. I crashed on to the hard floor and felt more hands tying my wrists up with parachute cord. A hessian sack, smelling strongly of hemp, was drawn over my head. I fought for air. The sack increased the feeling of suffocation. I was dragged several feet across the floor, still blind. Then water was sloshed over the sack. I gasped and tried desperately to draw breath through the fine hessian mesh. I was drowning. I was going under. I tried to crawl away, but someone kicked me viciously on the thigh.

At that moment a weird noise began. It was like static from a mistuned radio, formless, shapeless, a screeching, maddening, monotonous note which hovered endlessly in the room. I lay there as the sickening screech washed over me, not knowing whether to faint or vomit. I have no idea how long I was there. Suddenly there were hands on me again. 'You try anything and I'll kill ye!' a voice said. I was pulled up to my feet and hustled outside. My captors shoved me into the back of a vehicle, and I fell sprawling on to other supine bodies. One of them said 'OOOF!' as I fell on him. The engine started and a fume of diesel lufted through the back. There was a jolt as it set off.

It might have been half an hour before it stopped. Rough hands wrenched me out, untied my wrists and whipped off my hood. I was standing on the open road in front of an army Land Rover and a grinning Sergeant Norris.

'Here's a sketch-map,' he said, giving me what looked like a piece of lavatory-paper. 'You've got all night to get back to the Depot. Don't talk to civvies or police. I want to see you on first parade tomorrow morning!' The vehicle left me standing in the middle of nowhere. It took me until after midnight to find my way back to the Depot.

Corporal Stevens was a strong-looking Geordie from Sunderland, with expressionless blue eyes and a bum-fluff moustache. The next morning in the mess I noticed that one of his eyes was encircled by a shiny mauve bruise. After breakfast he sauntered past me. 'You're a punchy bastard, Asher!' he said. Then he went off to ask the cook for a piece of steak for his eye. I felt the fist-sized burning abrasion on my thigh where some unknown assailant had kicked me the previous evening, and remembered how Stevens had tipped me out of bed at Abingdon. I felt rather pleased with myself.

My thoughts were interrupted when Williams ran into the mess, shouting, 'Hey, Ash! Postings are up!' We all dashed over to the billets. There was a press of bodies around the notice-board. 'Where the fuck am I?' people were chanting. Craning over someone's neck I read, 'Adams: 3 Para, UN Force, Cyprus. Anderson: 3 Para, UN Force, Cyprus. Andrews: 3 Para . . .'

'Where the hell's Asher?' I asked out loud.

'Asher!' Williams's voice came from the front. 'You've got the Immaculate Second!' I fought my way to the front and found my name on a separate list. 'Asher,' it read: '2 Para, Peace-keeping duties, Belfast.' So that was my future. I was going to keep the peace.

We dropped on Hythe Beach at sunset. It was our final exercise, and Hythe had been chosen because it had the maze of terraced streets they called Little Belfast. The Hercules juddered through clumps of turbulence at 300 feet. As she climbed up to 1,000 for the drop, the RAF dispatcher opened the door. The stench of aviation fuel mixed with the seaweed smell of the Channel wafted through. Someone near me puked, and a pool of vile sick trickled along the cabin's vibrating floor. 'ACTION STATIONS!' the order came. As we waddled forward, weighed down by our kit, a familiar figure took up the Number One position by the door. It was Corporal Jekyll, and there was no mistaking the rigid fear written on his face as he looked down over the dark sea. I knew that everyone was frightened of parachuting. But after all the beasting and humiliation I had suffered at his hands, I couldn't resist a short moment of satisfaction. For even the gods have feet of clay.

'GOOOOO!' screamed the dispatcher. For a fraction of a second I glimpsed that long-hated face, bathed in green light and contorted by terror. Then the face was gone.

Our training would soon be over, and another phase of our careers would begin. Of the original hundred and twenty recruits who had paraded on that first day, only thirty-five had got through. I still missed Dave Walker. Williams and I both felt it was strange that after so many weeks we had heard nothing about the ballistics tests. Then, one evening, Williams came bustling in with some news.

'I got it from a Tom who worked in the officers' mess,' he said. 'You know who shot Walker?'

Oh, God! I said silently. Let it not be me!

'It was Captain Briggs!' Williams told me.

'What!'

'Yeah. The fatal shot came from Briggs's rifle. Of course, it was an accident!'

Of course, it was an accident. I felt sorry that such a good officer should have such a thing on his conscience for ever. Still, in my heart of hearts, I never quite trusted officers after that.

On the morning of our passing-out parade, Captain Briggs gave us a talk. 'All your training,' he said, 'has been geared to operating in the field for short, intense periods. You are the iron claw of the British army. You are trained and equipped to last only forty-eight hours. In that time a modern war will be won or lost. After your two days in the field, you are written off. Death with honour is the best fate you can expect in the Parachute Regiment!' We listened to the talk quietly and with swelling pride. We had never reckoned on being cannon-fodder. But the way he told it, it sounded like the highest honour. We had been chosen to die: *Dulce et decorum est pro patria mori.*

Parents and relations mobbed around the saluting base for the ceremony. The regimental flag was flying. The band marched on in their Number Ones, beating and blowing. After them came another soldier with the regimental mascot, a Shetland pony called Ringway, after the Manchester airfield where the first Paras had trained. Ringway was in disgrace. He had once held the rank of sergeant, but on a previous passing-out parade he had deposited a large and smelly heap of manure on the square. Nobby Arnold had reduced him to corporal. On the next parade he had registered his protest by repeating the action. The irate Nobby had busted him to lance-jack. If there were any such misdemeanors today, he would be a private like all the rest of us.

We strutted on to the parade-square, and the inspecting officer walked up and down the lines. He presented us with coloured lanyards: red for the 'Sporting First' battalion, blue for the 'Immaculate Second' and green for the 'Gungie Third'. He also presented the baton to the champion recruit. Then we fixed bayonets and marched forward in review order. We halted before the saluting base and presented arms with three crisp movements. The commandant took the salute and began a long and pompous speech. The crowd fidgeted. The band clung to their instruments and the regimental mascot snorted. The commandant went on and on. 'And never forget,' he said, drawing to a close, 'what Field Marshal Viscount Montgomery said about the Parachute Regiment! He said, "They are, in fact, men apart. Every man an emperor!"'

There was a visible stir amongst the spectators. The commandant looked gratified. But it was not his oratory that had stirred the crowd. They were craning their necks toward the little Shetland pony, who stood next to the band. A sudden cheer went up. Lance-corporal Ringway had done it again.

Nobby Arnold quickly stepped into the breach. His eyes narrowed. 'Platoon will march past in close column of salute!' he ordered. 'By the right, QUIIIICK MARCH!' As we marched, the band struck up the piece we had been waiting for all morning. It was Wagner's 'Ride of the Valkyries', our regimental march, always played last in the passing-out parade. We puffed out our chests, lifted our heads under our maroon-red berets, swung our arms up to shoulder height. I could see those winged horses pounding off from their mountain ledges, those slaughter-witches descending from Valhalla to carry off we dead heroes to the everlasting hall of fame. A thousand years. Ten thousand years and nothing had changed. The drums pounded. The brass played low and heavy. As our boots punched off the drill-square for the last time, I felt that I was really flying.

I carried my suitcase downstairs and stepped out of the building. By the door I met a sour-faced corporal. He was an inch shorter than me, and like me he wore a maroon-red beret. 'Watch out in 2 Para, Asher,' he said. 'They won't put up with what we put up with in the Depot.' All morning, and for many other mornings, I had been working out some cutting last remark for Jekyll. 'They're *real* soldiers in 2 Para, not Depot soldiers like you lot, *mate*,' I would say. But now I was faced with Jekyll, I was unable to say it. The conditioning I had gone through was too strong for that. I could never call Jekyll 'mate' ever again. That was what the training had all been about.

'Thank you for everything, corporal,' I said. Then I picked up my suitcase and carried it toward Normandy Barracks, the home of the Immaculate Second.

# 7

## *Shock Tactics*

———

My home in Belfast was a broken-down police station which had once been a base for the B-specials. It stood on the corner of Brown's Square and Peter's Hill, toward the lower end of the Shankill Road, a brooding red brick fortress with its windows and doors boarded up and sealed off and sand-bagged. There was an observation-post on the roof and another at the third-storey window, and a guard at the gate with a helmet and a flak jacket. He opened the gate as the four-tonner rattled into the yard.

I jumped out of the truck with the others and stood with my kit in the yard. Six men were tooling up for patrol. They were long-haired and soiled-looking, and wore masking tape over their badges and belt equipment. They wore flak jackets under their smocks, which gave them the look of sixteen-stone bruisers. They formed up briefly at the gate, and I heard the clicks as they loaded their magazines into place. Then they moved silently into the hostile street and disappeared.

'Asher, Fairley, Wilson!' a sergeant shouted. 'My platoon! Get your kit upstairs on the double! Get yourselves a bunk and a kit box, then report to me!' Upstairs, thirty bunks were crammed together in a small room. The floor was rotting, mildewed timber. The paint was peeling off the walls and dangling in papery segments. Over a vast old fireplace was the Red Hand of Ulster, the white and scarlet banner of the Protestant Loyalists. Beneath it was a poster showing a picturesque seascape, saying

WELCOME TO NORTHERN IRELAND. There were no open windows and the place smelled of savoury old socks and vintage unwashed bodies. Closer up, I saw some of the bodies, inert but fully clothed, with their boots on and their rifles crooked under their arms. They looked nothing like the smart soldiers I'd got used to seeing in the Depot.

My new platoon sergeant, Sergeant Beck, was an anxious-looking man with a tousle of curly black hair and a map of lines and wrinkles on his thin face. He presented each of us new-comers with the special kit we required in Northern Ireland: a flak jacket and a little yellow card marked INSTRUCTIONS FOR OPENING FIRE. 'No warning shots,' he told us. 'No cowboy stuff. It's too dicey. You might hit a passer-by. No shooting at hands or legs. You'd look a right tube if you missed and shot a little kid. That's what we don't need. Go for the big target. Shoot to kill.'

Then he told us to try out our body-armour. It was the same type the Americans had worn in Vietnam. 'Won't stop an HV bullet,' the sergeant said. 'But it might stop a pistol or a Thompson. Also, it keeps the bits of your body together if you get blown up. Not so messy when they have to clear you away!' He told us to wear the flak jacket beneath our smocks. 'Like that it makes you look bigger and stronger than you are,' he said. 'And it scares the Provos shitless, because they think you're not wearing one and anyone not wearing one must be a nutter. Nothing guarantees a tremor in the sniper's hands more than the feeling that he'll get taken out the minute he opens fire!' He gave us a few minutes to get scoff and sort out our kit.

'Asher, you're on patrol later with Corporal Cooper,' he said.

I found my way back to my bunk and examined my yellow card. It explained in very convoluted language what I already knew: that I was never to carry a round in the breech of my rifle; that I was always to shout out a warning before I cocked the weapon, and then another before I fired. I was to fire without warning only if there were a direct threat to life. I put down the card a few minutes later, none the wiser as to how I should really behave in a life-or-death situation.

'Are you the new bod?' a young officer asked me. 'I'm your platoon commander, Lieutenant Smythe.' He had sand-coloured hair that was greasy and unkempt, and mutton-chop sideburns that no one in the Depot would have got away with. 'I read your report from the Depot,' he said. 'You're an educated man. Someone I can *talk* to! For now, you're in Corporal Cooper's section. Cooper's been shot at a half a dozen times, and he knows what to do. You just follow him and you'll be OK!'

I expected Cooper to be a crusty veteran, but instead I found a weasel-faced boy, hardly older than myself. 'Can you operate a radio?' he demanded, and, as I nodded, he lugged the set and its man-pack over to me. 'Get that tuned in,' he said. 'About time we had some crows to do the donkeywork.'

'Excuse me, corporal,' I said, 'but I'm not a crow. Crows belong in the Depot. I'm out of that now!'

'Listen to the old sweat!' Cooper howled. 'First day in the battalion and he's a bleedin' hero! Look at the bugger! No sand under his foreskin yet! Still got the skidmarks on his arse! Why should Britain tremble with men such as these to defend her? Jesus Christ!' A few leering, unwashed hyena faces gathered around and chortled. I realized that the faces belonged to my new section. The only one who didn't laugh was a tall Welsh-man called Davis. He was a private, but he looked older than Cooper. Davis watched the corporal pointedly as he spoke. When Cooper moved away, he came to help me lace up my flak jacket. 'Don't worry about Cooper,' he told me. 'He's just got his first tape. He wants to show everyone that he's not the biggest crow in the platoon, that's all!'

'Get that radio on!' Cooper snapped. 'And let's move it!' I jerked the headset over my ears and listened to the sizzling mush of static. 'Radio silence till we're outside!' Cooper said. 'No point letting the buggers know we're coming, is there?' Then he stepped close to me and said, 'Out there your life depends on your mates, know what I mean? We don't want any cock-ups from crows. When the bullets are flying, you want to know who's on your side!'

'Get that patrol out, Corporal Cooper!' Lieutenant Smythe shouted, as he paced into the room. We hustled downstairs.

'What's Smythe like?' I asked Davis.

'Typical officer, boy,' he said. 'Plenty of brains, no common sense. Always on about his university degree. Educated idiot!'

The loading-bay was a semicircular wall of sand-bags set up like a shrine by the main gate. We pointed our rifles at it in supplication and slid our magazines into place. It was the first time I had ever loaded a gun knowing that I might have to kill.

'Right!' Cooper told me. 'We don't do any leaping about like the craphats. We don't do all that stuff they teach you at Hythe. That's for cowboys. We let them see the Maroon Machine. We walk out cool as if we own the place. But you keep your eyes peeled for everything. Stay behind me, five yards back, and watch the left of arc, specially upper-storey windows. If we get bumped, try and identify the flash and shoot back. Understand?'

Cooper gave a sign to the guard at the gate. The barrier lifted. Five Paras moved out into the battle zone.


I must have been insufferable after I got my wings. In the week's leave which followed our passing-out parade, I insisted on taking my Number Twos home and doing a circuit of the town. I referred to my father and my uncle as craphats, and only just stopped short of doing the same with poor old Tom Kew, my grandfather. I behaved as if I were afraid of nothing. I was a man apart, an emperor. I was about to go to Northern Ireland: they said it was 'peace-keeping', but everyone knew it was war. I was ready to sacrifice myself in war, and therefore a riotous and self-indulgent lifestyle seemed both excusable and necessary. I ran riot. I ate and drank beer and danced in discos, chatted up girls and insulted them if they were unfriendly. I even called a policeman a craphat and got away with it.

Deep down, I suppose I must have been afraid. But I don't remember it. On the contrary, I *wanted* to go to war, just like all those millions of young men who had marched out with Tommy Kew in 1914. No one talked about Ulster as a 'war', but there was still plenty to be nervous about. It was the most troubled year of the province's history. Almost a hundred British soldiers

had been killed there in less than twelve months, and the
number of reported shootings ran into tens of thousands. It was
a war, all right. The IRA had sworn revenge on the Paras over
Bloody Sunday, and the Loyalist Paramilitaries were rioting
over the abolition of the Stormont Parliament. The previous
August hundreds of IRA sympathizers had been interned without trial in Long Kesh. The IRA had removed all constraints
from its active service units. Internment had shifted world
opinion in their favour, and the fence-sitters among the Republicans came out on the IRA side for the first time. Everywhere the army went, its patrols were stoned, shot at and
petrol-bombed.

I felt better when my leave came to an end, and I headed
back to Aldershot. I had something definite to occupy myself
with. I collected my smock from the stores at Normandy Barracks, now embellished with the blue 'DZ' flashes which signified
my new battalion. 2 Para was already in the middle of its
second tour in Northern Ireland, and the battalion had suffered
only one fatality. In May 1971 Corporal Mick Willets, a popular soldier of the unit, had been standing at the entrance to
Springfield Road RUC station in Belfast. A terrorist had lobbed
in a suitcase containing a massive bomb. Willets's first reaction
had been to shield a Catholic family: he stood between them
and the bomb, while they ran past to safety. He had been blown
to pieces, and, according to other soldiers who had been there,
the Catholic crowd outside had danced and chanted all around
the pieces of his shattered body.

Our guide to Ulster was our former platoon sergeant, Tony
Norris. He had been posted back to his old company, and was
put in charge of us for our journey there. We drew our rifles
and collected essential kit. A bus took us to Liverpool docks,
where we boarded the ferry *Ulster Prince*, bound for Belfast. The
ship pulled out into the Irish Sea, which lapped and sucked
ominously at its hulk. The deck vibrated and squalls of wind-
borne rain fragmented grey and silver across the portholes.

'I don't want anyone getting pissed,' Norris said. 'The last
time I brought a platoon back from Belfast one of them fell arse

over tip into the briny. They stopped the ferry, but they never found him. It was the only bloody casualty my company had on that tour!' As the night wore on and we fought to stay awake, the ferry seemed the most drab and depressing place on earth.

Dawn came, uniformly bleak and weary over the city of Belfast, squatting like a gnome under its hills. Tiny figures moved on the docks like clockwork dolls. A gauze of mist lay on the mountains, and here and there chimneys smoked like flag-poles flying ragged white ribbons. A greasy tongue of rain licked across the lough, as the *Ulster Prince* manoeuvred awkwardly into the harbour. The mooring lines were thrown over bollards; the gangways were hoisted into place. Outside the terminal were the streets of a dreary dockland. There was nothing that seemed extraordinary about the scene except for a paratrooper in combat kit, crouching in a doorway with a loaded rifle. Another paratrooper escorted us to a four-tonner, and we clambered on. The tailboard went up; the guard sat down at the rear. The last thing I heard before the engine started was a magazine being clicked into place.


A private called Robbins was 'point', and Corporal Cooper followed him, five yards behind. I came after Cooper, and behind me was a big, thick-moustached man called Hensby. Davis was 'tail-end Charlie', the last man in the patrol. Half the time he had to walk backwards to cover the rear. They moved slowly, with precise, measured steps. There was an alertness about them that was almost menacing. They paced like easy, poaching predators, heads moving left and right, eyes ready and alert and watchful, as if they knew every inch of the street. They didn't look afraid. They didn't look anything but supremely confident. Their eyes scanned the buildings and cars and windows, one man looking left, another right, another behind, covering every possible approach. There was an asymmetrical logic to their movements as they glided along. It seemed that they moved and halted in silent consensus, picking up unseen cues from each other. They would drop into a doorway or crouch by a wall, covering each other in exposed places, around blind corners or across the road. Their rifles never left the alert position, and their boots whispered quietly across the pavements as they circled and stopped and moved on like parts of an oiled machine.

The crowds of shoppers we passed on the lower end of the Shankill hardly seemed to notice us. They hurried on with averted eyes or looked straight through us. Tides of women scuttled by with prams and push-chairs, dowdy, down-at-heel women with haggard white faces and whining children. There were men with greasy hair and slept-in trousers carrying shopping-bags, and youths with cut-off jeans and polished boots, swaggering up the street with their hands in their waistbands. Sometimes there were good-looking girls with long hair and tight jeans, and the patrol's eyes wandered lingeringly toward them for a second before returning to their scanning. No one spoke to us. No one wished us good morning. I had no idea if these people were Protestants or Catholics or both, but there seemed a sullen air of resentment about them. Some of them, I presumed, must have been glad that we were there, but none of them showed it. It seemed suddenly ludicrous to be walking through a perfectly ordinary street with a loaded rifle.

But that was a dangerous thought. Many soldiers had died here on these ordinary streets. To allow your attention to wander for a minute could be fatal. Any of these ordinary, down-at-heel people could have been an enemy. Any of these vacant windows could have concealed a sniper. Any passing car could be carrying a hit-team. Any doorway could contain a bomb. We crossed the main road, dashing from curb to curb, while the rest of the patrol covered. On the opposite side was the citadel of Unity Flats, and behind it the older complex of New Lodge. On our left was the Old Lodge Road, now no more than a diagonal runway through a site of derelicts in various stages of decomposition. The terraces were like a carcass rotting with the flies and the sun: a roof fallen in here, a window smashed there, a wall subsided or a floor caved in. Their smashed and mutilated windows stared at us accusingly as we hugged the shadows. It would have been a good place for a sniper to hide.

We moved into a kind of tunnel under Unity, and Cooper halted. He drew back the cocking-handle of his SLR and let the working parts move forward with a crash.

'Cock your weapon!' he told me, as the others did the same.

'That's against standing orders!' I said.

His reaction was faster than I could have imagined. He punched me in the ear with the speed of a professional boxer. The punch hurt.

'That's the first and last time you argue with an NCO in this platoon!' he said. 'Now cock your weapon!'

I flushed, and then I cocked. So after all my exultation at getting my wings, I was still the lowest of the low: still the despised crow, I thought. That blow shattered for me the illusion that we were all equal as 'brothers in arms'. Davis looked on from his position at the rear of the patrol. He said nothing.

Unity Flats had been built a few years previously as a mixing area for Catholics and Protestants. By now most of the Protestants had moved out, leaving Unity as a dangerous enclave of Republicanism on the edge of the Loyalist heartland of the Shankill. Often there had been confrontations here, as the Protestants marched past into the city-centre, and the Catholics poured out of the flats to jeer at them. The complex seemed desolate. The stairs and walkways were broken, and the walls scrawled with aerosol graffiti: KILL BRITS, PARAS = EVIL BASTARDS and FUCK THE QUEEN. The squares and underpasses were slimy with cooking-grease and chicken bones which no one had bothered to clear up. The waste disposal chutes were clogged. The lifts didn't work. Windows had been boarded up, and doors smashed in as a result of riots or stonings or army raids. At the back was a playground of fractured swings, twisted tubular steel like surreal modern sculptures, and half-derelict lock-up garages. People flitted in and out of doors quickly like ghostly apparitions. There were grey silhouettes behind unwashed lace curtains. There were screeching, drunken voices from behind closed doors. There were ominous twitchings of curtain corners as we walked by.

Once that morning, though, a woman opened her door and invited us in. She was small and ginger-haired and embarrassed-looking. 'Come on in for a cuppa,' she said. I felt reluctant, but the others trooped in happily. When I saw the Red Hand of Ulster hanging on her wall, I understood why she had invited us. Hers must have been one of the last Protestant families left on the estate.

We sat on her cheap sofa with its floral print, our big boots and rifle-butts dirtying the ragged carpet. The flat was clean and neatly kept. There was a pair of brass candlesticks on the mantlepiece, and above it an oil painting of a cherubic boy with a globular tear in his eye, that you could buy for five pounds from Boots.

'Sure it's desperate all this bombing and shooting every night, so it is!' the woman said. 'Sure youse boys should be out shooting those Fenian bastards, like you did in Londonderry!'

'We'd like to, missus,' Cooper said. 'But they won't let us!'

The woman brought us tea in mugs, but I hesitated before I drank it. Cooper noticed. 'They put ground glass in it,' he said, grinning and sipping his.

The woman looked offended. 'Sure you shouldn't be making crack like that with the wee boy, corporal,' she said. 'He doesn't look as if he's been here more than five minutes. You'll have him thinkin' we're all monsters, so you will!'

Cooper grinned more widely, enjoying my embarrassment and the woman's.

'I've got two wains of my own,' she went on. 'I don't know what'll become of them when they finish school. There's no work even for them that want it!'

'Just so long as they don't end up throwing bricks at us,' Cooper said. 'We don't want any more trouble with you Prods. We've got enough stick from the Fenians.'

The woman looked at him silently. 'We're respectable people here,' she said.

'That's what they all say,' said Cooper.

On the way back to base we came across a little dark-haired girl playing on the walkway with a doll. The girl was about four, very pretty, with eyes like brown saucers. I couldn't help bending down to speak to her as we passed. 'What are you doing, then?' I asked her, smiling.

She regarded me for a moment with her angelic brown eyes. 'Fuck orff, youse Brit bastards!' she said. It was so unexpected that I recoiled in horror. As I walked on, I saw that she had wrenched the doll's arms out of their sockets.

At the beginning of 1972 Director of Operations, General Sir Harry Tuzo, had predicted that the Provisional IRA would be defeated by March. On 6 March the Provies planted a bomb outside the Abercorn Restaurant in the centre of Belfast. It was a Saturday afternoon, and the place was crammed with women shoppers taking the weight off their feet, and noisy children. You could imagine the clink of the teacups and the squeak of the children and the grating of chairs on the wooden floor. And then the deafening roar of the explosion, and the blast spreading like a tidal wave through the building, and the bodies sailing over each other like burning dolls, and the stink of charred flesh. Two women died. A hundred and thirty were burned and mutilated. Two sisters out shopping for a wedding-dress both had their legs burned to bloody stumps. The IRA denied all knowledge of the incident, and blamed the Protestant paramilitaries.

Two weeks later another bomb blew the roof off the railway station in Great Victoria Street. Another hundred and thirty were injured. At that point Prime Minister Edward Heath abolished the Northern Ireland Parliament at Stormont and instead established direct rule by William Whitelaw, Secretary of State for Northern Ireland. The Loyalist paramilitaries thought the government would sell them out. 'Platoons' of the Ulster Defence Association were openly drilling in combat jackets and balaclavas on the Shankill Road. In east Belfast the Loyalists set up barriers blocking off their streets. Loyalist murder gangs were active again. William Craig, the fanatic leader of the Loyalist Vanguard movement, was talking openly of assassination. For a moment the province was poised on the brink of civil war.

Day by day the tannoy would buzz, 'Stand-by, platoon, ACTION STATIONS!' and we would shake off the sleep and dash downstairs in our smocks and flak jackets with our rifles tagged to our wrists by webbing. The vehicles, mostly open Land Rovers, would be gunning their engines and filling the yard with diesel fumes. Sergeant Beck would hand round pick-helves, riot helmets and rubber-bullet guns. The lads would pull their leather gloves on expectantly. 'No riot helmets unless we have to!' Sergeant Beck would say. 'Let them see the Maroon Machine!' The red beret was our amulet. We almost believed it bullet-proof. We would pile into the Land Rovers with our rifles and our pick-helves and our armoured vests. 'Let's hope there's some action this time!' the lads would say. 'Give us a chance to get stuck in!' No one wanted to miss a good riot. Even the cooks and bottle-washers would find some excuse to join in. The gate would open. The Land Rovers would roll out.

One day, it was the Tartan gangs gathering in Millfield. There were hundreds of youths wearing boots and bomber jackets and tartan scarves as their team colours. They scuttered about the streets, breaking up kerb-stones and pelting them at us. 'Let's get at them!' Cooper said. 'We'll settle these little bastards in two minutes!' But we held back and held back, crouching in doorways along the street. A picket of youths ran out of the ranks and threw a lighted petrol-bomb into a terraced house. The house belonged to a seventy-year-old Catholic. When we got there, the plastic sofa was already on fire. The old man was dead, overpowered by the fumes. As we carried the stretcher to an ambulance, the crowd hurled stones at us and cheered.

Then it was the Loyalists up the Shankill Road. They hijacked two buses and hauled them across the road, blocking the traffic. When we arrived, they had set the buses on fire and were huddling behind them in little balaclava-clad groups, a distorted mirror-image of ourselves. They wore combat jackets and DMS boots bought from army-surplus stores. Sometimes they broke out of their huddles to dash off a salvo of kerb-stones, to wave their Red Hand flags and to shout 'NO SURRENDER!' We strained to get at them like hungry dogs. The order to attack never came. When the buses had finally burned out, they cheered and waved their flags, shouted 'NO SURRENDER!' once more, and went off home for tea. We clambered back into our vehicles, heavy with disappointment and frustration. 'When are they going to let us get stuck in?' the boys would say.

The Provies wouldn't come out on the streets, but threw nail-bombs and took pot-shots. The Loyalists rioted, but the authorities wouldn't let us get at them. We gnawed at ourselves like leopards in a gin-trap. We wanted nothing more than to fight a war. Our attitude to the enemy was summed up in a new piece of graffiti which appeared on a nearby wall. Where someone had written PARAS = EVIL BASTARDS, an aerosol-packing para-trooper had added: THOUGH I WALK THROUGH THE VALLEY OF THE SHADOW OF DEATH, I WILL FEAR NO EVIL, FOR I AM THE EVILLEST BASTARD IN THE VALLEY. Signed, A PARA.

# 8

## Contact

———

Night was the fright-time, when death could hide in any doorway. We dodged quietly through the streets, avoiding sodium lights and lighted windows. We turned down the radio mush and darkened our faces with cam-cream. We fastened up all shiny bits and rattling pieces with masking tape. Once, as we moved along Upper Library Street, a man in a parked car switched his headlights on suddenly and pinpointed the entire patrol in their powerful glare. We ran and dropped and rolled as if we were still on the Brecon ranges. All except Cooper: he didn't budge. He pointed his rifle straight at the car, and for a second I thought he would fire. 'Put that fucking light out, or I'll put *you* out!' he screamed at the driver. The man didn't get a chance to explain. A moment later we had surrounded the car, dragged him out and spread-eagled him across the bonnet. We kicked open his legs and searched him roughly for firearms. 'I'll report ye for this!' the man gasped. Cooper kicked his feet still wider. 'You want to do it with a broken leg, Paddy?' he asked him. 'You got no more sense than to put your headlights on a patrol at night?'

Another time we were crossing Unity when there was a sudden surge of fire. 'THUMPA! THUMPA! THUMPA!' It was a Thompson sub-machine-gun firing from somewhere up in the fortress of Unity and dropping heavy 45-mm slugs on us. I fell into a doorway and brought my rifle up. Nothing stirred in the darkness. Cooper was crouching forward near some bins, a squat praying mantis in the shadows.

'Shit!' someone said. 'Were they firing at us?'

We lay there a moment, wondering and listening. We were itching to shoot at something, but there was nothing to shoot at. No one had even seen the flash.

'Shall I report a contact?' I asked Cooper.

'Just tell them we heard some shots,' he told me. 'Davis! You and Hensby get up on them walkways and clear them! I don't want any bugger bumping us when we pull out!' Davis and Hensby zigzagged across the base of the flats and were swallowed up in the darkness. I reported the incident to our ops room.

'Was it a contact or not?' the operator asked testily.

'We don't know!' I said.

'Tell Sunray to report immediately when you get back!' the irritated voice said.

As we moved off, someone began to crash a dustbin lid. Then another one started, like an answering voice. A third began, then another and another. The night was suddenly hot and alive with percussion. Rattling, smashing, crashing in the darkness, the drumming built up to an eerie crescendo. It was a primitive message of hate, ringing alive out of the hostile night. We were glad to get out of the shadows and back to Peter's Hill. Not until the gate closed behind me did I begin to shake.

Within a few days it happened again. This time I was on sentry duty in the third-floor OP. From the window I could see across the helter-skelter of roofs between Peter's Hill and the Falls Road, where the great, bloated pillars of Divis Flats winked over them like great periscopes. No matter how alert you were when you entered the box, within moments your mind would be wandering. Women, good food, beer, a warm beach and women again. On this occasion my daydreams were interrupted by the distinct sound of a rifle being cocked. A second later there was the crack of a bullet, and the thump and whizz as it glanced off the brickwork near me. It was so quick that I neither flinched nor reacted. Before I could lift the field-telephone, it buzzed.

'Did you see where that shot came from?' a voice warbled. It was the voice of Captain Darby, our company second-in-command. There was no inquiry after the state of my health, I noticed.

'No, sir,' I said.

'What are you doing in there, playing with yourself?' he demanded.

A few minutes later the door flew open and Captain Darby entered the OP.

'Do try and spot the flash!' he told me.

'There was no flash, sir,' I explained. 'But the shot came from right near, because I heard the rifle being cocked!'

He sniffed and looked at me in disbelief. 'How could it be, you idiot?' he asked. Then he marched out, irate. That was the 'man-management' skill we were always hearing about, I thought. I may have been an idiot, but I was less of one than General Sir Harry Tuzo. He had predicted that the IRA would be defeated by March. It was now April, and they were still shooting at us.

The day before my nineteenth birthday, one of our patrols was called to the Crumlin Road. There they found a taxi-driver bleeding to death in the cab of his own taxi. He was a Catholic called Gerald Donnelly, who had picked up two passengers for the Ardoyne, a solidly Catholic area. The passengers turned out to be members of a Loyalist terror squad. They forced him to drive into a back-street, where they beat him with their fists and then shot him five times with a pistol. He had no proven connection with the IRA. The terror gangs were on the rampage. They would pick up innocent Catholics who had wandered near their areas and take them to a house for what they called a 'romper-room' session. A gang of men would kick and beat the victim, slash him with knives and razor blades, or burn him with cigarette-ends, demanding information about the IRA. The 'interrogation' was just an excuse for unadulterated cruelty. After they had tortured him for hours or days, the victim would be shot. One man was found covered from head to foot in stab wounds.

The next day I received a birthday card from my parents and made the mistake of letting Cooper see it. 'How touching!' he scoffed. Later, in one of our OPs, a sangar on the corner of Unity Flats, he, Robbins and Hensby gave me a birthday present. While the two of them held me down, Cooper shaved all the hair off my body with a rusty razor. After he had shaved my abdomen, leaving a network of bad scratch marks from the blunt blade, Hensby suggested cutting off half my moustache. Hensby had once had the best moustache in the platoon, but one night Cooper and Robbins had shaved half of it off while he was sound asleep. The next morning he had been obliged to shave off the other half himself. Now he wanted to try the same thing on me.

'First we'll do the moustache, then the pubic hair!' Cooper grunted. 'Just like the romper-room, ain't it?' He applied the razor to my upper lip. It hurt, and its bluntness ripped the whiskers out rather than shaving them. Cooper was about to take a second chunk, when the door opened.

'That's enough, Cooper! He's only a kid!' Taffy Davis was standing by the door in his flak jacket.

Cooper hesitated. 'Your *pal*, is he, Davis?' he jeered. 'It's *Corporal* Cooper to you!'

'Yeah,' said Davis slowly. '*Corporal* Cooper. Sorry, I forgot.' He looked at the NCO so contemptuously that Cooper backed off.

'Get up, Asher!' Cooper said.

'Thanks, Taff,' I told Davis later. 'Cooper's got it in for me!'

'Cooper's tape has gone to his head,' he said. 'I've seen a thousand like him come and go. I've been in nine years. I got up to full-screw too, but they busted me.'

'What for?'

'For assaulting a senior NCO.'

Davis was one of several senior privates who had either refused promotion or had been busted. They were the real backbone of the platoon. Some of them went up and down in rank like yo-yos. There was a well-known saying that lance-corporal was the hardest rank to get and the easiest to lose.

'Spider' White was a senior private, a tall, silent man with James Bondish good looks. He never seemed to join in the beasting and the horse-play. He was one of those whose silence seems to reflect an inner power and intelligence. Half-way through the tour he was promoted to lance-jack.

One afternoon, Spider asked me to accompany his patrol as radio-op. I was due on fatigues that day, but even a foot patrol was better than scrubbing Dixies. The patrol turned out to be a 'funny'. Instead of patrolling the city-centre, as planned, Spider led us up the forbidden Shankill, past the place where buses had been set on fire, and into a Loyalist drinking-club. Spider bought us all pints of lager, and we sat down with our rifles, not quite knowing how to behave. The other drinkers were men in their twenties: the same arrogant types who paraded down the back-streets in balaclavas, shouting 'No surrender!' They weren't unfriendly, and Spider seemed perfectly at home. He sank his beer in great gulps and handed his rifle around for the civvies to play with. I wondered what would happen if they ran off with it.

'Our battalion is a load of crap!' Spider announced after two or three pints. 'Now, *1 Para*, they *had* the right idea! They shot all those Taigs down in Londonderry! They reckoned there was only thirteen dead. There was only thirteen *found*, is what there was. All the real IRA men were carried across the border and buried in shaller graves!'

The audience cheered. Someone passed Spider another pint. 'Ay, that's the spurut!' someone said.

'We know who the enemy are,' he went on. 'We should get 'em against the wall and top the lot! That's the only thing those bastards understand!'

It was at this point that I noticed something horrific. I had put the radio down on the floor without realizing that it was resting on the presser-switch. That meant we had been on the air for the previous half hour. Not only had we blocked out all other signals on that wavelength, but everything said in the bar had probably been relayed straight to the ops room.

I managed to persuade Spider to leave, and once we were outside I made a radio-check. I didn't tell him what the problem was. 'OK,' the base operator came back. 'Where have you been,

Zero-Bravo? We've been trying to contact you for the past half hour. Someone has been fouling up the net by keeping his presser-switch open!'

'Roger, Zero-One,' I replied. 'I've been having the same problem contacting you. Er, we're proceeding in your direction.'

'Zero-One, out,' he said. I heaved a secret sigh of relief.

'What was it?' Spider demanded.

'Some fool blocking the net!' I said.

Twenty minutes later we were unloading our rifles at the loading-bay, when Captain Darby came storming out of the ops room. 'Have you any idea who was blocking the net?' he demanded.

'No, sir,' I answered. 'Some operators have no idea. They sit on the presser-switch and forget about it!'

'Yes,' he agreed, somewhat mollified. 'But God knows where this one was. Sounded like some drunken Irishman rambling off about shooting Taigs!'

I managed to escape from the 2i/c, only to run into the company quarter-master sergeant, Colour McStevens. 'Weren't you lot meant to be in the city-centre?' he asked me.

'Yes, colour,' I said, hoping I wasn't blushing.

'Well I've just driven through the entire city-centre in a mobile, and I didn't see you!'

'Camouflage and concealment, colour!' I said.

When Spider asked me to accompany his patrol again the next week, I declined. I was very glad I had done: that afternoon a police mobile was called to a drinking-club on the Shankill Road. A drunken paratrooper had knocked down a Protestant youth and had to be pulled off him while holding a pistol to his head and screaming, 'I'll kill you, you Orange bastard!' The paratrooper was Lance-corporal Spider White. So much, I thought, for the strong, silent type.

Patrols were interspersed with vehicle check-points (VCPs), which we threw at random across major roads. They made local drivers livid. Crossing Belfast meant being stopped six or seven times by troops or police, and many drivers would vent their frustration on us. We loved it when they did. Any driver who was rude or irritable got the full treatment: taken out of the vehicle, spread-eagled, body-searched and made to watch while we went over his car with a fine-tooth comb. No one had taught us to be polite, and we weren't. We made things as awkward as possible. 'I've been through it all!' one old man told us. 'The Black and Tans and the B-specials: but youse Paras are the worst bastards of all!' That was the best compliment we'd ever received.

Often, standing for hours in the sopping rain, bored to death by the routine and the lack of action, we prayed for something to happen: for someone to shoot at us, for someone to make trouble. But the hours passed, and everything was stultifyingly normal. Our greatest dream was that the IRA would come out on the streets and fight us like a proper army. But they were far too clever for that. Instead, we had to make do with shouting abuse at women and clipping the ears of the cheeky urchins who walked past us in the street. The NCOs bore down on us to keep us in line. Once, as I returned from hours of waiting at a VCP in the pouring rain, CQMS McStevens inspected my rifle. I had been in his bad books since I'd made that unfortunate remark about 'camouflage and concealment'. 'This rifle is rusty!' he told me.

'It's raining, colour!' I said.

'I don't care if it's fucking snowing, your rifle should be clean at all times!' He put me on a charge and marched me in front of the OC. The charge was read out. The OC was a portly man with carroty hair and a beetroot-red face.

'Do you have anything to say?' he demanded.

'It was raining, sir,' I said.

'No excuse,' he told me. 'Fined twenty pounds!'

It all seemed a joke until I heard the size of the fine. When you get paid nineteen pounds a week, twenty is no joke.

'You can appeal to the colonel if you wish,' he said. 'But don't forget that he can make your sentence more severe!' He knew he'd got me. The idea of going before the colonel always put people off.

That was the first time I spoke to the OC. The second time

was a few weeks later, when I was on guard-duty at the gate. The guard-sangar was at ground level and opened into the street. Here, dressed in your helmet and flak jacket, you could watch the passers-by, mostly women pushing prams towards the Shankill Road. Some of them wished you a friendly 'Good morning'; others an acid 'Fuck off home, youse Para bastards!' On this morning two rather attractive teenage girls sauntered past.

'Hey, so'ja!' one of them shouted. 'Looks desperate borin' standing there on guard!'

'You wouldn't believe it!' I shouted back.

'Sure I'll come and talk to ye if you like!' the girl said sweetly, and moved nearer. She had a small oval face the shape of a peeled almond, and a swirl of rich dark hair.

'I like,' I said. 'But my officers don't!'

Right on cue the OC's Land Rover roared into the street and rattled to a halt by the gate. I shooed the girls away, but it was too late. The OC was dragging his heavyweight bulk from the front seat. He pounded up to me, enormously swollen by his flak jacket.

'What are you doing talking to those girls on guard?' he demanded.

'I was just about to tell them to clear off, sir!' I said.

'Just about!' the big man repeated, almost choking. 'Listen! We're fighting a war, sonny Jim!' He put me on restricted privileges for the rest of the tour.

Of course, he was quite right. I thought myself tough, but the first pretty face I saw could knock the wind out of me. But I couldn't help laughing at the idea of 'restricted privileges'. It was difficult to see what 'privileges' I was supposed to have. We were never allowed out of the base, never wore civilian clothes, never officially entered a shop or pub. And the base was no larger than a large house. There were a few stables at the back converted into a kind of Naafi shop, run by a quiet Pakistani. In the shop you could buy Mars Bars, fizzy drinks and 'banjos', our word for fried-egg sandwiches. But that was the bounds of our freedom. We weren't there for the good of our health.

These restrictions existed for a purpose. Up to the previous year soldiers had been allowed into the city-centre in civvies during off-duty hours. Then three young men from the Royal Highland Fusiliers had been murdered in horrendous circumstances. Joseph McCaig, his brother John and another Fusilier called Douglas McCaughey were drinking in a Belfast pub called Mooney's Bar, when three men began chatting to them. One of the men claimed to have served in the British army, and the Fusiliers thought them sympathetic. In fact, they were Provisional IRA. The Provies led the unsuspecting soldiers to another pub, where they proposed that all six of them should move on to a party. There would be women at the party, the men said. They all piled into two cars and drove up into the Belfast Hills, where the soldiers had to get out to relieve themselves. As they did so, their 'companions' shot them all in the back. The McCaig brothers were found lying on top of each other; McCaughey was found sitting on the kerb with his beer-glass in his hand.

We were expected to make our own entertainment, and frequently it consisted of fist-fights. The platoon would gather round and cheer whichever contestant they favoured. A word or a glance out of place was enough to spark the thing off. I got into an argument with a squat little private called Sykes, whose distinguishing feature was a flat nose splayed out like a gorilla's.

Cooper had ordered Sykes to carry the radio, but Sykes resented it. He tried to assert his seniority by passing it on to me. 'You're carrying it, Asher!' he told me.

'Drop dead!' I said. 'It's your turn!'

'Listen,' he said. 'I'm a private third class and you're a crow!'

'You're as much a crow as I am. At least I didn't take three goes to pass out of the Depot! You got back-squadded twice!'

'You're a bleedin' poof, Asher, that's what you are! Reading big books, thinkin' you're clever! *Lord of the Rings*: more like Lord of the flaming arseholes!'

'At least I *can* read!'

'You won't be able to when I gouge your fuckin' eyes out!'

'Yeah?'

We were already squaring up to each other, neither of us quite knowing how the argument had got so bad. 'Go on, Sykes!' someone said. 'Knock his twat in!'

Sykes advanced with wide nostrils flaring. He was small and powerful, and his muscles flexed determinedly. I was ready for him, knowing that whatever happened couldn't be much worse than milling. Just before contact, Taff Davis interposed himself between us.

'This is a waste of time!' he said. 'We're due out in two minutes!'

Sykes groped past him. 'I'll knock the crow's head in!' he said. At that moment the door opened, and the platoon commander, Lieutenant Smythe, entered.

'Corporal Cooper!' he said. 'Where's your patrol?' Then he noticed our aggressive postures and demanded, 'What's going on?'

'Nothing, sir!' I lied.

'A little disagreement, sir,' Davis contradicted me.

Smythe looked hard at Cooper. 'You're supposed to stop this kind of thing, corporal!' he said. 'If these fights don't stop, you'll be down to private again. And I shall ask the OC to hold a milling competition so you can work some steam off!'

Cooper was almost white with rage when the lieutenant closed the door. He looked meaningfully at Davis, and then made a V-sign at it. 'I hope I draw *you* in a milling competition, sir,' he said under his breath. 'I'll rip your fucking nose off!'

The fights were understandable. They were what happens in most exclusively male societies: fights to determine the pecking order and who can boss who. But they weren't the only exotic form of entertainment. One group of soldiers would hold so-called 'gunge' contests. They sat round in a circle and tried to outdo each other in acts of gross obscenity, like eating shit and drinking urine. During house searches they vented their anger on their victims, smashing down doors and breaking up furniture, kicking and rifle-butting anyone who resisted, making lewd suggestions to the women of the house and threatening the children. Some of them tormented the quiet Pakistani in the

shop until he threw a chip-pan of boiling fat at them. They
battered to death a stray cat that wandered past the OP and
held up its mangled corpse to the children who came looking for
it. Several of them boasted of dragging a mentally deficient girl
into the OP and forcing her to perform oral sex. They said she
enjoyed it.

The circumstances of our training, coupled with the peculiar
nature of our existence in Northern Ireland – a blend of bore-
dom, frustration and occasional terror – turned us into savages.
We begged and prayed for a chance to fight, to smash, to kill, to
destroy: we were fire-eating berserkers, a hurricane of human
brutality ready to burst forth on anyone or anything that stood
in our way. We were unreligious, apolitical and remorseless, a
caste of warrior-janizaries who worshipped at the high-altar of
violence and wanted nothing more.

The animal inside us had been deliberately unchained, deliberately starved and made hungry to kill. Our training had been an
apprenticeship in violence. In any other circumstances my colleagues might have been quite ordinary: perfect gentlemen,
good friends, loving husbands, gentle fathers. But they had been
conditioned by shared suffering to think of themselves as an
elite. They had been brain-washed into believing that cruelty
and aggression were the most desirable qualities. When you
place human beings in such conditions, this is how they behave.

The Provisional IRA believed themselves to be defenders of
their people, an elite force held together by suffering and courage. They thought of British soldiers as 'uniforms', not as people
with mothers, wives and children. If they had regarded us as
human beings, they would never have been able to kill us. Our
worship of violence insulated us from guilt or fear. It prevented
us from remembering that the IRA were human beings like us.
The ability of people to dehumanize anyone outside their own
'tribe' is the sole cause of war. It is also, paradoxically, the
reason for human survival. The world exists in harmony, but
everywhere nature is in conflict, tooth and claw. Conflict is
what gives nature its structure.

Half-way through that tour, something happened which

changed things for me. We were on patrol in Unity, moving along the streets with that shark-like, predatory sense of purpose which had now become second nature. It was almost sunset, and a web of dull grey cloud was stretching its claw across the sky. I was tail-end Charlie of the patrol, and little Sykes was ahead of me, carrying the radio. As my gaze swept the upper-storey windows nearest to us, I picked out one of them that was being slowly and surreptitiously opened. I had trained myself to look out for such things over the weeks, and the slow deliberation of the movement brought an immediate cold sweat to my temples. Just then, something grey and elongated was pushed through the window. It was unmistakably the barrel of a rifle, pointing at Sykes in front of me. A pulse of adrenalin shot through me. My yellow card was forgotten. I dropped on one knee with the rifle up, held my breath, took the first pressure. I must have been a fraction of a second away from firing, when I recognized the bobbing head of a little boy behind the open window. He was holding a plastic rifle, just like one I'd once been given for Christmas. 'BANG! BANG! Youse Paras are dead!' the boy shouted merrily. A woman appeared behind him as I clicked the safety-catch on. It was only then that I noticed the rest of the patrol in covering positions: they had dropped into them without a sound at the moment I had brought my rifle up, and I realized that I had shouted to them without even knowing it.

'You nearly had a dead kid, missis!' I shouted angrily to the woman.

'Yeah!' she shouted back. 'Youse Para bastards are good at shooting kids!' The window slammed shut, and when I got up I found that I was trembling like a leaf. I had been within a fraction of a second of a horrific mistake.

'I nearly shot the kid!' I shouted to Cooper. 'A little kid!'

'Pity you didn't!' was the corporal's reply. 'The less of them the better!'

But I worried about it more as the hours passed. I had been ready to kill, with an illegal round in the breech and without a proper warning. I had been lucky. No one else knew quite how near I'd come to opening fire. I realized then that I had come up against the true horror of Northern Ireland: I had entered that infinitely brief limbo which lay between the hero and the murderer, the survivor and the victim.

Put yourself for a moment in the position of the soldier suddenly confronted with an individual who appears to be threatening life. You can shoot him outright or you can deliver a series of two warnings, then arm your weapon, then warn him a third time, then fire. If the individual is threatening life, then he has ample time to react. He can kill you, he can kill others, he can set off a massive bomb and kill scores. If you shoot him, though, and he is *not* afterwards found to have been threatening life, you will be guilty of murder. Remember, you have less than a second to make up your mind.

Back in the base Taff Davis told me, 'Don't worry about that kid. You didn't fire, that's the main thing. If you spend your time worrying about that kind of thing, you'll crack up!'

'It's against standing orders to have a round up the breech!' I said.

'Yeah,' he said, 'old General Tuzo writes out his yellow cards, but he doesn't have to patrol the streets. All you're doing is evening the chances a bit. You've got to stay alive, that's the important thing. They stack the odds against you. They train you to kill, then they let the Provies use you as a shooting-gallery. The Provies can hit us anywhere, any time, on or off duty. We're an offensive unit, and we should be able to do the same to them. That's what we're trained for!'

'Then why don't they let us do it?'

'Proof! They've got to make it look legal-like. We know who the IRA are, but we can't treat them like an army, because this is Britain, not Yemen or Borneo. You've got to catch them shooting before you can touch them!'

'If I'd shot that kid, I'd never forget it!'

'Then you shouldn't be here!' he said.

I suppose, deep down, I knew he was right.

# 9

## *Violent Streets*

———

One night an incendiary bomb wrecked Belfast's biggest store, the Co-op. No one knew exactly how the incendiary device had been smuggled in. Vehicles were now excluded from the city-centre and all shoppers searched when entering stores, but still the Provies managed to get in explosives hidden on the person. Women wearing long skirts might carry a bomb no bigger than a cassette-tape hidden between their legs, where few searchers would have the courage to feel. The bomber would deposit the device amongst some combustible material like paint or plastic, which would be certain to ignite when the timer set it off.

The night the Co-op went up, the entire city-centre was choked with smoke and the sickening smell of melting plastic. By the time the fire brigade had extinguished it the following morning, the building was no more than a shell, punctured and reeling, but with some upper floors still intact. Cooper, Robbins, Hensby, Davis and I prowled around the smoking ruins, covering some policemen who were erecting barriers to seal it off.

'Forensic will be in there all day,' one of them told us.

'I don't suppose there's much left inside?' Cooper said.

'Sure you're joking!' the policeman told him. 'Half the floors are still hanging. The stuff is smoke-ruined, sure, but there's plenty left: leather jackets, cigarettes, even washing-machines and fridges!'

Cooper listened with satisfaction. 'So forensic are there till sunset?' he asked.

That evening Cooper and the rest of the patrol brought their rucksacks with them and stashed them in the OP on Unity corner. When it was dark, and the traffic almost cleared, they donned their bergens and blacked their faces. 'You stay here,' Cooper told me. 'You do your two-hour stag on OP, and if anyone wants to know where we are, we've gone to investigate a possible shooting.' I watched them as they padded across Upper Library Street with their bergens dark humps on their backs. I hoped very much they wouldn't get bumped. I should have a difficult time explaining their presence in the city-centre.

Minutes passed. I stared out into the night, watching the traffic-lights change monotonously from green to red to amber. A few cars and delivery-vans roared past. Suddenly the radio sprang to life.

'Whisky Two-One Alpha, over?'

'Whisky Two-One Alpha.'

'This is Zero-Alpha. Call Sunray, over.'

I hesitated nervously. 'Sunray' was the usual code for 'commander', which in this case meant the patrol-leader, Cooper. 'Oh God!' I whispered. Then I pressed the press-all. 'Whisky Zero-Alpha, Sunray has gone to investigate a possible shooting incident. He will be back shortly, over.'

'Roger, Whisky Two-One Alpha, tell him to report as soon as he gets in.'

'Roger, wilco, out.'

I put the press-all down and began to drum my fingers on the wooden sill impatiently. The patrol had been away almost an hour. What the hell were they doing? Another fifteen minutes passed with no sign of them.

The radio buzzed again, making me jump. 'Any sign of Sunray yet?' the operator asked me. I looked up. At that moment the patrol came padding across the road, carrying bergens that were bulging with something.

I hit the press-all. 'Wait, wait, out!' I said, giving the procedure for a temporary delay.

Two minutes later the patrol was unloading at the door. Cooper grabbed the radio. 'No,' I heard him say, 'there was nothing in it. Yes, wilco, out.' Turning to me, he said, 'The Paki's requesting his mess-bill! You'd think they could wait till I got back to base!'

The others were already tipping out the contents of their bergens. 'Look!' Robbins said, 'cigarettes, watches, leather jackets, Mars Bars! You can't imagine it!'

'Weren't there any police about?' I asked.

'Police!' Davis scoffed. 'They were helping themselves the same as us!'

'Why not?' Robbins said. 'It's all insured. The Co-op doesn't lose a penny. All the stock is written off!'

The next night they went off for another harvest, and the night after that. I wondered if Sergeant Beck would notice their sudden enthusiasm for night patrols and suss out what was happening. When I mentioned this to Davis, he laughed.

After a few days our base was packed with goods looted from the store, crammed into lockers, chests and cardboard boxes. The most difficult part was smuggling it past the ops room, where an officer or the CSM might be on duty. Despite Davis's assurance that everyone was involved, none of them seemed willing to risk being caught red-handed. After a few days the Co-op was boarded up. The fuss died down. Things got back to normal.

That week I was assigned duty with the Special Patrol Group in west Belfast. It was a special anti-terrorist force raised from the police, skilled, tough and taciturn men without the destructive bravado of the Paras. Or so I thought then. 'We have to live here!' one of the SPG men told me. 'You Paras just descend on the place, beat up the men, slag off the women and move out. I was born here. These streets are my streets. I'll have to live here after you've gone!' These SPG men knew the city. With them we tracked from street to street, lurching past the wedge of the Ardoyne in our shrapnel-proof Makralon Land Rovers, and swerving into the Old Park Road, where only a few nights previously there had been a savage gun-battle between the IRA and the army. We drove past rows of terraced houses like bad teeth, past the square towers of the old flax mills, their roofs caved in and their windows smashed, past old mill ponds stewing in effluence, where rusty prams and bicycles protruded from the pallid mud.

I got to know the city more during that week than I had in the previous six. It was an evil, gloating presence. It was a vicious, dying carcass with its entrails slashed open, dripping pools of blood and filth and vomit and lashing out in its death throes. There was no excitement here. There was no adventure. This was an evil place, the embodiment of evil, like a disturbed ant-hill turned on itself. A stink hung over the city, a smell of death, of dying places, of the damp-sodden rags of civilization, of animal pens in a vast market, of an enormous concentration camp guarded with barbed wire, search-lights, towers, machine-guns, guards with batons and barred windows. A place where there were secret societies plotting murder, where there were dark alleys and secret houses, and savage tortures in back-rooms, and huddled whiskey-smeared groups who croaked in whispers and held court and pointed the finger of death, and terrorized children and old people, who watched us from dirt-spattered windows with the red eye of hate and the talons of revenge, assessing our chances of living and dying like squalid gods.

Everywhere we went people shouted and children threw stones. 'Black bastards!' they screamed at the SPG. There was trouble brewing in the Protestant ghettos, across the Lagan. In the Woodstock Road the UDA had barricaded themselves in and were defying the police. The city was at boiling point. People stayed in their own areas and were afraid to venture out. A Catholic brewery rep called Bernard Moane was kidnapped from a bar in the Shankill by three Loyalists: they took him into the hills above the city and shot him three times. In Andersonstown a woman was injured in cross-fire between troops and IRA men. As soldiers helped her to the ambulance, a second sniper opened up on them. A 13-year-old girl was killed in a gun-battle in Ballymurphy, and a 64-year-old grandmother was killed by an explosion in Oxford Street.

In the following week I was back to routine duties with my

platoon. I was on night-patrol with Cooper, Hensby and Robbins and another Tom called Peasgood, in an armoured Pig. It was the first time I had done Pig-patrol, and Cooper said that he had asked for it because of the danger from car-bombs. That was the official reason. I soon found out the real one.

'I spotted a place this morning on a recce,' he told the others. 'A little shop down a back-street. Some good stuff there!'

'What are you up to?' I asked.

'You fucking shut your mouth and keep it shut!' Cooper told me. 'Just wait in the Pig with the driver and answer the radio till we get back!'

The armoured car lurched awkwardly into an alley, and the soldiers jumped out. We heard their soft boots running down the alley. Ten minutes passed. Then fifteen.

'I wish they'd hurry up!' the driver said. 'I don't want some bugger hanging a blast-bomb on our wheels!'

'What are they up to?' I asked.

'Ask no questions!' he told me, shrugging.

A few minutes later they were back, beaming with satisfaction. 'GO!' Cooper told the driver. 'Went like a dream,' he said. 'Door caved in like butter! It took us five minutes to get what we wanted. You want to see it?'

The driver shook his head. 'Don't tell me, I don't want to know!'

The Pig pulled into the base at five in the morning. Dawn was glowing like a cigarette-end through a haze of cloud thickened by the sea-fog which had drifted off the lough. Cooper and the others carried their booty sneakily past the ops room and buried it in their equipment chests, which they locked firmly with giant padlocks. Then we stripped off our smocks and flak jackets and, cradling our rifles as usual, went to sleep.

'GET UP, YOU LUCKY LOT!' Sergeant Beck was calling. It was 8.30 a.m., and I had been asleep for only three hours. I yawned as I dragged myself out of my bunk. I still had my boots on, and my sheets and pillows were stained an unhealthy grease-grey where my unwashed clothes had touched them. 'Listen!' Beck told us. 'There's going to be an SIB investigation this morning.' He looked round at the assembled faces: not one of them displayed any emotion. 'There've been a lot of burglaries in the city in the past week,' he said, 'and the police think they're army jobs. They've found imprints of DMS boots outside the premises. Now, I'm not saying it's anything to do with us, but since we're responsible for the city-centre, they're searching us first. I want you to get this place clean as a whistle, you understand?' I watched him for a sign, a wink or a nudge, but his face was perfectly poker.

As soon as he had gone, the lads leapt into action. 'Get rid of everything!' Cooper said.

'Where?' Peasgood asked.

'The walls!' Cooper told him. 'The walls are hollow, so is the ceiling. This place is about a thousand years old and there are nooks and crannies all over. There's at least a foot of space between the panelling and the wall, we can stash it all in there!'

'We'll have to seal it,' Davis cut in. 'I'll go and see the carpenter and get some plastic seal.'

'No,' Cooper said, stopping him. 'If they see new plaster-work, they'll be suspicious!' Then he stopped in his tracks. 'Hey! Where's Hensby and Robbins?'

'They went out early,' somebody said. 'Beck got them up for a prisoner-escort!'

'Christ!' Cooper grunted. 'They've got the keys to their boxes with them. I'd better get down to the ops room and ask the duty operator to call them in.'

Cooper hurried off, while the lads scrambled to get what they had collected from the Co-op into the nooks and apertures behind the walls, the fireplace and the ceiling. The crack in the wall was covered with the poster WELCOME TO NORTHERN IRELAND and the Red Hand of Ulster flag. We had only just managed to pack everything in, when Sergeant Beck appeared again. 'They're here!' he said. 'Stand by your beds!'

Cooper appeared behind him, looking breathless. As Beck went off to fetch the SIB men, he asked, 'Did you get rid of it all?' A second later three plain clothes detectives entered. They were all ex-Redcaps, calm, disinterested men like the ones I had met at Brecon. They searched Cooper's kitbox and found nothing. They rummaged in Sykes's kit, then mine. They searched only our boxes, not even glancing at the walls or ceilings, or even under mattresses or pillows. It was suspicious. Almost as if they knew where and where not to look.

The detectives reached Robbins's and Hensby's boxes. 'Whose are these?' one of them asked.

'Out on duty, those two men,' Sergeant Beck answered. 'But they'll be back before long.'

'I hope so,' the tallest detective said, 'because we haven't got much time!'

The three detectives searched the rest of the boxes and found nothing. The tall one halted in front of the fireplace and glanced at the WELCOME TO NORTHERN IRELAND poster. Then he turned his back on it.

'Well, that just about wraps it up!' said Beck.

'Looks like it,' the tall SIB man agreed.

The tension relaxed. Perhaps Robbins and Hensby would be out for hours. The SIB men wouldn't wait that long.

The detectives walked back along the bunks toward the door. It opened just as they reached it, and Hensby and Robbins stood there with open mouths, looking at the three policemen. 'Would you mind opening your boxes?' the tall detective asked politely. Robbins got his keys out and fumbled with the lock. Hensby followed suit. The tall detective sorted through Robbins's dirty clothes and spare webbing. He came up suddenly with a brand-new watch, holding it aloft as if it were a fresh-caught fish. He looked at Robbins with fish-eyes, but said nothing. Then he dipped his big hand back into the box and came out with a second, third, fourth and fifth watch. 'You have been having a ball, haven't you?' he said finally, holding up the five glittering watches and balancing them, while he checked their numbers against a list he took from his pocket.

Behind him, his two companions were pulling watches out of Hensby's kit. They displayed no triumph. They only looked at the soldier reproachfully as if to say, 'Couldn't you have found a better hiding place?' When they had checked all the numbers, the tall one took their names and said, 'You are not obliged to say anything, but what you say may be taken down in writing and used against you.'

Robbins smiled sweetly and Hensby grunted, 'I ain't saying nothing!'

After they had marched the two soldiers away, Beck strode in, glowering. 'I told you to get this place clean as a whistle!' he stormed. 'I gave you plenty of warning. Bloody morons! That's the end of everyone's freedom! From now on we do everything by the book!'

When the door had closed, Cooper flicked a V-sign after him. 'Those bloody dildos!' he said. 'Keeping their keys with them! We could have avoided it all!'

'They nearly blew it for you, didn't they?' Taff Davis grinned.

'They nearly blew it for all of us!'

'No they didn't. It wasn't the Co-op stuff they were looking for. It was you who started doing other joints, Cooper!'

'*Corporal* Cooper! I've told you before, Davis!'

'Yeah, I heard! So what?'

'I'll have you on a charge for insubordination!'

'You've got plenty of mouth, but no guts, *Cooper*!' Davis said. 'You may have a tape, but you're still a bloody *crow*!'

This was too much for the corporal. He roared and threw himself at the Welshman. Davis had just drawn his fist back to deliver a walloping round-house blow, when the tannoy buzzed: 'STAND BY, ACTION STATIONS!' The punch froze in mid-flight, as everyone scrambled for their flak jackets. Lieutenant Smythe came rushing in, already dressed. 'Get yourselves tooled up!' he said. 'We're going to break through the barricades in Woodstock!'

The argument was lost in the excitement. 'At last!' the lads said, waving their fists. We tagged on our rifles and drew on our leather gloves. Sergeant Beck scurried about with three rubber-bullet guns and an armful of pick-helves. He handed one of the rubber-bullet guns to Sykes.

'I'm not carrying it, sergeant!' the little man said. 'There's going to be shooting today. I've got a right to carry me rifle. You can't carry a baton-gun and an SLR together!'

Beck looked exhausted. 'I don't suppose *you* would have any objections to carrying it, would you?' he asked me with heavy irony.

'Asher can't carry it, sarn't,' Cooper cut in. 'He's not been trained in it. Let Davis carry it!'

The sergeant handed it to Davis. A question mark spread across the Welshman's features, as Cooper grinned. 'Don't worry, Davis,' he said. 'If anyone starts shooting, I'll look after you!'

The Green Howards had been fighting the UDA all morning. Now they were crouching in doorways along the road, looking like great two-legged insects in their helmets and respirators. 'They're using CS gas!' Sergeant Beck gasped in amazement. 'We haven't brought our respirators!' The Howards withdrew, as our Pigs raced down the Woodstock Road. We sniffed the gas through the slits in the armour, and someone jeered 'Green Cowards!' at the retreating soldiers outside. The Pig I was in pulled suddenly into a side-street, and we glimpsed Red Hand flags and balaclava-heads before the driver pulled up the battle-hatches and a shower of bricks and bottles crashed against the vehicle. Beck opened the doors. 'GO!' he yelled. We piled out so eagerly that we tripped over one another. Sykes fell swearing into the gutter, and another paratrooper tripped over him and cut open his face on the muzzle of his rifle. The CS gas drifted over us, stinging our eyes and making us blunder into each other. Through the smoke, we could hear the Green Howards laughing at us.

'Fucking craphats!' Sykes shouted, getting up.

'They're not the enemy!' Beck grunted, pointing towards the barricade. 'There's the enemy!'

We formed into a dog-leg. Terraced houses reared above us like the sheer sides of a canyon. Suddenly there was a crack from up in the roof-tops. Then a crackle of rifle-fire whizzed over us, as some paratroopers from another company shot back. There was smog and gas and noise and confusion. In front of us was a barricade of orange-boxes, rusty bed-frames and old furniture. Behind it a rank of men in balaclavas bristled forward with sticks and Red Hands, chanting, 'NO SURRENDER!' A fusillade of bottles and stones rattled over us, clunking and smashing against the Pig. I saw Davis hit by a piece of paving-stone, his face drawn and white, before he leapt suddenly forward in full view of the rioters and fired.

'VROOOM!' A livid wave of fire splashed out across the barricade. 'GO!' someone shouted. 'KILL THE BASTARDS!' Then I was running along the street with the others, running like dogs. The Pig lurched through the barricade, smashing the furniture and scattering the balaclava-clad men in all directions. Another rubber-bullet blammed out and someone screamed. A chunk of paving-stone hit me, then a bottle. I hardly noticed it. Any fear I might have had was swept away in the excitement. I was over the barricade. I was lashing out with my rifle-butt. Flesh was reeling back in front of me. The phalanx of balaclavas broke. The men ran back up the street, no longer shouting, 'NO SURRENDER!' They began to disappear into doorways which opened up magically to receive them. Davis was clamping another black sausage into the breech. Cooper had cornered a youth in a doorway. He belted the youth on the arm with his rifle-butt, and heard the bone snap. Two balaclavas stepped toward him with swinging sticks. 'Get out of the way!' Davis shouted to me, pointing the rubber-bullet gun directly at Cooper's back. For a second I was sure he would shoot the corporal. Then there was an ear-splitting bang and the balaclava near Cooper fell over with a strangled cry. The other ran like a greyhound for the nearest door.

The street was almost empty now. The Green Howards were walking along it in silence, kicking the debris aside. The medics were wrapping up the injured. Someone said that two snipers had been shot. The Pigs pulled up and we embussed. As the Pigs turned and we drove back past the Green Howards, Cooper put his mouth to the slit and shouted, 'YAH! CRAPHATS!' There wasn't a single Para on the vehicle who failed to cheer.

# 10

## *Secret Squirrel*

———

The sky was full of canopies like schools of jellyfish. All around me parachutes bellied and collapsed, as the parachutists touched the ground. I rolled on to my stomach and began to haul my chute in by the rigging lines. 'MEDIC! MEDIC!' someone was yelling. 'Shut up!' came the reply. I punched the harness release and crawled out of the straps, took my rifle and loaded it. I replaced my helmet with my maroon-red beret, which I had stuffed beneath my smock. 'MEDIC! WHERE'S THE MEDIC!' the desperate voice continued. I packed my chute into its nylon and piled it up with my helmet and reserve, a neat little monument to mark where I had landed. Already scores of paratroopers were tabbing off the DZ, making for their rendezvous points, each one leaving behind his small cairn of helmet and two parachutes. 'COME ON, MEDIC!' I heard again. As I stood up, I saw two Paras with red-cross arm-bands helping a bulky figure not ten metres from me. It was the OC.

We had been back from our tour of duty in Belfast only a few weeks, and this exercise on Salisbury Plain was intended to whip us back into shape for *real* soldiering. The Royal Marines had taken over from us in the city-centre, but their first few weeks there had already been dogged by ill fortune. First, two of their patrols had mistaken each other for the IRA in Smithfield Market at night, and in the firefight that followed a marine had been killed. Next, one of them had accidentally discharged an 84-mm rocket-launcher at their base in Girdwood Park, which had passed through four walls and destroyed half the building.

Off the DZ, I found Cooper and Davis, and the rest of the platoon. They were lying in a brake of blackthorn, in an all-round defensive formation, while the platoon commander brewed himself tea. I dropped into the bushes near Davis. 'Did you see the OC?' he asked me, grinning all over his narrow face. 'Broke his bloody arm, if you ask me, boy! He got twisted right up to the maker's nameplate and couldn't kick them out! Bleeding officers! Educated idiots!'

We moved out of the RV in full darkness. There was no moon, and the stars were veiled in a sheen of mist. For hours we tabbed on across the moor, changing direction and wheeling round until Cooper told us to dig in. Davis and I worked together on a shell-scrape while Cooper supervised, lying in the bushes. The ground was summer-hard, and the work was back-breaking.

'To hell with this for a game of soldiers!' Davis complained. 'Give me a good war any day!'

'That's not what you'd say if they called us back to Belfast tomorrow!' I said.

'You don't call that a *real* war!' he said. 'That's more like playing demo platoon for the IRA. Here I am! Shoot me!'

'Shut up and keep digging!' Cooper's voice came.

We had almost finished the shell-scrape when the radio cackled. I had to climb out of the trench to answer it. 'All stations, this is Zero!' the voice said. 'All units withdraw and RV at . . .' There followed a grid number. I rogered the message and relayed it to Cooper.

He stood up, yawning. 'OK,' he said. 'Fill her in and bug out!'

Davis collapsed in the shell-scrape. 'There's something funny going on!' he said.

He was right. There was a mysterious hush over the company when we arrived at the RV. The 'tactical mode' of the exercise had evidently been abandoned. The men were clumped together in knots, talking quietly. When everyone had assembled, the company sergeant-major addressed us. 'That's it for you, lads!' he said. 'We're going into action. I don't know where, but this is the real thing. Tonight you hand in blanks and draw live ammo. You're going to need it!'

Action ... the real thing: visions of Anguilla, Belize, Hong Kong, Oman, filtered through my mind. The real thing! Before the CSM had finished talking, the men were jumping up and down and throwing their berets in the air and doing a wild war-dance across the ancient sod of Salisbury Plain.

The next evening we boarded HMS *Intrepid* at Chatham, under the cover of darkness. The vessel was an assault-ship, designed for carrying troops. There was a palpable spirit of excitement amongst the battalion. From this backwater we could be bound anywhere in the world, I thought: this silent, dark river led to the shores of glory and adventure, like Conrad's *Heart of Darkness*. As we pulled out of the docks, I stood on deck, drinking in the cloak-and-dagger atmosphere like wine, listening to the thumping gyration of the engine, smelling the heavy scent of oil and watching the amber lights glittering like eyes out on the black waters of the Medway. The evening was cool and sea-damp, and the waves beneath us were a pattern of dark eddies rippling out between the dim headlands of Sheppey and Sheerness.

Taff Davis came bristling into the cabin later. 'Guess what this baby's carrying in the hold?' he gasped. 'Centurion tanks, that's what! I tell you, boy, this is going to be the real thing! At least the Middle East!'

'Must be the Middle East,' Sykes agreed. 'Why else leave from Chatham?'

'Could be a bluff,' Peasgood cut in. 'If we were going to the Middle East, they'd have made an operational drop, like Suez.'

The Colonel called us all together that night to end the misery. The air of expectancy was almost at bursting point. He stood up and cleared his throat. 'Well lads,' he began, 'I suppose some of you are wondering where we're going?'

'Get on with it!' Davis whispered urgently.

'We're going to Belfast,' he said. 'To Ballymurphy.'

There was a visible sag amongst the audience. Someone booed. 'What a shit!' Davis said.

'Quiet!' said the Colonel. 'This is a top-secret operation, Operation Motorman, the biggest op ever to take place in Northern

Ireland. The object is to open up the "no-go" areas in Belfast
and Londonderry. The IRA has promised to fight to the death,
so we might have a good scrap at last! The Murph is the worst
area in Belfast, and the Provisionals there are well armed. The
last unit in there got ambushed a hundred times in a single day.
Now we're going to let them see red berets on the ground.
We're really going to get stuck in! I expect the highest standard
of professionalism from this battalion!'


We sailed into Belfast Lough the next day, 30 July, and were
whisked away from the docks to a disused warehouse on the
outskirts of the city. We oiled our weapons and our magazine-
springs, smoked cigarettes one after the other, nervously
chewed gum and prepared ourselves mentally for the coming
battle. As I climbed into my sleeping-bag that night, I had a
visitor. He was a thick-set captain with long sideburns and an
almost oriental face.

'Captain Bush, Int.,' he said. 'I hear you're very intelligent,
Asher.'

'I've got a couple of A-levels, sir.'

'That means nothing,' he sneered. Quite, I thought. You can
get to captain with two O-levels.

'Listen,' he said, 'I need a bod for the Int. Section. You've
been recommended. Report to the Int. Room ASAP.'

'Yes, sir,' I said. There was nothing so good as volunteering, I
thought.

The 'Int. Room' had been set up in a small antechamber. The
first thing that I noticed was a sign on the door showing a
disjointed eye, and a cartoon of a squirrel wearing a trench-coat
and a Homburg. INT. SECT. – SECRET SQUIRREL was written
underneath it.

There was chaos inside. A gypsy-dark sergeant was speaking
fast into a field telephone. 'New bod?' he asked with upraised
eyebrows as I entered, speaking to me and to the telephone at
once. 'Sarn't Dawson, Int. Sarn't. Asher? I see. Wait a tick. Yes,
sir. Yes, sir. We're getting it ready now, sir. Very good, sir.' He

put the phone down. 'Corp'l Dunbar,' he said, pointing to a good-looking NCO who was busy sorting out maps on the floor. 'York, Crieff, Mitchell,' he went on, indicating three oldish privates who were helping him. 'Asher, new bod! IO'll brief us in a tick. Help clear those maps up! Always good to have an extra pair of hands!'

When the IO came in, we squatted on the floor to listen to him. 'There's been a change of thinking about this war,' he said. 'This war won't be won by brute force. The Provisionals won't come out on the streets, whatever the lads might think. This war will be won by low-grade intelligence. You set up OPs, you use surveillance equipment. You talk to people. You build up a complete picture of the terrorist organizations, their personnel, their command structure. The new emphasis will be on covert ops. We will immerse ourselves in the comings and goings of everyone. Our job is to assemble a complete picture of the Provisionals in our area. Now, jobs. Corp'l Dunbar is Int. Corporal. Asher and York, collating clerks. Crieff is photographer, Mitchell is driver-radio-op. Sarn't Dawson is in charge of screening. I'm in overall charge.'

A collating clerk! I was suddenly stunned. It sounded like an office job. 'Int.' had sounded very romantic at first, now I saw that it meant missing the action. My old platoon was poised for the biggest battle of their lives, and I would be stuck with a lot of desk-wallahs and bottle-washers. I didn't believe the Provisionals wouldn't fight. When I went back to my sleeping-bag, Cooper, Davis and the others were still chatting nervously and smoking cigarettes. 'So you're in Int. now?' Cooper said mockingly. 'Anything to get out of a fight!'

'"Int." is what you get when you go to Eton!' Davis said. 'We buckshee Toms don't have it! We only have beasting!'

The lights went out, but nobody slept. The men were stretched like bowstrings waiting to be released. At three o'clock the lights went on again. We rolled and packed our sleeping-bags silently. On went our webbing and masking-tape. On went the cam-cream. The platoons and companies grouped. There were muffled voices in the halls, and the muted clicks of magazines being pressed on to rifles. Sergeant Dawson issued me with a Stirling sub-machine-gun to mark my new status. There was no further talking as we mounted Land Rovers and trucks. The men chewed chewing-gum and sucked Polo-mints. The engines were gunned. The great gates opened. The convoy rolled out into the black streets of Belfast.

The vehicles moved without lights and with muffled motors. We drove down the Crumlin Road, through Woodvale and Ballygomartin. It was still dark and the ragged buildings glowed in their smearings of sea-mist off the lough. Rows of sodium lights, amber and phosphorus green, were islands of brightness in the night. The city smelt damp and foetid, the familiar carcass smell of the long-dead beast. The maze of streets was a hostile forest of shadows where unknown terrors lurked. I sat in an open Land Rover between York and Crieff, with my SMG ready. I felt strangely vulnerable without the familiar weight of my SLR. We were hunched in our flak jackets, our faces streaked with cam-cream moistened by the morning dampness and the salty dew of the sea. Our eyes hunted out the nooks and crannies for the sudden interjection of hand, face, rifle-barrel, but the people of Belfast slept on behind closed doors. The streets were as silent as the grave.

It was almost dawn when we came to Whiterock. The first redness was smarting like a sore across the lough, and the lumps of the hills slowly assumed shape and detail: Divis, Black Mountain, Wolfhill. Ballymurphy was below us, a curious coil of streets arranged around the central 'bull ring', a medieval town of modern council houses. But the houses and streets looked ordinary in the cold grey light of dawn. There was no welcoming committee, no barricades, no active service units. The IRA had got wind of Motorman. Their active volunteers had melted away like snow.

We set up our HQ in the primary school at Black Mountain. Almost at once there were reports from our units on the ground. The patrols had landed on the streets like D-Day commandos, with their night-sights and snipers' rifles. But there was no shoot-out. The good citizens of Ballymurphy slept through it all and woke to find cohorts of face-blacked para-troopers standing-to on their little plots of lawn with nothing to shoot at. The Paras weren't pleased that things had folded so easily. They found rifles and bits of machine-guns in the hedges where people had thrown them away. 'Not a bloody shot fired!' said Davis when I saw him later. 'The craphats got shot at ninety-four times in one day when they were here. For us, nothing.' That was the price of fame.

In Londonderry 1 Para and the Green Jackets had smashed through the barricades of Creggan and Bogside with the Centurion tanks Davis had seen on the *Intrepid*. Two armed youths were shot dead, but the massive armed resistance the IRA had threatened never materialized. All but one of the Provisionals' leaders had slipped out, alerted by the build-up of armour. The one who remained, Martin McGuinness, managed to escape from under the soldiers' noses in disguise.

Meanwhile, in Ballymurphy, the new 'Int.' plan was put into operation. Hundreds of men and youths were gathered into the net by patrols on the ground and brought into the Int. Section HQ for questioning: the 'notorious screening process', as one pro-Republican paper put it. The men were searched by the patrols, then bundled into Pigs or Saracens for transport to the base. Often, it seemed, they resisted. Sometimes they 'fell over the step' of the armoured car and arrived at the school with bruises or even broken bones. The patrols would then drag them to the 'screening rooms', where two enormous provost corporals would take down their details, photograph them and push them around a bit if they showed any fight. After that, Sergeant Dawson would question them. Actually, the questioning was quite mild. Dawson would ask, 'Who are your friends?' or 'What do you do in your spare time?', carefully noting down names and details. None of those screened were IRA activists, but some had IRA associations and almost all of them had some knowledge of the comings and goings of the IRA. It was the job of York and I to collate all the information received and to build up a picture of the IRA's structure. Piece by piece, mug shot by mug shot, the skeleton of the IRA's second battalion took shape on our wall.

Part of my job was to collect newspaper clippings which concerned our area, and, as the pile grew, I saw a clear picture of the way 2 Para's invasion was glimpsed from the other side:

Residents of Belfast's Ballymurphy Estate claimed last night that paratroopers 'went berserk' after a blast-bomb exploded near the school. No troops were injured, but a number of estate residents were hurt during subsequent military action. Among the injured was sixteen-year-old clerical student Thomas Ward, who is at home on holiday from his college. Thomas said he was going home with a friend after making arrangements for an outing for handicapped children whom they helped care for. He said he was stopped by paratroopers in Divismore Crescent. 'They called me an Irish bastard and said that Irish bastards like me shouldn't be on the street,' said Thomas. 'They made us stand against a wall and searched us. Then they kicked our legs. I fell and got up again and one of them hit me with a gun-butt in my face. They kicked my friend three times in the ribs while he was lying on the ground.' Thomas's lips were cut by the blow and his teeth loosened. A spokesman said that the behaviour of some of the paratroopers indicated that they were either drunk or drugged. 'They're even threatening to shoot women. Young lads can't walk the street without being attacked by them.'

The home of Mr and Mrs P. Corrigan has been raided fifteen times since the Paras arrived. 'They just won't leave this family alone,' said the Republican Club. 'The language of the soldiers and their behaviour have been atrocious. They never knock, just kick in the door and knock everybody about. On one occasion the Paras threatened two of the Corrigan children, aged six and nine, and told them they would shoot them along with everyone else in the house. One showed the children a gun and told them the bullet was for them.

They stop men and ask them to go to the back of the houses for a fight, and when the men refuse, they are beaten about the head with rifle-butts and also subjected to verbal abuse.

One young girl was arrested because she would not open her coat and the soldiers trailed her along the ground.

Their continuous harassment and belligerence have now reached
new levels. Not content with the usual pushing and thumping of
people during street searches, they have now also taken to biting
people, as occurred with two members of the clubs recently. Their
stronghold at Black Mountain School is another 'Holywood Barracks', as stated to a young man by a Special Branch hack when
he was taken there for the notorious screening process. In many
cases this involves a beating and a lonely, dangerous walk back
through the UDA-controlled Springmartin Estate.

We accuse Mr Whitelaw of having absolutely no control over the
Parachute Regiment, who have saturated our area. We demand
their immediate withdrawal from our streets, and an assurance
that never again will these stormtroopers terrorize our people.

Many parishioners witnessed this brutality and have made statements recording what happened. These are the so-called 'peace-
keeping' troops who are supposed to safeguard the local residents,
yet every day there are new instances of paratrooper brutality.
They burst into houses and arrest and coerce innocent people.
These are the degenerates of the British army who waylay and
terrorize innocent people. One wonders how long local people can
tolerate this oppression.

The Paras are educationally sub-normal thugs used by British
imperialism as a killer-force.

Most of these statements were made by the so-called 'Republican
Clubs' in and around the Ballymurphy area which were a front
for the IRA. The Provisional IRA saw itself as the protector of
the Catholic people, and therefore needed to emphasize the
threat to the Catholic community in order to underline its
importance as a protective force. The curious thing was that
when I showed these cuttings to the lads of my old company,
they were proud of them. 'If they're squealing, it means we're
doing a good job!' Davis told me. 'How do the Provies get away
with it? I'll tell you – by terror. Anyone steps out of line, they
get kneecapped. Any girl makes eyes at a squaddie gets tarred
and feathered. Anyone who says a word to the army gets
topped. We put pressure on them. We have to make them more

scared of us than they are of the Provies. Terror works!' 'What happened when we moved into the Murph?' Cooper once said. 'All the villains went across the border or to England on holiday. That's because they knew the Paras were coming. Before we got here, they used to bump the craphats every day because the craphats treated them with velvet gloves. You've got to make people scared of you, then they run away!'

Once I met a patrol returning from a walkabout in Bally-murphy. The corporal in charge was complaining that his rifle-butt was broken.

'How did it happen?' I asked.

'Beasted three blokes in the Murph,' one of them told me. 'Made 'em lie down in a garden. One of them got up and the corporal hit him so hard with his rifle-butt that it broke off! "You move again and we'll zap you!" he told them. They didn't budge again! I wonder if they're still there?'

Ten days before Motorman, the Belfast IRA set off fifteen bombs in the space of seventy-five minutes. The bombs caused utter confusion in the city. A crowd, hearing that there was a bomb on the Albert Bridge, took refuge in Oxford Street Bus Station, only to be blasted by another bomb which had been planted there. It killed six people including two soldiers of the Welsh Guards. On the day we moved into Ballymurphy, a bomb exploded in the village of Claudy, ten miles from Londonderry, killing seven people. On 7 August a young trooper of the Royal Dragoon Guards was killed in Armagh when the scout car he was driving turned over after being stoned by schoolchildren. The trooper was crushed to death. On 14 August two soldiers, one a major, were blown to pieces by a claymore mine in the Roger Casement Football Ground in Andersonstown. On the eighteenth two more soldiers were shot dead by snipers in Belfast. On the nineteenth two soldiers were injured by a mine on the Falls Road: one of them lost both legs.

As the days passed, a menagerie of curious characters began to turn up at Black Mountain. Some of them were Ulstermen,

Special Branch detectives with beery red faces and frayed tweed jackets, who seemed to live in a permanent alcoholic haze. Most of them were from Castlereagh, the notorious detention and interrogation centre, where the first-rank terrorists ended up. The SB dealt in information: it was their currency, and they had built up gilt-edged reserves of it from their methodical interrogations at Castlereagh. Under the Special Powers Act, they could hold a suspect for seven days without charge, and in that time they could make things very uncomfortable for him. They used methods perfected by the Chinese in the Korean war: disorientation produced by lack of sleep, sensory deprivation and the use of white noise. Suspects were made to stand against a wall in search position, on fingertips and toes with sacks over their heads, and were fed on Weetabix and water at irregular intervals. Such techniques filled the SB's coffers with information, but it led directly to the European Court of Human Rights.

The army had its own shady characters. They were long-haired hippies in jeans and bomber jackets, and when they appeared at Black Mountain, it was rumoured that they were SAS hit-squads. 'Two-hundred-quid-a-head-blokes,' the lads would say. The government at that time denied that the SAS was operating in the province. The Civil Rights Association claimed that such undercover squads were the authors of a number of unexplained murders which had taken place since April. The truth, as always, was less exotic. One day I recognized one of these undercover characters as a corporal from 2 Para named Charlie Simms. He told me that he was a member of the MRF, the Military Reconnaissance Force, who were ordinary soldiers recruited from the twenty-nine battalions then working in Northern Ireland. 'As soon as there's a sniff of anything covert, the civil rights people scream SAS!' he said. 'There's no SAS on the ground, only us!' The MRF was made up of volunteers, each battalion being required to provide two. As battalion commanders were frequently loath to give up their best men, it tended to be the most expendable who were 'volunteered'. Charlie Simms was the battalion carpenter.

The MRF had been raised a year earlier under the aegis of the army's counter-insurgency expert, Mau Mau man Frank Kitson. The army had arrested ten former IRA men and persuaded them by a combination of threats and promises to turn informers. The 'Freds' lived with a section of ten MRF soldiers at Holywood Barracks. Their objective was to penetrate hard-line Republican areas, which they toured in plain cars, pointing out former colleagues, arms caches and safe houses. It was a dangerous job for the Freds, many of whom were tortured and murdered when they tried to return home. If the MRF had been responsible for the unexplained murders the CRA claimed, then it had wasted its time. Not one of the victims of these mysterious killings was a proven member of the IRA. In fact, such killings of unknown passers-by fitted the pattern of sectarian murders which had been taking place for several months. All except for one.

On 22 June, a Catholic called Patrick McVeigh was manning a civilian road-block in the Republican area of Andersonstown. Such 'vigilante' actions were common in those days, in view of the number of abductions being perpetrated by Loyalist terror gangs. The vigilantes hailed a passing car, whereupon one of its occupants produced a Thompson machine-gun and mowed them down. McVeigh was killed and several others injured. The police began searching for a Loyalist gang, but soon discovered that the car belonged to the army. The occupants of the car had been a team of MRF. Eventually, one of the MRF men was tried for McVeigh's murder. He was acquitted, having proved that the MRF team thought they had been fired at first.

A similar event occurred on 28 August, with a less drastic outcome. Some Republican vigilantes who were guarding the Dawnmore Estate noticed a car behaving suspiciously. They stopped the vehicle and realized that the two men in the front seat spoke with English accents. The men claimed to be members of the security forces, but they offered no proof, and the vigilantes managed to pull a third man out of the back seat. They snatched a 9-mm pistol he was carrying and punched and kicked him. At this point one of the other occupants of the car fired a shot at them, and the men drove off, leaving their colleague. As the *Republican News* told it:

The CRA claimed that the man held by vigilantes gave his name and said that he was a member of the SAS from Holywood Barracks. When troops of 40 Commando appeared on the scene, one of the soldiers cursed him and arrested him. The man refused to answer any questions and was taken away in a military vehicle. Later, a major from 40 Commando reluctantly admitted that it was all a military operation that went wrong. The CRA sought clarification on what restraints were on these admittedly undercover British army operatives. 'These questions must be answered in the light of the current spate of unexplained murders.' An army spokesman said last night that such allegations were 'nonsense'. 'The army is not here to shoot anyone except when he is shooting at us. Plain clothes soldiers never fire on unarmed civilians, but they have responded when fired on.' Questioned about the incident, the spokesman said a patrol was stopped by a crowd which became hostile and prevented its movements. The car was rocked, the door forced open and a soldier dragged out. Other members of the patrol saw a person in the crowd with a pistol, and the patrol commander fired a warning shot into the ground. The vehicle was able to extricate itself and reinforcements were called to rescue the soldier.

The article concluded:

The CRA yesterday challenged the Secretary of State, Mr White-law, to 'come clean' with the people of Northern Ireland and say whether the SAS is operating there.

But I was sure the men in the car weren't SAS. For a start, the SAS never fire 'warning shots into the ground', which every crow infantryman knows is against all professional rules. 'If you have to fire, fire only aimed shots' is the yellow card's cardinal statement. But I was certain for another reason that the man they pulled out of the car and 'roughed up' wasn't SAS. The man I saw with broken teeth at Black Mountain School a few days later was none other than poor old Charlie Simms, the battalion carpenter.

The MRF's greatest success was their 'Four-star Laundry' project. They ran a laundry service door to door in the Republican areas, washing laundry at cut-throat prices. The operatives gathered information with the mounds of soiled clothes in two ways: first, by chatting to the housewives who provided them, and second by presenting the clothes to forensic experts for examination. However, the laundry's cover was eventually blown by a former Fred and the van was ambushed in Twinbrook by the IRA. The driver was killed.

In Ballymurphy, these Freds brought to light dozens of hidden weapons and thousands of rounds of ammunition, which were later picked up by our foot-patrols. All the arms ended up on my desk for recording. There were Russian and Chinese AK47s, American Armalites and a pot-pourri of ancient Tokarevs, Garands and Lee-Enfields. Each of them had to be identified and traced. The Armalites had almost certainly originated from a consignment of 500, bought in Philadelphia by a group of American IRA sympathizers.

These consignments were smuggled to the Republic in ships and aircraft, often with the connivance of the crew. They were usually packed inside furniture: sofas, mattresses and armchairs. The furniture would be loaded into containers and eventually arrive at the border town of Dundalk, a well-known centre for Provisionals on the run from the North. The weapons would be hidden in trees, orchards and flower-nurseries to await pick up by IRA volunteers from across the border. The IRA would send women-drivers with crowds of rowdy schoolchildren in rented cars. The weapons would be stashed under the seats, and the cars would sneak across the border on a Saturday afternoon when the customs posts were busy. Next step was Belfast, where the arms went on the streets, pointed in our direction.

The RPG rocket-launchers we found created the biggest stir. They fired an anti-tank grenade and could bring down a helicopter in flight. They looked good on the Provisionals' propaganda photos, but, in fact, the IRA never really learned to use them correctly. Far from being a weapon easily concealed, the RPG produces a powerful back-blast when fired, a tongue of bright orange flame thirty feet long. The first IRA men to try the RPG against a police-station evidently didn't realize this. They fired the launcher from the back of an enclosed van and were both roasted to death in the back-blast. We traced the RPGs to the Middle East, where they had probably been obtained from the Palestine Liberation Organization. Their country of origin was Soviet Russia, and the Soviet Embassy in London was eventually asked to help explain how these sophisticated weapons came to be in IRA hands. The Soviets replied acidly, railing against a 'slanderous campaign' carried on in Britain with regard to Soviet weapons in Northern Ireland.

Another of my jobs was recording injuries and shooting incidents in the battalion. One of them was amongst my own section. Jock Crieff, the battalion photographer, shot himself in the foot. 'Always good to shoot yourself in the foot!' Sergeant Dawson told me. 'There he was, Int. man on his way to an important IRA funeral. Gets chatting to the local vicar. Balances his SLR on his foot, muzzle down. Against regulations. Always good. Next thing, CRACK! Middle toe's gone. Shot off. Bloody fool!'

Soon afterwards I learned that my old sparring-partner, Sykes, had been injured in the face. I went to see him to obtain details. I found him nursing a head swollen like a melon, with an atrocious purple slash across the lips and cheek. The wound was held together by six or seven stitches.

'Sittin' in the back of the Rover, wasn't I,' Sykes told me, 'when these kids start lobbin' bits of pavin' stone at us. Got one smack in the mush! Size of a football, it was! These kids were only nine or ten years old. The first thing they must teach 'em is lobbin' a pavin' stone!'

'Hard luck,' I said.

'Hard luck nothin',' he replied. 'Best bit of luck I've had all year. See these stitches? Worth fifty quid each they are! Compensation. The doc added on a couple. Good bloke, he is. This little lot's worth over three hundred nicker!' He waddled off happily with a tender little hand on his newly acquired fortune.

Such incidents happened when you least expected them. I was once assigned to plain clothes duty, escorting the Int. Officer, Captain Bush, in a plain car. It was a dicey affair, I knew. Two men in plain clothes had no firepower if ambushed, and little chance of bringing up reinforcements quickly. Moreover, the city was riddled with illegal 'vigilante' road-blocks, where you had the choice of trying to escape and attracting attention, or stopping and being recognized as 'Brits'. The experience of the MRF showed that this was an extremely sensitive business.

Sergeant Dawson issued me with a 9-mm Browning pistol, which I lodged in the waistband of my jeans.

'Crotch!' the IO told me.

'Pardon, sir?'

'Crotch, not waistband. If we get stopped you can get the weapon out quicker. And no seat-belt. You might want to get out in a hurry!'

Driving along the Springfield Road, I felt the eyes of every pedestrian upon us. I was sure we must stick out like sore thumbs. 'Relax!' the IO said. 'The more tense you look, the more you stand out. Don't worry about the car number. The numbers are changed all the time. The IRA can't keep track of it. And the cars get resprayed regularly.'

'When was this one last resprayed, sir?'

'Actually, it's due for respraying any day now.'

I wondered why the captain drove so fast, swerving around corners and beetling up to sixty on the flat. 'In case there are any bombs about,' he told me. 'We get out of the blast area quickly.' 'I see, sir,' I said. But I didn't. If we were as inconspicuous as all that, how could they ambush us with a bomb? 'Just relax and enjoy it!' Captain Bush said.

We were halted by a vehicle check-point on the edge of the city, four belligerent-looking Green Jackets who pointed their SLRs at the car and looked very alert. 'Oh!' said the corporal, when the IO handed him his ID card. 'I *thought* you looked like a couple of squaddies. Thank you, sir!' And he waved us on. We burst out into green hedgerows with fields and trees and the sun bright across rippling blue waters of the lough. The countryside seemed to explode with life after grim days stuck in the city. 'You could live your whole life inside that place and never realize what a beautiful country this is!' the IO said.

'Makes you wonder what they're fighting about, doesn't it, sir?'

'I suppose this is what they're fighting about,' he said.

We drove to the RUC base at Carrickfergus, and then back into the city. The Green Jackets at the check-point recognized us and waved us on. The second time round I felt better. I had got used to the plain car and the lack of uniform. We drove back up the Springfield Road, and we were just turning into the Spring-martin Estate, when there was a thud. A lump of paving-stone hit the wing of the car, and a little boy of about ten waved his fist at us. 'Youse Para bastards, ye!' he cried.

Occasionally, we got an evening's 'rest and recuperation' at a pub in Lisburn. Lisburn pubs were reckoned to be relatively safe, but 'just in case' we were issued with 9-mm pistols for protection during our night's boozing. 'And don't get paralytic!' Sergeant Dawson told us, when he dropped York and me off. The pub was narrow and dark and full of hard-faced men who looked us up and down as we entered. We stood with our backs to the wall and downed pints of beer till the place looked a little less gloomy. York was a northerner, an elfin-featured man who had served in the Paras for years but had never got higher than private. 'If my missis could see me now!' he said. 'You know she's a Belfast lass? I met her on our last tour. Well, it were all different then, discos and dances. Plenty of *fraternizing*, know what I mean? Packed with crumpet! So many of the lads made girlfriends, it were like Heartbreak Hotel when we pulled out. Anyway, I married my missis the first leave I got. She thought it were great, getting out of Belfast. Till she got to Aldershot, and found out it were just the same: same faces, same shit. So many Paras married Irish girls, they call the Paras' married-quarters "Little Belfast"!'

In Lisburn town centre there is a statue of a man with a sword. I don't remember whom the statue depicts. I only re-member that I was half-way up it that evening when a police Land Rover pulled in, and I was suddenly being threatened with a sub-machine-gun. It took York and I some moments of dis-cussion to get out of that one.

Careful intelligence work was beginning to pay off. Martin
Meehan was arrested in the Ardoyne. Cornelius McHugh was
captured in Andersonstown. The Loyalist assassin Gusty Spence
was lifted in the Shankhill Road. Twenty-five top Provos were
arrested in September and October. Secret surveillance posts
watched the IRA's every move. They were riddled with Freds
and informers. Their volunteers became younger and less dedicated. Their security and inner discipline declined. One of our
battalion was shot dead by a sniper in Ballymurphy. 'Textbook
snipe,' Sergeant Dawson said. 'Professional shot. Straight to the
head!' The lads were infuriated, and broke down a few more
front doors. But the slogging Int. work went on. And soon after
I had a good lesson in the sensitive nature of Int. operations.

One morning a patrol from my former company brought in
an old man, who was pushed out of the Pig holding his nose.
He had been lifted on the IO's orders, because he was father to
an IRA volunteer who had been killed the previous week. The
son, Iain Dermott, aged nineteen, and his girlfriend, aged eighteen, had been sent to plant a bomb somewhere in the city-
centre. The bomb had exploded prematurely, and the van they
had been driving had been blown to smithereens. The bodies
were so badly mutilated they were virtually unrecognizable. I
saw a photo of the boy's corpse. It was like a piece of charcoal, a
twisted, blackened lump with shapeless appendages: a giant
cockroach scorched to death by a flame-thrower. 'Always good
to have these pics,' Sergeant Dawson said. 'We'll get the father
in, show him. Bad stuff, might just turn him. He's not pro-IRA.
Your brilliant son forced to plant bomb, pretty girlfriend fried to
a frazzle! That's what we'll give him!'

When the old man staggered into the screening room, I saw
that his nose was bleeding. He moved his hand away, and I
noticed five distinct human tooth-marks in the flesh. 'They bit
me nose!' he said in amazement. 'Those pigs bit me fuckin'
nose!'

'I think you'd better have a look at this, sarn't,' I told
Dawson. He came back a few minutes later and put away his
carefully prepared photos. 'Idiots!' he said disgustedly. 'Biting

bloody noses now! Always good to beast people and spoil the
whole bloody show!' He ordered me to fetch the corporal in
charge. It was none other than Lance-Corporal Cooper. 'Not
going to ask who bit Dermott's nose,' Sergeant Dawson began.
'Don't laugh, bloody fool! Don't you know what we could have
done with that man? Kick in ribs. Butt in face. Biting noses.
Any bloody fool can do it, but it won't win this war! Waste of
energy. Int., that's what we want, corporal, int.'

'It's different at the sharp end, sarn't,' Cooper said uneasily.
'They shot Smith, and it made the lads a bit angry, like.'

'Listen,' Dawson said, more angry than I'd ever seen him.
'The only way to get the bugger who shot Smith is by Int. If you
don't understand that, you're a bloody moron. If you beast ONE
more detainee, I shall personally shit on you from a great
height!'

But Dawson's words didn't stop the beasting. There was an
unbridgeable gulf between the 'warriors' and the 'watchers'.
When the story of Dermott's nose spread around the battalion,
the lads thought it so amusing that it started a new fashion.

# 11

## *Home From The Wars*

---

The thing about fighting for a living is that it becomes a habit. While you are in the war you long for peace, but when peace comes you long for the intensity of life you experienced in the war. The army had raised us as a fighting elite, and many of us couldn't settle down to living ordinary peace-time lives. As a unit we were fanatically xenophobic. We regarded anyone outside our ranks as an enemy. We had few friends among the craphats, because we looked down on them, and none of us respected the police because they represented an authority which hadn't 'proved itself' the way we had.

Aldershot became the new battle-field. We roved it in groups, turning up uninvited to dances and discos held by the Royal Corps of Transport and almost inevitably beating the place up. There were no night-clubs in Aldershot. Someone had opened a night-club once, and the Paras had smashed it up on the opening night. The Naafi social club on the corner of Gun Hill was closed. It had been closed since the night some Paras threw the juke-box out of the first-floor window, closely followed by several craphats.

The Paras had their own games and amusements in Aldershot. A regular feature of a Paras 'night out' was suicidal boozing, followed by an event called the Dance of the Flaming Arseholes. During this feature, one of the group would dance on a pub table, while the others chanted a grunting song called 'The Zulu Warrior'. The performer would remove his clothes garment by garment, throwing them into the audience. When he was completely naked, he would thrust a rolled-up newspaper into his anus, and someone would set light to it. The nearer the flame got to his anus before he removed it, the more 'class' he showed. None of the publicans ever stopped them doing it. If they made a complaint to the brigade, their pub would be put out of bounds to all Paras, and there were several thousand very thirsty Paras in Aldershot.

The Paras' favourite enemies were the Hell's Angels. They reserved for them the special hate that you feel for those like you but different. Despite their long hair, urine-stained jeans and motorcycles, they were curiously similar to the Paras. They were an aggressive male society with a penchant for violence. They had a 'dare-devil' attitude to life, celebrated by wild motorcycle-runs and fierce bacchanalian drinking sessions; they could attain their 'wings' only by performing certain acts of nameless obscenity, and they had absolute loyalty to their tribal 'colours'. Yet they were so few in number that they stood little chance of holding their own. The Paras had but to glimpse Hell's Angels in a pub to start on them, and the fight would continue outside the pub, with the Paras pulling their long hair and smashing up their motorcycles with iron bars. The one group the Paras never fought was the Gurkhas. They were silent, aloof men who were conspicuous by their old-fashioned smartness. I think it must have been standing orders in a Gurkha battalion that the men weren't allowed out without a white shirt, dark tie and dark jacket. Their formal little beer-drinking groups were a marked contrast to the other rowdy squaddies in their jeans and running-shoes.

There were other monstrous games played by the Paras. Apart from the obscene 'gunge contests', some of them would hold a so-called 'grot contest'. The lads would meet together in an Aldershot pub and have a few drinks, then scatter round the town searching for women. The object was to see who could pick up the most nauseatingly ugly girl. No one was immune from the Paras' humour. They would bring their escorts back to a certain pub at a certain time, and over the next round of drinks would judge the 'grot' of the evening. The crowning act of utter obscenity was to obtain a woman's hand-bag under some pretext and defecate into it. The real Hell's Angels were the Paras.

I remained 'Int.', but I occasionally came across my former colleagues from the 'Rifle' company. One of them, recently out of gaol, celebrated his release by getting almost paralytically drunk, stealing a car, driving it to London, and smashing it, apparently deliberately, into a gate. When a police-constable came to arrest him, Robbins calmly drew a 9-mm pistol and told him, 'You're just a fucking craphat!' That was the end of him in the Parachute Regiment.

And other members of my old platoon had their moments with the police. Hensby, Sykes and Peasgood were caught trying to break into the Womens' Royal Army Corps barracks one night. It took four policemen, a police-woman and a police-dog to get them into the Black Maria. All four of the policemen were injured. The police-woman suffered a black-eye, and the dog got a broken leg. On another occasion the police came for a private called Peel. He had been identified as a peeping-tom who had been terrorizing the married-quarters. A lad called Bryant was peaceably lying on his bunk writing a letter to his fiancée, when another Para came in drunk from the next billet and stabbed him in the chest with a bayonet. Bryant was on the critical list for a week. Several Toms who had passed out with me went AWOL. I didn't blame them. Living with that platoon was like living with a bunch of lunatics.

I remember the *Starry Plough* newspaper which had described the Paras as 'educationally sub-normal thugs'. The horror of it was that they weren't sub-normal. They were perfectly normal people who had been given a little power and encouraged to think of themselves as an elite. They had been trained to cope with extreme hardship and they did it admirably. Their training was harder than any prison sentence: they had a special spirit which came from a combination of shared suffering and a fanatic loyalty to their colours. The Maroon Machine was their totem of war, for which they would suffer hardship and death.

The Paras knew their job. In a conventional war, like the Falklands, they proved themselves to be simply the best and bravest infantry unit in the British army. On the battlefield they were everything Montgomery said they were. In peace-time they were *murder*.

In what seemed like desperation the battalion was moved to Singapore and billeted at the ANZUK base at Nee Soon. The change saved us. The fascinating work of the Far East drew us together and provided a new outlet for our energies. These days of jungle-training were the best times I had in the army. In the rain-forests of Kota Tinggi, Sergeant Dawson led the section on an expedition to map out vehicle- and foot-tracks for a battalion exercise. We drove through plantations of rubber trees on the edge of the wild forest, and once, just as the sun set, the Rover got bogged down in a pit of mud. We jumped out and heaved the chassis, as the wheels spun uselessly and splattered us with mud. At precisely that moment there was a boom of thunder, and the monsoon began. The rain was like a billion jiggling insects moving through the thick undergrowth. It beat on our backs like rods of cold iron. It sizzled into the soft ground and churned up the muck like a plough. It gurgled across the awning of the Land Rover. The engine strained in agony as the wheels sank deeper and deeper into the mud. Corporal Dunbar cut a length of wood with his panga, and we tried to lever the wheels up, but with every jerk the vehicle wedged itself further in. In desperation we abandoned the vehicle and set up our hammocks in the trees, as the rain whipped around us and the leaves of the forest moved with swishing life. 'Always good to get your kit soaked before you get into your sleeping-bag!' Dawson said. 'Just like *Force Ten from Navarone*, isn't it?'

We dived into our hammocks and lay under our ponchos, swinging gently. We listened to the swish and slither of the water until dawn. The rain stopped and dappled light fell through the canopy of leaves. Insects began to buzz like electronic alarms. There was the squeak and scamper of unseen monkeys high in the trees and the jitter of tree-frogs and jungle-rats. Dampness and humid heat rose smoking from the forest floor.

At sunrise Dawson sent Dunbar back to the kampong we had passed, to get help. A couple of hours later a Malay turned up in a battered Land Rover and pulled our vehicle out of the quagmire with a tow-line. We followed him back to his village, where the villagers crowded around us, staring at our jungle-white faces and touching our sodden bush-shirts. The man who had pulled us out of the mud was as oval as an egg, wearing a Western-style shirt and a checked sarong. He invited us to his long-house, where we sat round in a circle and drank tea. 'Dig out your rations,' Dawson told us. 'It's always good to give them something.' We piled tins of chicken-curry and beef-stew and tubes of jam on the floor like sacrificial offerings. The rotund man seemed pleased. The villagers mobbed us again as we mounted our Land Rover. It was a brief but intense vision of a world quite different to the one I knew.

Afterwards, we penetrated the jungle on foot. It was a fresh, untamed world. The great trees rose up above us like phantom beanstalks, as tall as skyscrapers with their fluted buttress roots like rocket-fins. The bush was alive. A cobra hissed and reared up in our path, inflating its head-pouches and flicking its tongue. Then with eye-dazzling speed it coiled into the undergrowth like a whiplash. Once, we discovered fresh tiger-tracks and felt glad of the live rounds in our rifles. Often we had to cut through the bush with our pangas. The leaves were infested with black ants which dropped unavoidably down our necks and burrowed into our bergens. There were leeches like little yellow maggots which perched on the wet leaves and attached themselves to us as we pushed through. Once they were hooked on to your skin, the only way to get rid of them was by applying a cigarette-end or some salt. If you just pulled them out, the head would remain embedded, while its decoagulating saliva allowed your blood to flow. One man in the battalion was hospitalized when a leech crawled into the canal of his penis and expanded there, gorged with his blood. That must have been one of the most painful experiences imaginable. The large bull-leeches were the worst: they could quaff large quantities of blood. Dawson told us the story of a Gurkha NCO who had fallen into a monsoon-ditch drunk one night, and had been found dead the next morning, pints of his blood having been sucked by a dozen bloated bull-leeches.

The ants and leeches were there constantly and you grew accustomed to them, but what I feared most were the great bird-eating spiders. They spun webs with a six-foot span between the trees and lurked in the centre, horrific creatures of black and yellow, as large as a hand. I was always afraid of blundering into a web in the shadows and having that horrendous animal fall down my neck.

At night I never ceased to be amazed by the deafening wall of sounds which poured out of the darkness. There were tiny cicadas which rattled like an electric drill and frogs which called out to each other in the grass with voices like trumpets. 'BURP! BURP!' the male called, far away. 'BUUURP!' came the answering female, just below my hammock. 'BURP! BURP!' came the male again. No answer. 'BURP! BURP!' He was getting closer, coming to investigate. 'BURP! BURP!' His call was frantic now. I smiled to myself, thinking his lady-friend had left him. 'BUUUURP!' came her farting refrain, almost in my ear.

The ants penetrated our mosquito-nets in marching caravans. Tree-rats scuttled about beneath our trees and wrinkled their way into our bergens and webbing. One morning Sergeant Dawson approached my hammock warily and said, 'Don't move!' in a low voice.

'Come on, sarn't!' I said, thinking he was joking.

'Shut up! Bloody fool! Big black snake in the end of your hammock!'

'Get out of it!' I told him, not believing it. I swept my mosquito-net aside and leapt out of the hammock. At once a huge black snake splattered to the ground and coiled away into the jungle.

Those days in Malaysia seemed a far cry from the grim streets of Belfast. Here was the adventure which I had dreamed of

when I joined the army, but failed to find amongst the bleak
hills of Ulster. The jungle was the wilderness I had lusted after
as a small boy, an untouched exotic world of strange plants and
mysterious animals. At the jungle-warfare school in Pulada, we
were trained by Australian and New Zealand instructors fresh
from the war in Vietnam. They taught us how to blend into the
jungle, to become animal, to interpret the sounds and smells of
tracks. In the jungle you never washed or shaved: the smell of
soap could carry for miles. Jungle warfare was a close-quarter
war where the enemy could be lurking six feet away, entirely
unseen.

When we came out of the jungle, there was the fascinating
world of Singapore waiting for us: the fish markets and the
trishaws and the bars where girls in sequinned bikinis sidled up
and asked you to buy them a drink. There was Bugis Street,
with its pavement cafés where you drank Tiger beer and could
spend hours watching the catamites. They were alluring creatures: blonds, brunettes, black-haired beauties from all over the
world. They seemed gloriously seductive with their luxuriant
tresses, smooth skin and curvacious figures. It was only when
they spoke in gruff voices that you realized they were men. Here
was the perfect correlation for the Paras' 'grot contests' in
Aldershot. But, inevitably, some of my colleagues went home
with the catamites 'just for the experience'.

One evening I was sitting at a table in Bugis Street with
Corporal Dunbar and another corporal, when a dark little
Malay in a spotless white shirt came along. 'You want girls,
John?' he asked.

'Have you ever been to a brothel?' Dunbar asked me.

'I bet he's never even been with a woman!' the other corporal
said.

'Well, we'll make sure he gets one tonight,' Dunbar said. 'We
only want men in the Paras!'

Before I could argue, he told the little man, 'Take us to them!'

The man led us to a black diesel Mercedes, and we hopped
inside. He switched on the radio as we drove off. The Beatles
were singing 'And I Love Her'. Only minutes later we arrived at

a tall, stately house in its own grounds. It was hardly the back-alley I had imagined. In a wide reception-hall sat the mama-san, an old lady in a brightly coloured sari with a face like a dried banana-leaf. 'Welcome!' she said. 'Sit down! You have Coca-Cola or tea?' As we sat there, nervously swigging from bottles of Coke, the mama-san led the girls in. They were Chinese and Malay, black and tanned, with long straight black hair or curly afro-hair. They stood self-consciously in a line waiting for us to choose.

'You have the first choice!' Dunbar told me.

I blushed with embarrassment. 'No,' I said. 'You choose first.'

'Come on, Yellow,' the other corporal said. 'We only came here for your sake. Now choose!' I wanted to run and hide. Anything to escape from the eyes of those women. It was as emotionless as choosing a new shirt. There was a wonderfully attractive Chinese girl, but her beauty intimidated me. Instead, I just pointed to the nearest girl, a dark-skinned Malay, and said lamely, 'I'll take that one!'

The girl led me to a dingy room with a divan and a wash-basin. The door closed behind us. She wiggled her slim black body in front of me and removed her bra. Just then the door snapped open, and the dark little man who had driven us there appeared with his hand out. 'That'll be eight dollars, please!' he said. I gave him the eight dollars, and he withdrew discreetly. The girl was naked. I looked at her and felt no desire at all. I took my clothes off, but still felt nothing. 'Look', I said heavily, 'this is my first time in a place like this.' The girl giggled. 'Can't we just talk?' I said. The girl giggled again. I sat down on the bed and asked her name. She told me. 'Do you like your job?' I asked her. 'It's very good!' she laughed.

Twenty minutes later she escorted me back to the foyer. 'Look,' I said, 'you won't tell *them* about this, will you?'

'No worry, John,' she said, and linked her arm through mine. 'You paid!' She was really a nice girl, I thought.

'Here's the hero!' Dunbar shouted when he arrived and found me sitting with the girl on my knee. She bounced up and down and sang, 'Johnnie's first time! Johnnie's first time!'

'How does it feel to be a man?' Dunbar asked me, as if I'd just been admitted to a very exclusive club.

'Great!' I told him toughly.

At weekends we took out the army's motor-launch and water-skied to a tiny island with palm-trees and ivory sands, like a glossy-magazine paradise. The only drawback was the number of sharks about, which made you feel very uncomfortable sitting on the skis in the murky water and waiting for the launch to pick you up. My old friend Butcher was drowned when an underwater current carried him out to sea. They found the remains of his body a few days later: his arms and legs had been bitten off by sharks. Not long after his death someone showed me our platoon photo: the one on which Jekyll had taken such delight in scratching out faces. 'I hope you're not superstitious!' my companion said. On the photo Dave Walker and Butcher were sitting together. The third recruit along was me. And, ironically, death by water visited another man whose face was on that card within a year. Bernie Hosking, a member of Chay Blyth's yacht crew in the Round-the-World Yacht Race, was washed overboard and lost at sea. Blyth and his team of Paras, several of them from my former platoon, went on to win the race in their yacht *Great Britain II*.

A week after we arrived back in Aldershot, we were briefed for a parachute drop in Denmark. It was to be a massive exercise, the biggest drop since the war, and a demonstration that airborne troops could still be of use in a conventional theatre. Just before the drop, I had to report to the stores to collect a new steel helmet. It was not until I had got the helmet back to my billet that I noticed whose it had been. The name BUTCHER was stencilled on the inside in white paint.

I was still 'Int.', and our role in Denmark was to man the colonel's operations centre. It was located near a barn on the plain of Zeeland. The barn was infested with very large Danish rats which prevented us sleeping at night with their scampering and squeaking. I was the command-post runner, and once during the long night I was sent to wake up the regimental sergeant-major. Like all RSMs, he was a fearsome man, a boxing champion and a karate black-belt. When I found him, he was rolled tightly in his sleeping-bag and sleeping like a baby. How do you wake an RSM? The normal Para method was a sharp kick in the ribs, but this was not recommended for a karate black-belt. I shook him timorously by the arm and nothing happened. I shook him again. Suddenly his eyes opened and the great gnarled face formed into a resentful snarl. 'What do you want?' he said.

'Excuse me, sir,' I said, stammering, 'but the regimental sergeant-major wants to see you!'

'WHAT!' the big man wheezed, sitting up and staring at me incredulously. 'But I AM the regimental sergeant-major!'

I didn't last long in 'Int.' after that. The whole battalion returned from Denmark under a cloud, having knifed Danish tracker-dogs, threatened Danish part-time soldiers with bayonets, and generally descended on Copenhagen afterwards like a plague of locusts until **NO BRITISH SOLDIERS SERVED HERE!** notices appeared at the windows of shops and bars. I was posted back to a rifle company, but, somewhat to my relief, it was not amongst the likes of Cooper, Robbins and Hensby. And there was another surprise waiting for me when we got back to Aldershot. Once, walking across the drill-square, I saw a new second lieutenant coming towards me. I lifted my hand to salute automatically and then froze. The new officer was none other than my old schoolfriend Geoffrey Deacon, now commissioned in 2 Para.

Deacon invited me to his room in the officers' mess. It must have been quite unusual for a Tom to have been taken there. I compared its comfort with that of my cramped billet.

'This is where you should be, Mike,' he told me. 'Don't you feel envious?'

'No,' I told him truthfully. 'I'm there, with the men, and you're here where you deserve to be.' That was absolutely true.

'That's what I was afraid you'd say,' he told me. 'You should be envious. You've forgotten that you joined the army to become an officer. Instead, you've become exactly like a squaddie. Now, there's nothing wrong with squaddies, but for most of them this is the only life they'll ever know. You're different. You'll never really be one of them. If I were you, I'd retake the Commissions Board.'

'I don't know if I want to be an officer any more,' I said.

'Then my advice is get out!'

But before I could reapply for the RCB, the battalion got its marching orders. Our destination was the most feared area of Northern Ireland: the Armagh border, the place they called Bandit Country.

# 12

## *We Cease to be Amazed*

———

The Scout rose to 3,000 feet, and the pilot switched to auto-gyrate. The helicopter hung in the sky for a moment, then began to descend gently, circling like a sea-bird on a pillar of air, a maddeningly slow vortex. My feet were resting on the skis, and my rifle was across my knees. A safety harness was all that kept me in place. The sky was diaphanous blue glass painted with flurries of white cirrus. Below the two peninsulars of my boots the fields and moors of Armagh were laid out like an emerald-green tableau, a tapestry of pine-woods and turf-brown fields dissected by dry stone walls and spiky hedgerows of gorse. Glistening streams snaked through stunted hills and roads of asphalt-silver trickled from farmstead to homestead, from bridge to field to forest. Somewhere down there was the border of the Irish Republic, a drunken line on a map which sliced up fields, streams and hedgerows. From where I sat, it all looked the same country.

An eagle swirled below us, free and easy, carrying the sky on its spread wings as it circled gracefully. For a second I recognized an unreasoning impulse to throw myself out of the helicopter and soar across the blueness with it. Then the crash of the rotors drew me out: the chopper swooped out of the sky and skimmed over fields and farmland, dodged some dangerous telephone wires and looped back in a somersault so that I felt my bowels hanging somewhere above me.

'Whatsa matter?' the pilot grinned through the intercom,

looking round at the pale face of my section commander in the seat next to him.

'Is all that necessary?' the corporal asked.

'Uncertain trajectory foils pot-shots!' the pilot said, simply. 'They can't get you in their sights. Anyway, it's fun, isn't it?'

The chopper hovered lower for our exit. We poised ourselves for the moment of truth. The patrol and the helicopter were at their most vulnerable during debussing and embussing, especially if the local IRA had rocket-launchers. No helicopters had been shot down yet, but there was always a chance that one might be. We jumped out and sprinted for cover with our weapons and equipment. The pilot gave us a thumbs-up, and the chopper leapt into the sky. Seconds later it was a small black insect silhouetted against the clouds and a faint thump of rotors, trailing oil fumes on the fresh summer morning.

Despite my five companions, I suddenly felt isolated. We were like a small commando group in enemy territory. Reinforcements were far away, and everyone and everything was suspicious. Only last week, one of our patrols had been passing a farm when a milk-churn had exploded. The nearest man had turned into a fireball. The blast had seared off his skin and melted his rifle. His flak jacket with its plastic plates had dissolved into boiling liquid. The man next to him had also been pole-axed as if he had been hit by a flame-thrower. Both men had died from their wounds. 'Bandit Country' did not sum up the fear and the terror which existed here on the border. Every time you went out on patrol, every time the chopper disappeared into the blue yonder, it was like a rendezvous with death.

I hefted the radio on and the rest of the patrol donned their bergens. 'Spread out!' Corporal Geordie Bates said. 'Let's move!' We paced cautiously in a zigzag pattern around the spiny cactus-growth of the gorse. It was covered with bloom: brilliant yellow flowers which filled the air with chocolatey scent. We moved ten yards apart: too far for a sniper to kill more than one of us with a single shot. But the danger in this border country came not from snipers but from bombs hidden in culverts and milk-churns and hay lorries, detonated by enemies hidden half a

mile away. We moved off carefully, searching the horizon for
any flash of metal or whirr of movement, knowing that if
anything happened we would have only seconds to make a
decision – that is, if we were still alive. Ahead of us were three
or four days in enemy territory. Our main objective for those
few days was to survive.

Our base in Armagh was at Bessbrook, where my company had
been billeted in the infants' school. We were crammed into
what had once been the staff-room, still equipped with black-
board, a whole platoon in double bunks, six inches apart. We
worked round the clock, sixteen hours a day, coming and going
constantly. There was always noise and quarrelling, and the
lights were always on. We never removed our uniforms or our
boots. Once, coming off guard at six in the morning, I staggered
into the washroom to shave. It was like entering the washroom
of Snow White and the Seven Dwarfs. The washbasins and
mirrors had been designed for infants, so you had to squat
down to wash and shave. The urinals and WCs were only knee-
high and presented an even more delicate problem. On this
occasion, frustrated and bleary-eyed, I managed to stagger back
to the billet, having left my SLR propped against the wall. I
dashed back almost at once, but my weapon had gone. It
turned up in the possession of the company sergeant-major, Ted
Eliot. 'A professional soldier never leaves his rifle!' he told me,
quite rightly. That afternoon I was on OC's orders, and was
fined another twenty pounds. I didn't opt to go before the
colonel.

The school was like a Foreign Legion fortress in the desert. It
was encircled by high walls and a higher mesh of rocket-fence
to protect it from onslaught by IRA rocket-launchers and mor-
tars. It had a guard-sangar at each corner, and at the rear a
tower on thirty-foot metal stilts. The tower looked over a stag-
nant mill-pond of malarial yellow water, through which the
rusty saw-edges of submerged corrugated-iron sheets pushed
insuppressibly. One night I was on guard in the tower when a

human head presented itself at the window. This struck me as odd, since the window was thirty feet above the uninviting waters of the pond. I blinked and jumped with shock to find the head still there. I pressed myself up against the window. The head dissolved slowly into the night, revealing itself as the hallucination it had to be. Something told me I was working too hard.

The school football-field had been converted into a heli-pad, where Scouts and the smaller bubble-like Sioux helicopters took off from piles of railway sleepers on scaffolding. Every time a chopper took off, the roof of the school rattled with the vibrations. There was little enough to the town of Bessbrook: a single main street like a cowboy town, a pub, a couple of shops and, further up, the square block-house of Bessbrook Mill, where the battalion HQ was stationed.

Geordie Bates was my new section corporal, and I was glad of it. Bates was a veteran, an ex-SAS man who seemed as much at home in the cuds as the foxes and the badgers. He was a superb tracker and could read spoor and signs written on the moors and woods like a book. In appearance he was mildly studious. His head seemed too large for his wiry frame, and he wore gold-rimmed spectacles which gave him the look of a more aggressive John Lennon. His eyesight was, in fact, Geordie's *bête noire*. 'The SAS threw me out for poor eyesight,' he said. 'Now I've got my glasses, I'm the best shot in the battalion!' Geordie was the mainstay of the Bisley team. But he found the pettiness of 2 Para irksome after the SAS. 'It's a different world, the SAS,' he would say. 'There's no beasting. On the selection course you either make it or you don't. If you don't, you're out.' Geordie was relaxed about discipline. So relaxed that at night he would defecate in the corner. Perhaps he imagined, half asleep, that he was still at his post in the cuds. An SAS soldier never leaves his post. Once, he even defecated in the showers, sending another of our NCOs, Corporal Mike Lambert, into a twitch of rage.

'You're an animal, Bates!' he commented.

'That's right,' Geordie told him calmly. 'I am. You are. We're all animals here!' He talked incessantly about the SAS, and how he hoped to get back into it now he had his glasses. But I wondered if it was really his eyesight or his curious toilet habits which had led to his downfall there.

His most prominent feature was the neat row of indentations from some sharp human molars which encircled the tip of his nose like a necklace. They said that years ago someone had tried to bite his nose off in a brawl. By the look of the nose, they had very nearly succeeded. Since then, they said, Geordie had become obsessed with 'chewing'. 'Never get into a fight with Geordie,' the other NCOs warned. 'He's not the full shilling. He'll have your nose off before you can say Jack Robinson. Geordie's as queer as a concrete parachute!' Most of the NCOs were frightened of Geordie because of those teeth marks, but Mike Lambert was a great lumber-jack of a man and wasn't scared of anyone. 'It's not the ones with the teeth marks!' he used to say. 'It's the ones who haven't got 'em that are hard!' Geordie was notorious for chewing the heads off live rats and chickens. It was a party-piece he would perform gladly at platoon gatherings. Once at Bisley, bored during a lull in the shooting, Geordie had filled a spare moment by shooting a squirrel in a tree. It was a wonderful shot, but some competitors from the Green Jackets had surrounded him as he picked the animal up. 'Big, tough paratrooper!' they jeered. 'Shooting squirrels!' Geordie had been so piqued that he had bitten the squirrel's head off in front of them. 'There's nothing so odd about it!' Geordie would answer when taken to task for his unusual pastime. 'There are people in Morocco who bite the heads off snakes for money! I do it for free!'

Once, when we were on patrol near Warrenpoint, he tracked down a badger and fought with it, beating the animal to death with his rifle. He then ordered me to carry it in the radio-manpack. During the next few hours the animal's fleas steadily abandoned its carcass and invaded my clothes. I imagined that Geordie intended to eat the creature: I knew SAS men were trained to 'live off the land'. But when we bivvied-up that night, he told me to bring the dead badger, and when I dropped it thankfully in front of him, he dropped his pants and defecated

on its head. Whether or not this was some secret ritual symboliz-
ing his mastery over the beasts, I never had the nerve to ask.

But I liked Geordie, despite his strange habits. Unlike almost
every other NCO, he wasn't a bully. He was aggressive and
tough when necessary, but in his book that didn't mean treating
the Toms roughly. And he was the best field-soldier in the
company. 'And that's what counts,' he would say. 'Not what
you say after a few pints in the bar. Too many "bar soldiers" in
this army! It's what you do in the *ulu* that counts!' He had
picked up unorthodox habits in the SAS, like calling the platoon
commander 'boss' instead of 'sir'. The platoon commander was
a short-service officer who seemed more flattered than annoyed.
This infuriated Mike Lambert, whose father was a regular officer
and who had been brought up to believe that army ways were
the unchanging cornerstones of the universe. But Geordie went
too far when he started calling CSM Ted Eliot, 'sarn't major'.
Ted was hardly a giggling subaltern; he was a blooded professional who had won the MM in Borneo. 'I've seen the SAS in
action,' he would say. 'And from that day on it's them who
have to convince *me* that they're better than our patrol company!' He resented Geordie's assumption of SAS informality. 'In
the *real* army only officers call CSMs "sarn't major", corporal,'
Ted told him. 'You're not an officer, so it's fucking SIR to you!'
Mike Lambert was delighted.

We worked ten days' guard-duty, ten days' vehicle check-
points and ten days' patrols. Patrols might include setting up
observation-posts, and this was the most dreaded job, since it
meant lying in one place for several days.

It was curious how often Geordie's patrol was assigned OP
duties. 'But sarn't!' Geordie once complained to the platoon
sergeant, Martin Serle. 'We did the *last* OP! It's Corporal Lambert's turn.'

'Corporal Lambert's section are on chopper-patrol,' Sergeant
Serle said. Chopper-patrol was the plum job. 'So there's no one
but you to do it.'

'Anyway, you're good at it!' Corporal Lambert said, grinning.

'About time you learned to be good at it too!'

'That's enough!' the sergeant said. 'You're doing the OP, Bates, and Lambert's party will be the search section. You'll be watching a *shebeen* in Belleek.'

Within minutes we had collected our machine-gun, night-sights and binoculars, cobbled together the radio and its spares, and assembled our menu of chicken-stew and tinned bacon-burgers. The Scout gunned its engine on the heli-pad, and we ran out to embuss.

We climbed a wall and moved in patrol formation down a gorse-covered convex slope towards a stream. A hundred yards beyond it, stuck on the side of a bald hill, was a white-washed farmhouse. We trod carefully through the broom and brambles, avoiding the track. We had no wish to leave clear DMS prints for IRA trackers to read, or to step on a mine left deliberately for an occasion like this. Our eyes flickered over everything, clearing it mentally: the gates, the ditches, the tiny bridge, the dry stone walls. Was there any sign of recent disturbance or digging? Had part of a fallow field been ploughed up for no reason? Were there cigarette-ends or sweetpapers about, suggesting recent occupation? Were there broken twigs or grass or leaves, or concentrations of footprints? Noticing such minutiae could keep you alive.

We had just reached the stream-bed, when Geordie made the 'down' sign. We dropped like silent skittles. My trunk was on wet, mossy turf, and my legs were still trailing the water. A fruity smell of warm dung reached my nostrils, and, looking down, I saw that I had put my elbow through a cow-pat. Beyond the gorse, I could make out the figure of a man, standing by the farmhouse and smoking a cigarette. I could smell the faint scent of the tobacco on the air. After a moment the man disappeared, and we began to crawl one by one along the base of the wall and into the pine-plantation which lay beyond. While we made a defensive formation around the machine-gun, Geordie and a tall private called Chandler went off to clear the wood. In a few moments they came monkey-walking

back on knees and hands, and Geordie called us on silently into
the belly of the wood, where we laid down our equipment. 'No
good pressing on till sunset,' he said in a low voice. 'We'll be
spotted and maybe bumped. I don't want anyone getting a lead
on our OP. Now, we'll put up the gun and a sentry and you'll
do stags. No talking, no smoking and no cooking. No noise of
any kind!'

It was in situations like this that Geordie was at his best.
There was nothing more dangerous than putting an OP into
hostile territory. He knew how to avoid nasty incidents like the
one which killed two Royal Marines in this area the following
year. The marines' OP was on a hill overlooking the border and
had been compromised. The IRA had laid a hundred pounds of
industrial gelignite in the earth directly beneath it. After the
patrol had settled in, the IRA unit had detonated the device by
radio control. The ground had erupted directly beneath the
patrol, tearing two of them to pieces. Two others had been
badly injured.

The war in south Armagh was a different war from the one we
had grown accustomed to in Belfast. Belfast was the war of the
Secret Squirrel: an intelligence war that could be won or lost on
information. But here in Armagh there were no Freds. The
Catholic population lent tacit support to the IRA. They were the
eyes and ears of the insurgents, keeping them up to date with
our movements. It was the classic 'war of the flea', which the
British army could not hope to win until they had the support
of the Republican majority. The proximity of the border and its
arbitrary design made it unlikely that such support would ever
be forthcoming. The British needed the roads for their vehicles,
so the IRA mined the roads. In some areas it was almost
suicidal to drive. The colonel himself, together with the regimental sergeant-major, had been driving near Newtownhamilton, his party spread into two Land Rovers, when a mine
exploded between them. A few seconds earlier and the battalion's commanding officer would have been taken out.

Helicopter-patrols or foot-patrols were the best alternatives,
but even these were vulnerable. A team from our patrol

company, the elite unit of the battalion, had been patrolling a country lane near the border when a culvert-mine had exploded. John Hughes, company sergeant-major and a jungle veteran, had been virtually vapourized. The culvert-bomb had been set off by a radio-control device similar to the type used to fly model aircraft. The bomber, hidden on the brow of a hill, with a pair of binoculars, had watched the patrol getting nearer and nearer to the mine. When CSM Hughes was directly over the culvert, the bomber pressed the control button. The surface of the road had buckled and ripped open, sending chunks of molten asphalt into space. John Hughes's flak jacket had landed in the road a hundred yards away, but John was no longer in it. What was left of his body was hanging from the gorse and the blackthorn trees in bloody slivers. The only recognizable piece of him was his upper lip with the moustache still on it. The back-up team found a foot in a DMS boot in a field some yards away. On the following morning a farmer turned up with his left hand, still wearing its wedding-ring.

We put in the OP near sunset, on the top of a stumpy hill, overlooking the pub on the main street of Belleek. We lay in a camouflaged position amongst the thornbush all night and throughout the next day. Below us, the town of Belleek was grey and silent. We did not talk, nor smoke, nor cook. We took our stag from one another with hand-signals, and if we felt the need to relieve ourselves, we just rolled over and did it on the ground. About mid-day rain began to fall, plinking on to our ponchos and fluttering on to the gorse and the blackthorn leaves. Cars slushed through the street below us with their windscreen wipers working. Just before sunset on the second day, two new call-signs checked on to the air, and we knew that Lambert's section and another had been dropped by helicopter. They would make their way into the village on foot and raid the bar, hoping to catch some IRA men.

The binos were replaced by a starlight-scope, which allowed us to see in the dark. As night fell, cars began to draw up outside the bar. I watched carefully through the starlight-scope as two patrols, the bulky figure of Mike Lambert in the lead, moved into the main street. The big corporal just kicked at the bar door, until it gave in. Then, while the other patrol gave cover, Lambert's section rushed into the building. Even from where I lay, I could hear shouting and the smashing of glasses. Lambert appeared at the door, dragging a stout bearded figure, whom he thrust up against the wall, spread-eagled on his fingers and toes. More men trickled out, still clasping beer-glasses. They talked and joked with each other in jaunty, sing-song voices, as if this kind of thing happened every day. The Paras spread-eagled all the men against the wall, but most of them sagged and fell in seconds. They looked as drunk as lords. 'Brit bastards!' someone yelled. 'Shut up!' I heard Lambert's voice shouting. One of the Paras kicked at a man's legs and the man collapsed, laughing. He got to his feet again, and as they returned him to the 'search position', he started to sing. I couldn't catch the words, although the tune sounded something like 'Paddy McGinty's Goat'. 'Shut up!' said Lambert, but the singing went on. Two more men fell down and were picked up again. The singing stopped, but the cheerful banter went on. The men were so drunk that nothing could hurt them. They seemed so easy-going and good natured that I felt sorry we had disturbed their Saturday evening drinking session. Yet some of these men had almost certainly connived in the blowing to pieces of British soldiers. In the end, Lambert just took their names and let them go. They staggered back into the pub, still singing the song that sounded like 'Paddy McGinty's Goat'.

Lambert stormed into the debriefing session. 'McVeery was there and you let him go!' he shouted at Geordie.

'McVeery wasn't there,' Geordie told him. 'We watched that place for twenty-four hours and no one came out or went in without us seeing them, and I tell you he never came near it!'

'He came and went under your nose, Geordie!' Lambert insisted. Then he laughed. 'What's left of it!' he said.

'Yours could do with some cutting down to size,' Geordie told him. 'It's big enough to stick in any other business but your fucking own!'

Just then Sergeant Searle came running into the billet. 'Get your kit on, lads,' he said. 'There's just been a bombing near Newtownhamilton. Three of our men killed!' We pulled on our equipment, expecting to be flown out in the Scout. 'No,' Sergeant Searle told us. 'You're going in a Saracen.'

'A Saracen!' Geordie exclaimed. 'That's suicide. What's wrong with the chopper?'

'Corporal Lambert's section is going out in the chopper!'

'Of course, how could I have forgotten!'

The Saracen pulled into the danger zone. News reached us on the radio that the first back-up team to arrive, from another company, had also lost three men. They were helping the casualties from the first explosion, when one of them, clearing the area, had set off a trip-wire which had detonated a booby-trap. The flesh had been slashed from their bodies in the blast. Now, here we were approaching in a Saracen armoured car. It was little protection. A large enough bomb could bowl it over like a ninepin, crushing the occupants to death. We sat hunched in our seats, our brains ticking over like clocks. Every casualty we had suffered on this tour had come from radio-controlled bombs on the roads. Even Geordie went white. 'I don't call this soldiering,' he said. 'This is just stupidity. It's like asking them to top you!' 'We cease to be amazed!' one of the Toms said, so solemnly that we laughed. The tension eased a little. At precisely that moment there was a tremendous bang, and the armoured car rattled and sprang into the air. A bead of sweat dripped from my forehead. The Tom opposite me blanched. 'Jesus fucking Christ!' somebody swore. The driver turned and grinned at us. 'Sorry about that!' he laughed. 'Went into a dirty great pot-hole!'

We lived on nervous energy, fighting an unseen enemy and popping Dexedrine pills to stay awake. The pills made us buzz around like punctured balloons. Half the platoon were sucking their tongues and teeth, and hurtling around like blue-bottles. When the Dexedrine ran out, we crammed ourselves with caffeine pills and plodded on for another sixteen-hour day.

Vehicle check-points on the Dublin Road or on Carlingford Lough were the most tedious pastime. Once, on check-point duty I stopped a middle-aged balding man who seemed very nervous. 'I think this one's hiding something, corporal,' I told Geordie secretly. 'Give him the works!' Geordie said. While the man showed his driving-licence to my companion, I searched inside the car, the dashboard, the seats, under the chassis, and finally inside the boot. There was a large suitcase tied with string. 'Can you open that?' I asked the man.

'Sure there's nothing in there but me private things!' he objected.

'Get it open!' Geordie said.

Reluctantly the man untied the string and opened the case. Inside were ten gross of Durex.

The man blushed. 'Ten gross!' Geordie said. 'Either you're very optimistic or you're more of a goer than you look!'

'Nah!' the man said. 'They're not for me. They're for sale in the Republic. People can't get them there!' A few days later a sniper opened up on us as we checked a car on the shore of Carlingford Lough. I wondered if it might be the Southerners protecting their supply of condoms.

After a while, the pressure began to tell on us. You couldn't take one step on patrol without imagining a mine blowing your legs off. You couldn't set up a vehicle check-point without fearing an ambush. Two more soldiers of the battalion were killed near Crossmaglen, when a bomb exploded in a culvert and sent their Land Rover crashing into a concrete pillar. In frustration at not being able to turn on the enemy, we turned on ourselves. A Tom from Geordie's section refused an order from another NCO, who promptly hit him with a chair. I quarrelled with the radio-operator of Lambert's section over who should have the spare battery, and ended up punching him in the face. The next day the same man argued with the radio-operator of a third section, who broke his nose. People threw tins of chicken-stew at each other. Lambert reported Bates for defecating in the showers, and Bates was sent off before the OC. The platoon commander accused me of negligence after ordering me to give the spare battery to the same man whom I'd fought for it, and then being surprised that I hadn't got it. Geordie told the platoon commander to 'get stuffed' and called the CSM 'sarn't major' until he was put on orders for insubordination. Before the OC he offered to go down voluntarily to private, but the OC told him that he couldn't be spared.

In the midst of all this madness, I got a call to report to the battalion HQ at Bessbrook Mill.

'What's all this about, sergeant?' I asked Searle.

'Officers' selection,' he said. 'I didn't know you wanted to be an officer, Asher!'

'I don't,' I told him.

The second-in-command was waiting to talk to me when I arrived. 'You've been recommended for the Regular Commissions Board,' he said. 'With certain reservations.'

'Thank you, sir,' I replied.

Only a few days after the battalion returned to Aldershot, I was called to Westbury in Wiltshire for the RCB. It was unchanged, yet somehow the shine had worn off. The generals and colonels in their red staff-gorgettes no longer looked like heroes. The candidates included many rankers: chatty corporals from the Pay Corps and the Royal Signals who had been on special pre-RCB courses. My pre-RCB course had been in 'Bandit Country'. The course supervisor who gathered us in the candidates' mess on the first night said, 'If you're not accepted by the RCB, don't imagine that it means you're useless. It just means that we don't think you're suited to be an officer, that's all!' I sat in the mess with the other candidates, wearing my coloured apron which numbered me as '25', addressing them by their numbers and being similarly addressed. The entire affair suddenly seemed pathetic and meaningless. I couldn't even remember why I had wanted to be an officer. When the interviewing officer asked me, 'How was Northern Ireland?', I replied, 'I was tired, bored, on edge; sixteen hours a day staring into space!' He didn't look impressed.

On the day I received my rejection slip, I had a visit from my old schoolfriend Geoffrey Deacon. We went out together for a drink. 'Well, what are you going to do?' he asked.

'God knows,' I said. 'The Paras was all I had!'

'You don't need it,' he said. 'You can do better. You could even go to university.'

'And become a long-haired pansy?'

'Yes,' he said. 'Only there aren't any long-haired pansies. That's just the Maroon Machine speaking!'

'What do you think I should do?'

'Get out. Leave. The regular army's not for you. Don't waste your time!'

Good old Geoffrey Deacon. He was the only person who ever gave me an ounce of sound advice.

The next week I handed my kit back into the stores. I handed back the 'Smock, Dennison, Airborne', the 'Boots, Dunlop-moulded Soles', the 'Trousers, Olive-green', and all the rest of it, now soiled and worn by continuous use. I kept my red beret, stable-belt and wings – all I had to show for my military service. Then I walked back to my billet to collect my civilian clothes: two pairs of jeans, two shirts, a book, washing and shaving-kit. I placed my maroon beret in with them. There was no one in the billet. The entire battalion had gone off to attend a briefing for a new drop in Turkey that was soon to take place. I said goodbye to no one. No one slapped me on the back or said 'nice to know you' or 'keep in touch'. I closed the door on the billet; a barrack-room, like all the other barrack-rooms, and I carried my bag across the drill-square. No one shouted to me or tried to call me back. I passed the guard at the main gate in his maroon-red beret, carrying a pick-helve and staring into mid-space. The red and white barrier closed behind me, and I walked towards Aldershot and the railway station. Free.

# PART TWO
*The SAS*

# 13

## A Different Army

———

I was twenty-one years of age, still young and only slightly pickled by my experiences in the Paras. I hitch-hiked up to Leeds to stay with an old schoolfriend called John. I felt like some latter-day Dick Whittington, all my wordly goods in a plastic grip, thumbing the long-distance trucks on the verge of the A1. The driver who took me to Leeds was expansive. 'This is the richest city in Britain,' he told me. 'You've got everything here, lad. You'll have a job in twenty-four hours.' He was right. The very next day I was employed by Leeds Corporation as a lifeguard in their International Swimming Pool. 'A man of your education could go far in this job,' the manager said.

My new uniform was a sky-blue tracksuit with a broad scarlet stripe. Except that its universe was confined to that one building, my new job was not unlike my old one: patrol the poolside, enforce the rules, expel the trouble-makers. My new colleagues were an interesting mixture. There were two half-brothers who had both been 'Daddies' in Borstal, where they had served time for armed robbery. The last I heard of them, they had gone down for robbing a Leeds sub-post-office with a sawn-off shotgun. One of the brothers was recognized by a tattoo that he had forgotten to cover up. I thought I had seen life, but my education really began in Leeds. My shift included a lesbian woman who fell in love with the manager's wife and walked out in a huff when her advances were repulsed, and another

ex-Borstal boy who had a flourishing business buying expensive
stereos with stolen credit cards. He was so obsessed with chess
that everything in his flat was painted black or white. There
was a man who had once won a fortune on the football-pools
and had blown it all in a few years. 'It's easier going up than it
is coming down!' he told me. There was also a hippy who made
the same complaint about taking LSD. He was sacked for 'com-
muning with the waters' when he should have been patrolling
the pool.

My home life was no less colourful. I came to an arrangement
with John to share what he called his 'penthouse apartment'. It
turned out to be an attic in a three-storey terraced house in
down-at-heel Headingley. The 'penthouse' referred to the fact
that the ceiling sloped down at an acute angle: you had to stoop
to avoid banging your head. There were no windows, but light
came in through an opaque 'skylight' which opened like a
battle-hatch among the slates of the roof. Part of our arrangement
included the single bed. It was a bow-shaped Victorian structure
that rattled like a full biscuit-tin when you laid on it. We took
turns sleeping on the floor, and I slept in the kitchenette next
door when John entertained his girlfriend.

There was no hot water in the flat. In winter, when snow lay
over the skylight we kept warm with a single-bar electric fire.
One compensation was that we soon learned how to obtain
electricity free: the meter, when removed from its nail and laid
gently on the floor, failed to register. We fed it the occasional
two-shillings for appearances and hung it back on the nail when
we heard footsteps on the stairs.

The only bathroom in the house was on the first floor. To get
there we had to brave a steep, slippery staircase guarded by an
ogre-like married couple. Neither of them ever spoke to me, and
the wife spoke to John only once. That was when he opened the
bathroom door to be confronted by her large pink receding
posterior. A bath was a rare treat, since it involved slotting a
whole sixpence into the water-heater and waiting for an hour
while the feeble machine rattled into life. During that hour, the
ogre-like couple might easily take possession. I was guarding my

sixpenny investment one day, when a lovely, slim slip of a girl with long jet-black hair wafted up from the ground floor. She asked in a soft, seductive voice if she could use the bathroom. Naturally, I agreed.

The next day, John and I were invited to the ground-floor flat by Margaret, the dark-haired girl. She shared it with Stephanie, a pint-sized nurse with flame-coloured hair. The flat was decorated by nude studies of both girls, done in charcoals. They had been drawn by an artist whose favours they shared. A characteristic which the girls had in common was their physical childishness. Stephanie's height made her look like a twelve-year-old; Margaret, though taller, was completely flat-chested. Their artist lover was particularly interested in the childish aspect of women, it seemed: he had recently been arrested for molesting schoolgirls.

That first night we shared several bottles of cheap sherry, bought by the pint from the local branch of Patel's. It proved so overpowering that I woke up the following morning with Margaret beside me in the bow-shaped bed. Thereafter, our relationship ran down. One night, over a drink in a local pub, I told her that we should stop seeing one another. Her reaction was astonishing. She leapt up and directed at me a string of shrivelling abuse which she certainly hadn't learned at her convent school. She hurled a knobbly half-pint beer mug across the pub, narrowly missing an old lady propped against a glass of Guinness at the bar. I followed her back to the house and just caught a glimpse of her disappearing into the bathroom where I'd first laid eyes on her. 'Bye, Mick!' she shouted at me.

A few moments later she staggered out of the bathroom, scarlet blood squirting from the artery she'd severed in her wrist with a broken wine-glass. The blood splashed over the walls and the ceiling, but we managed to drag her upstairs and sit her on the bed. While my friend ripped up the landlord's sheet for a tourniquet, I rang for an ambulance from the nearest phone-booth. When the ambulance-men arrived, there was a fearful scene, as Margaret fought them off. She was an orphan and continual rejection was the one thing she couldn't stand. It was the sixth time she had tried to commit suicide.

But for me, life still held its fascination, and I grew my hair long, dressed casually, rode a motorcycle and thought my military self submerged by the new experience. Occasionally there would be dreams of Jekyll swearing at me on a deserted parade-ground, where I stood at attention with my long hair stuffed vainly into my red beret.

My foreman was a veteran of the Korean war. 'If I ask you to do something, you don't do it,' he once told me. 'If I order you to do it, you jump. I've seen men like you before. You're still brain-washed!' One day I received a small packet through the post. It was a silver campaign medal bearing the Queen's head, with a green and purple ribbon. On the ribbon was a bar inscribed 'Northern Ireland' and on the back was carved '24246810, Pte Asher, M.J.'. To see my name and number written like that gave me a jolt.

I knew that I should have to get myself organized. John had been on a six-month industrial training course, and would shortly be returning to Bradford University. I still wanted to be a journalist, and applied for the current training course on the *Yorkshire Post*. There were no vacancies. As a matter of routine I applied for various teachers' training institutions to read for a degree in education. 'Do you really feel you have a *vocation* to be a teacher?' one dragon-like lady registrar asked me. 'Because if not, you're wasting your time.' I mumbled that I wasn't too sure. 'Then you'd be far better applying for university!' she told me. I had hardly even considered the possibility. That woman gave me the second good piece of advice of my career. I left her office determined to apply for a university place, and the same day I filled in a UCCA form.

As I had writing in mind, English was the natural choice of subject. I sent off my form, complete with a reference from my old headmaster, who seemed to have mellowed towards me since I had left school. But I heard nothing. In desperation, thinking I should be stuck in the swimming-pool for ever, I went to the opposite extreme. I applied to fight in various African countries as a mercenary and even considered the French Foreign Legion. Very luckily for me, my applications came to nothing. Instead I was invited to an interview at the University of Leeds.

I donned a jacket and tie for the first time in months and walked across the park to the School of English. It was part of an ultra-modern complex of elegant prestressed concrete and glass. An attractive female undergraduate met me at the door. I suppose she had been enlisted to put me at ease, although at this she proved to be less than effective. 'You don't have to wear a jacket and tie for interviews these days!' she said. I was interviewed by a member of staff who told me that he liked candidates with experience of what he called 'the outside world'. He questioned me about my time in the Paras, and then we talked about Shakespeare and twentieth-century literature. At the end of the interview he gave me an unconditional offer.

A few months later I was queueing up for registration with the rest of the freshers. I collected my Union card and was immediately pounced on by an undergraduate in military uniform. I was so surprised that I only just prevented myself from standing to attention. 'Why not join the Officers' Training Corps?' he asked me. 'You get free uniform and good pay!' He handed me a recruitment booklet and was about to march on to the next prospective recruit, when a troop of goggle-eyed hippies waltzed down the corridor, shouting, 'TROOPS OUT! TROOPS OUT! TROOPS OUT!' One of them carried a placard on which was scrawled GET THE OTC KILLERS OFF THE CAMPUS! Later, one of a similar bunch tried to sell me a thin newspaper called the *Red Star*. 'It's got pictures of bombings in Northern Ireland!' he told me, with all the prurient avidity of a porno-salesman. I looked at the pictures. They showed the results of terrible explosions in places I had visited, where pieces of human bodies were being shovelled into plastic bags. 'Have you ever been to Northern Ireland?' I asked him, with a feeling of nausea. 'I only sell them, comrade!' he replied.

Autumn 1974 was a time when few people in Britain could continue to ignore the crisis across the Irish Sea. The Provisionals had moved their campaign to the mainland and were scurrying about laying charges in Brookes Club and Harrow

School. The Prime Minister was bombed in his house in Bel-
gravia; Guinness book editor Ross McWhirter was gunned down
on his doorstep. Every week there were new murders and
bombings, and every week the Student Executive of Leeds University seemed keener on giving the IRA moral support. One day, I
found my way across the campus barred by a crowd of students
toting banners saying SUPPORT THE IRA! I learned that it was a
Special General Meeting of the Union. A bearded undergraduate
thrust a booklet into my hand. I noticed he was wearing a Sinn
Fein badge, though his accent was as English as mine. 'Support
the Provisionals!' he shouted at me. 'Get stuffed!' I said. Later I
heard that the Executive had passed a motion of support for the
Provisionals' cause. I don't suppose the Provisionals actually
gave a tinker's cuss for the opinions of a lot of English middle-
class undergrads, neither do I imagine that many of these
undergrads would have been there if they had witnessed the
effect of an IRA bombing. But at the time they all considered it
jolly good fun.

I wasn't interested in politics. I was too busy grappling with
Anglo-Saxon grammar, semantic shift and principles of Indo-European philology. If I had spare time, it was devoted to a social life
which was livened by a very favourable ratio of female-to-male
undergraduates on my course: eight to one. Eventually I fell in
love with a girl called Anne, tall, black haired and very bright.
She was the only person I ever met who turned down an offer
of a place at Oxford to go to Leeds. The daughter of a solid
Lancashire police-constable, her ambition was to become a
detective. After a time we moved into a house together with
several other students, male and female. I was busy socially,
and intellectually my course was rewarding. Yet I still felt that
there was something missing. My life lacked the physical challenge I had known in the Paras: there was little danger, no
pressure on me to bring out the primitive instincts of raw
survival which I had found so satisfying in my army days.
Perhaps I should have been satisfied with the University Explora-
tion Society, or in taking up some challenging sport like
mountaineering or pot-holing. The truth is that, after my

experiences in the 'outside world', I looked down on such undergraduate clubs as being Boy Scoutish. I formed rather the same impression of the Officers' Training Corps, and the constant political games in the Union only confirmed my impression of undergraduates as impetuous children playing at life. I realized afterwards, of course, that this was quite normal. I was the odd one out. But my unusual and intense life in the Paras had made a lasting impression on me which was difficult to throw off despite the long hair I cultivated.

I was sitting in a basement wine-bar in Leeds Headrow, when someone touched me on the arm. The face which presented itself was immediately familiar, yet I had to struggle to recognize it. I knew at once that it belonged to part of my life which now seemed a far-off dream. 'Robbins,' the face said. 'You haven't forgotten? 2 Para!' Then I recalled the same face capped with a maroon-red beret, the day the SIB marched him off to prison for stealing watches in Belfast. The last I'd heard he had been discharged for threatening a policeman with a pistol. 'It wasn't even a real pistol!' he told me over a drink later. 'It was only a replica. But the penalty's the same these days!' He looked prosperous, I thought, with his expensive three-piece pin-stripe suit and gold cufflinks. 'Got my own security business now,' he told me. 'Business is booming in West Yorkshire. You want a job?'

'No thanks,' I said. 'But I do miss the action.'

'So do I,' he said. 'After I got out of the pokey I went to Rhodesia and enlisted in the Rhodesian Light Infantry. All Dutch and Germans, it is. Still, I got decorated for bravery in the war.' He took out a wallet and proudly showed me a citation. 'But things went bad. I had to get out.' He sipped his drink thoughtfully and said, 'You should join the Territorials.'

'Like the OTC?' I answered. 'Bunch of Boy Scouts!'

'What about the SAS?' he asked.

'In Leeds?'

'Why not? There's a sabre squadron of the SAS volunteers here. There's no amateurs in the SAS. They might be TA, but they do the same type of selection course as the regulars. It's

tough to get in, though. They don't take any old Tom, Dick or
Harry. You'd have to get fitter than you are now. And get rid of
that long hair. You look like a bleeding pansy!' At the end of
that evening, many drinks later, I knew I had found the missing
challenge.

The SAS barracks was tucked away at the end of a suitably
nondescript side-street, and entered by a tumble-down gateway
watched by hidden cameras. On my first nervous visit there I
was interviewed by a small, very fit-looking Yorkshireman who
spoke quietly and acted informally. I learned later he was a
captain. Raymond Dart impressed me. He had none of the
superior air of the officers I had met in the regular army. 'Don't
come here expecting to turn into James Bond,' he told me.
'There are a lot of myths about the SAS. There are no piano-
wires or exploding cigarette-lighters. What we're looking for
first and last is good soldiers who can work alone or in small
groups rather than the big battalions. You'll find it a bit different
from the Paras. There's no bull and no screaming NCOs. If a
man can't keep himself smart, he's out. Discipline here is self-
discipline. SAS selection is hard, but it's not beyond the powers
of the ordinary, alert man with proper determination. You can
forget about gadgets and false-bottomed suitcases. The things
you'll exercise most in the SAS are brain, lungs and feet!'

Captain Dart explained that the selection course consisted of
nothing more mysterious than a series of marches over wild
country, alone and carrying heavy equipment, responsible for
your own navigation. Put like that, it didn't sound too hard.
'The SAS won't train you up to it,' he said. 'Fitness is your
responsibility. If you aren't fit on the day, you'll fail!' I left the
SAS barracks that day determined at least I should be fit on the
day.

The sabre squadron of which I would soon become a prospective member was part of 23 SAS (Volunteers), the same battalion that my old acquaintance Bradley had described to me as
'a different army'. It was the youngest star in the SAS trinity.
Raised in 1959, it was descended from a wartime intelligence
mob, MI9, which had been responsible for organizing the escape

lines amongst the Resistance. MI9 agents ferried home escaped RAF pilots, whom the government considered expensive equipment to lose. Their boss had been Major Airey Neave, later Conservative MP and spokesman on Northern Ireland, but then famous as the first escapee from the notorious Colditz castle.

By 1959, however, it looked very unlikely that in a future nuclear war there would be any escaped pilots to ferry home. Instead, the unit was converted to an SAS unit with its primary job insurgency behind enemy lines. It joined the two existing SAS battalions, 21 SAS (Artists'), descended from the wartime SAS, and 22 SAS, based in Hereford, raised as the Malayan Scouts, from a motley collection of elements. By the time of my application in 1975 the SAS was a miniature brigade group, still virtually unknown by the public and bearing very little resemblance to the gung-ho desert commandos of the wartime SAS. Sadly, Colditz hero Airey Neave did not live to see the SAS rise to stardom. The Irish National Liberation Army blew him up in 1979, outside the House of Commons.

I realized that I should have to be careful about revealing my new interest to my campus colleagues. The climate there was unsympathetic, to say the least. Actually, I didn't know a Marxist from a Malekite or a Socialist Worker from a social worker. Sometimes I thought my fellow undergraduates didn't either. This feeling was confirmed much later when Sue Slipman, the former Leeds University Union Marxist President, was elected to the Commons as a Social Democrat MP. However, there was a hard-core of activists behind them, hangers-on rather than students, who did. I decided that in the SAS case, discretion was by far the better form of valour.

Now there was no Jekyll to goad me into giving my best. It was all up to me. I had several months to get myself ready for SAS selection, and I had to devise my own programme of fitness. I had put on weight since leaving the Paras, and my heart and lungs were full of cobwebs. I went for a preliminary run around the block and came back puffing and sweating after only fifteen minutes. I knew something drastic had to be done.

First of all I begged, borrowed or bought all the books I could find on the principles of physical training. I learned that fitness was basically a matter of accustoming the heart and lungs to accept overload. I tested my heart-rate and its recovery time after a bout of activity. It was too high, and the recovery time too long. I plotted a systematic course of 'aerobics', beginning with a run and walk over two miles in twelve minutes. I bought a map and measured the distance around Woodhouse Moor, the park near my home. I began a steady programme of jogging there three times a week before lectures, through rain and slush and snow. The excess weight slowly began to burn off. My heart-rate started to drop, my recovery time to shorten. I upped the distance to three miles and the frequency from three times a week to four. Soon, I was back on intimate terms with my old friend the pain barrier. Every second clipped off my time was a small victory, every extra lap of the course a major triumph. I soon found that I didn't need Jekyll to urge me on. He was there inside me anyway, deep in my subconscious, goading, cursing and screaming in my head, telling me that I was a useless tube, that I would never attain the most hallowed totem of war in the British army: the Winged Dagger and the motto 'Who Dares Wins'.

# 14

## *Winged Dagger*

————

In 1940, when the Italian army and the German Afrika Korps were pushing the British desert rats back towards Alexandria and Cairo, a young lieutenant from the Scots Guards was lying in a Cairo hospital with both legs paralysed. The officer, a sixteen-stone mountaineer called David Stirling, had injured himself during an illicit parachute-jump. His canopy had snagged on the tailplane of the aircraft, causing him to Roman-candle into the rocky desert ground.

Stirling detested being inactive. While his legs slowly recovered, he considered ways in which a small force of British parachutists could attack the enemy at their weakest point: in their overstretched supply lines. Dropped behind enemy lines, a trained force of saboteurs could destroy enemy planes, fuel-dumps and supply depots, inflicting damage far out of proportion to their numbers. Stirling left hospital on crutches two months later, and made an unannounced visit to the commander-in-chief of the British forces. Not long afterwards his plan was accepted, and the Special Air Service brigade was born.

In practice, part of Stirling's plan proved unsuccessful. The unpredictable winds and storms of the desert made parachuting a dangerous option. Instead, the new SAS unit was eventually equipped with armed jeeps in which it penetrated deep into enemy territory, blowing up vehicles, machine-gunning camps, destroying aircraft. By the end of the war in North Africa, the SAS had destroyed more than 400 enemy planes. As the war moved on into the Mediterranean and Europe, the unit became two regiments, 1 and 2 SAS. They fought with the Resistance and Partisans until 1945, when they were disbanded. It is precisely at this point that the curious history of the modern SAS begins.

1 and 2 SAS became a Territorial unit, whose number '21' was simply a reversal of their two numerals. It was amalgamated with an eccentric London officer-training battalion, the Artists' Rifles, whose ranks had included such characters as William Morris. 21 SAS (Artists' Volunteers) became the first modern SAS unit. It was the Malayan crisis in 1949 which provided 21 SAS with its first opportunity for action. The British army was up against experienced guerrillas who operated in the rain-forest. It could be reached only by small patrols operating independently. Captain Mike Calvert, given the job of assessing the situation, decided that what was needed in the jungle was a formation whose patrols could stay there indefinitely as the guerrillas did. They would, in fact, be conventional troops who fought like insurgents. And, since no insurgency could succeed without the consent of the local population, the patrolling force would have to be able to win over the 'hearts and minds' of the jungle aborigines.

Calvert cobbled together three squadrons: one from 21 SAS, another from local veterans and a third recruited in Rhodesia. The three squadrons became the Malayan Scouts (SAS), but not until the communist insurgency was won and it was added to the army's official order of battle as 22 SAS. The success of the regiment in Malaya and its subsequent efficiency in almost everything it took on was based squarely on its selection philosophy. Men were not chosen on hearsay, the 'he's a good chap' method of most elite units. Nor were they chosen for the size of their biceps, their propensity for bar-room brawls or even their scores on the weapon-training tests.

The SAS selection looked for a special type of individual: one who could stand up to long periods of loneliness, had a high degree of self-discipline and self-motivation, and didn't require the support of the 'big battalions' to bring out his courage. SAS men were required to work alone or in four-man patrols, usually deep inside country controlled by the enemy. They were not hit-and-run commandos but long-term deep penetration troops.

The year 1957 was a troubled one for the British army. The government made drastic cuts, getting rid of distinguished old regiments and phasing out national service. The army was made a professional body. It was streamlined to cope with the petty wars of decolonialization, already occurring throughout the Third World, and the possible future scenario of nuclear conflict in Europe. The SAS was uneasy. A committee was formed to look into the workings of Special Forces and decide if they were necessary. The final verdict was: yes. The SAS had a role in a future European war. Its job would be to operate far behind enemy lines, gathering intelligence and striking at important targets. But the new SAS was to be more sophisticated than anything dreamed of by its wartime members. The new SAS had to assimilate quickly a vast menu of technical skills: communications, field-medicine, demolitions, languages, recognition and many others. In a world where technology was becoming daily more sophisticated, they had to become increasingly efficient as its eyes, ears and striking arm.

All of this was unknown to me as I prepared myself for the selection course. I enrolled in a city fitness-club. Every other day I would be there grunting beside the 'Mr Universe' contenders, with my sets of sit-ups, barbell squats, bicep-curls and all the other extraordinary configurations of flesh and iron. I watched the 'body beautiful' crowd with amazement, not believing that the human body could become so unnaturally grotesque. There was a definite pecking-order at these places, in which he of the biggest biceps ruled the roost. I knew that some of these body-builders could have broken my arm with a single snap, yet still they amused me. For all their fitness and strength, their liver-pills and their yoghurt, they still trained only for appearance. It was pure vanity. Yet we were all united in the pursuit of excellence through bodily exertion, pushing that barbell once

more and yet again through the red mist of agony, pumping
that dumb-bell for the last repetition through the saw-tooth
edge of shrieking ligaments. In each repetition completed, each
new set achieved, each kilogramme added to the barbell, there
was the same pattern of the mind's domination over resistance.
It was the opposite of man's bestial nature. No animal will
voluntarily endure pain and suffering to reach a future abstract
goal. Each movement, each exercise of muscle, lungs and heart,
was in itself a perfect cipher for the completion of the greater
task to which I was working.

Already the physical challenge had given me new life and
purpose which seemed to relegate even my studies and social
life to the second league. A new, obsessive side of my nature,
glimpsed only dimly in the Paras and never fully understood,
was emerging. Something in my make-up had imbued me with
this need for physical challenge. As my muscles lost their
softness, I began jogging to the fitness centre instead of using
my motorcycle. I finished a two-hour work-out with a Swedish
sauna, relaxing naked in the sizzling heat and plunging afterwards into an ice-cold shower. The body I saw in the mirror
when I rubbed myself with a towel looked tougher, squatter and
more streamlined. Often now I jogged to the International pool,
my old workplace, where I set myself a mini-programme of
swimming. I started with a quarter-mile and worked steadily to
a half-mile and then a mile at each session. I enrolled in the
University Sports Club, where I practised power-lifting and
trained intensely on the circuits laid out in the gym; rope-
climbing, medicine-balls, step-ups and sprints. At weekends,
while Anne was studying dutifully, I would be out in the Dales,
running the peaks of Whernside, Pen-y-ghent and Ribblesdale.
At first the distance defeated me. Then I tried again, navigating
with my own map and compass, and bypassing the booted and
cagouled climbers in my shorts and running-shoes.

Back in Leeds, I was jogging twenty miles a week in boots,
carrying an old rucksack. I was hefting more than 300 pounds
on the bench-press and squatting with more than 500. I even
found time to take up my old school interest, fencing, represent-

ing the university in both épée and foil. When the long vacation came up, I managed to find a job in a small district swimming-pool, where I could swim as much as I pleased. Here, I was back in the 'outside world' again. My new colleagues included a Scotsman who had done three years in Barlinnie Prison for grievous bodily harm, a former lighthouse-keeper and a strange man called the 'Deeker' because of his obsession with peeping into the changing-cubicles of young girls.

The pool was part of a traditional public baths, designed for an era when few Leeds citizens possessed a bathroom of their own. It was an interesting Edwardian building, complete with stained glass, glazed bricks and brass plates and pipes which we polished daily. As well as the swimming-pool, the baths contained a Turkish steam-bath and conventional baths, each fitted with an enormous brass tap, known in the trade as 'slipper-baths'. Water was heated by a bloated old boiler known as 'Mary Ann'. It was a noisy caterpillar of cast-iron, much given to sudden bangs and bumps and emissions of steam. We took it in turns to 'bank up' Mary Ann, delivering tons of broken coal into her mechanical maw on a spatula-like shovel. Under the pool was a sinuous inspection-tunnel which led beneath the changing cubicles. In one of them, No. 45, there was an iron grille with a small hole in the centre, allowing someone in the inspection-tunnel to peer up into the cubicle above.

The Deeker's trick was to stand at the door until an attractive woman entered, take her ticket and give her the key to No. 45. As soon as she had closed the cubicle door, he would make an excuse, rush down to the inspection-tunnel beneath and watch her undress. The foreman suspected him, but never managed to catch him in the tunnel. Since no woman ever made a complaint, it was difficult to prove that he had made a nuisance of himself. One day, however, he went too far. He climbed up on the roof of the baths and 'deeked' through the glass skylight into the women's slipper-bath, where a very large and forthright West Indian lady was enjoying a bath. She burst out with only a towel around her and informed the manager. He caught the Deeker in the act of descending, and summarily dismissed him.

But the comedy ended in tragedy. Only a week later the Deeker was arrested for murder. He had raped a girl by a railway embankment and at the same time smashed her head in with a house-brick.

Towards the end of the summer, Anne and I decided to drive a motorcycle from Britain to Istanbul. The motorcycle got us as far as Ferrara in Italy. We left it in a garage and hitch-hiked or rode trains through Yugoslavia, Greece, Bulgaria, Turkey and back. I returned to find that I had passed my positive vetting and was accepted as a recruit in 23 SAS.

Everything I saw amongst the SAS confirmed what I had heard about them in the Paras. There was a convivial, mutually supportive atmosphere rather than a belligerent air of conflict. If the Paras were shock-troops, then the SAS were 'softly-softly' men. There were no loud-mouths or bar-soldiers. There was a palpable sense of quiet determination about them, a seriousness which dealt with each obstacle as an interesting problem. There was no aspect of training which was too trivial to examine in detail: nothing was waved aside in the pressure of achieving the goal. These SAS men looked very fit, but as a matter of course rather than as a means to prove themselves 'tough' or superior. You could tell at a glance that they were above 'beasting' for its own sake. They were not truculent or sadistic, as the Paras had been. You could see that they might kill easily, but never for the love of it.

In the Paras, recruits had been mostly young working-class men in their late teens or early twenties. Here, I was amongst married men in their late twenties or early thirties, from all walks of life and with plenty of experience. Recruit wing included amongst its members a national karate champion, a pioneer free-fall parachutist and a former professional footballer. Training with me were an officer, Robert Byfield, a former Australian commando sergeant, John Leese, a post-office manager, Bill Tetley, an insurance clerk called Mike Porter, an ex-REME corporal called Trevor Wyman and a former marine called Ed Scott. No one in the SAS talked about craphats. Some of the most distinguished SAS soldiers were ex-craphats, coming from such humble parent-units as the Army Catering Corps and the trusty old Pioneer Corps, the army's navvies. The ex-Paras, and there were plenty of them, were conspicuously lacking in the old chauvinism. They had evidently given complete loyalty to their new badge.

'No special gadgets,' Captain Dart had said in my first interview, and this proved to be a magnificent understatement. Everything the SAS issued me with was pleasingly prosaic. There was no formal dress, jungle-hats, bum-rolls, long johns, kit-bags or spares. I was simply given a wind-proof smock, a shirt, a pullover, a pair of denims, socks, puttees, a woollen hat called a 'cap-comforter', and a pair of DMS boots chosen with great care and deliberation from the stock in the stores. There was a poncho, a sleeping-bag, a belt with two ammo-pouches, a water-bottle and mug, two mess tins, a towel, a field-dressing, and most important of all, a bergen which would take everything else inside it with room to spare. After the masses of kit I had had in the Paras, this was really the basics. The instruction manual for recruits summed up 'Discipline' in three clipped paragraphs:

1. All clothing is to be kept clean and in a good state of repair.
2. Hair is to be kept reasonably short and tidy. No sideburns, mutton-chops, beards, wigs, etc. Unfortunately, the public judge a man more by his appearance than his abilities. While we know you are 'mustard', they do not, and the unit can well do without adverse publicity.
3. There is no bull in the SAS, but personnel are expected to keep themselves reasonably clean and tidy without prompting.

Their attitude to 'special gadgets' was summed up by a notice on the wall of the stores: 'A Spartan mother's advice to her son who complained that his sword was too short: "Take a step forward!"'

Looking back even now, I can still remember the excitement and awe I felt on being accepted as a recruit in the SAS. It was 'only TA', I knew, but there was an unmistakable feel about the men and the place, that here you were part of something very

special, very serious, very aloof. There was the feeling that
nothing had been left to chance: everything had been measured
and considered and evaluated over the decades by men who
were much more than the 'dogs of war' I had been amongst in
the Parachute Regiment. The Paras were fanatically brave,
peerlessly stalwart and superlatively aggressive, but you always
had the feeling that they were like clockwork toys being wound
up and pointed in the right direction. The Paras had talked
about 'every man being an emperor', but the SAS lived it. The
SAS was without class and every officer had first to serve in the
ranks and to earn the respect of his men. The SAS was almost a
separate army, a caste in itself, a family in which every member
was valued. SAS soldiers were anything but 'cannon fodder':
they were thinking men who wouldn't hesitate to question an
operational procedure if they thought it wrong. It was this
element of free thinking, of application to a problem, coupled
with the stark simplicity of approach, the informality of relationships, the mutual respect for men who had passed the same
selection course, which gave me a lasting affection for 23 SAS.

The first instalment of my training took place in a cramped
classroom, and consisted entirely of map-reading. I thought I
knew maps, but again I was astonished by the purposeful and
painstaking method employed by the SAS. We started from
square one: grid north, magnetic north, true north, magnetic
variation, horizontal equivalent, vertical interval, basins, cols,
saddles, spurs, contours, watersheds and re-entrants. The instructor, Pete Green, had the patience of Job. No shouting. No
swearing. No press-ups. The instruction sessions had the hushed
and academic atmosphere of a Sunday school. If you failed to
understand, he simply explained again and again, until the
lesson had been absorbed.

Every weekend would find us in the hills in various parts of
Britain, with a bergen, a map and a compass and a set distance
to cover. From the beginning I needed all the strength and
fitness I'd acquired during my training period. The distances
were long and the weights we carried relentlessly heavy. At first
we were set off in groups of two or three and asked to reach an

objective ten miles away. The objective, or 'RV', was usually sited deep in the most difficult country, on a mountain peak or in the middle of a marsh, or at least you had to cross the most difficult terrain in order to reach it. The emphasis was on accuracy of map-reading and compass work. We had to learn to select a bold route across the hills or valleys to attain our objectives even in the foulest weather. And the weather was almost always foul. There was snow, there was clinging fog which hid the landmarks from view. There was freezing rain which turned the mountain streams into raging torrents and winds so high and violent that they threatened to hurl you off the peaks. Bad weather was never an excuse for cancelling training: it was a desirable factor as far as the SAS was concerned. Part of the regiment's ethos was the ability to operate in any conditions, a factor well illustrated by 22 SAS's landing on south Georgia during the Falklands War in 1982. To make the selection of your route more difficult, you were forbidden to use tracks or roads, from passing through villages, hamlets or farmsteads, from making contact with or asking directions from anyone, from crossing bridges or cultivated land. The instruction brief was final when it stated: 'If you break any of the above rules, goodbye.'

The first march sorted out the sheep from the goats. The big ex-marine, Ed Scott, was a bruiser in the Para mould: tall and bullish, his head was like a knob of granite, his expression one of permanent ferocity. The weight of his bergen was nothing to him, but the task of map-reading was different. On the very first leg of the march, he got lost and was four hours overdue at the RV. On the second leg, having been patiently orientated by Sergeant Green, he sat down and sliced through an orange with his razor-sharp commando knife. In his eagerness he sliced through most of the palm of his hand too. He managed to hike back to the previous RV, clutching a hand that was still dripping with blood. He hadn't even thought to slap a field-dressing on it. Scott was not SAS material.

Mike Porter, the insurance clerk, was the next to go. He was as fit as any of us, and had been an enthusiastic fell-walker

for years. He even brought along his own boots, which the
instructors had allowed him to wear as a matter of course. He
simply gave up one day on reaching an RV sited on top of a
steep slope. 'I thought you were used to walking,' one of the
other recruits commented. 'Not the SAS way, I'm not!' he
replied. 'I walk for pleasure: this is torture!'

Gradually, both the distance and the weight of your bergen
were increased. The nights drew in. Lashings of snow lay on the
Dales and it took a vice-like determination just to get out of the
cosy warmth of the Land Rover and set off into the wilds. The
instructors never goaded you. Whether you went or stayed was
your own decision. When you bivvied out in the valleys, lying
sleepless all night from the cold, no one ordered you to get up.
The motivation had to come from you. There was no bravado,
as there had been in the Paras, no taboos against stopping to
rest or eat or drink. No one called you a pansy if you happened
to wipe your nose. The only essential thing was that you
reached your objective on time, without breaking the rules, and
in a fit enough state to carry on to the next one. In the Paras,
fitness had been an end in itself. Your officer or section commander did the map-reading, and as a Tom it was sufficient to
follow with 'your thumb up your bum and your mind in
neutral', as the instructors put it. There were no 'thumbs up
bums' in the SAS. Whether ravaged by cold or blisters or
exhaustion you had to stay alert, reading the ground, reading
the map, selecting the best and quickest route, conserving
your energy, surviving the elements. Gradually the map ceased
to be a piece of paper with words and symbols on it and
started to assume its 'real' shape: a perfect mental model of the
ground you had to cross. It wasn't enough to look at the map:
you had to be able to visualize the ground from it in your
mind's eye, so that when you came to obstacles it was as if you
were seeing them for the second time.

In the Paras the attitude had been 'march or die'. You were a
machine: no attention was given to details of bodily comfort,
the small tricks the soldier could adopt to make the way a little
easier. In the Depot, such tricks had been regarded as almost

'cheating'. In the SAS, the approach was the opposite. Nothing was beneath consideration, from the calorific content of your food to the best method of applying a plaster to a blister, from the best way of putting on socks to the most energy-saving way to climb a slope. On the surface the SAS seemed almost Boy Scoutish. In fact, it was supremely professional: the SAS knew that blistered, painful feet or lack of sufficient nutrition in wild country far from base could mean death: moreover, it could mean the difference between the success or failure of a mission. The contrast between the two approaches seems well summed up in their respective recruit literature. The Paras are fire and brimstone: 'The parachute soldier must be of high quality, both in mind and body, fit to fight and fighting fit. Training is hard and only the best is good enough. Parachute soldiers need intelligence, common sense, determination and will-power.' The SAS booklet ran: 'As an SAS soldier you will have many exacting tasks to perform in the field. To keep going you need to eat, drink, rest and maintain your equipment in good working condition. If you look after yourself properly, you will not only be more comfortable, you will also be a better, more efficient soldier.'

This more positive approach I found well suited to my personality, perhaps more so than the 'blood, sweat, toil and tears' method of the Paras. But there was plenty of sweat, toil and tears in the SAS. The marches were more excruciatingly vicious than anything I had done in the Paras, yet they were unaccompanied by beasting or abuse. You felt that the instructors actually wanted you to succeed. Each training weekend was a small endurance test. No matter how fit you were, it was impossible to sail through. There came a point for every recruit, ex-soldier and civilian alike, when the body was at its last gasp and the mind had to take over control. There came a moment when the bravado and the fighting-spirit were torn away, when a veil was pulled from your eyes and you saw yourself as you really were, a weak and inconsequential worm with a poor and inadequate body, struggling ineffectually to take on a task that was too great. That was the real moment of selection. It was then that you decided how much you wanted the Winged

Dagger. I had been through the pain barrier often in the Paras, but then team spirit, the *élan* of the platoon, had helped to carry me through. The weaker and stronger elements of the unit had melted and fused together to create something stronger than the sum of its parts. But here there was only yourself and your untrustworthy body, which seemed to be in the continual process of coming apart at the seams: burning, blistered feet gave way to aching shoulders and back, which were in turn overwhelmed by chafed thighs, freezing fingers and gasping, straining heart and lungs. Your body told you to stop, to lay down, to remove the dead weight on your back, but you fought the revolt down, tottered across the raging cold torrent, jiggered yourself on hands and knees up the bank, slithered across loose screes, ploughed on, clawing hand over hand up the slope through the lashing tongue of the rain and the freezing clutch of the wind, on and on until the RV was in sight, then on and on again to the one after that. And when you finally made it back to the warm comfort of your vehicle with thirty miles of Britain's most rugged country behind you, you forgot the pain and the blistered feet and prepared to do it all again.

Each Sunday evening I arrived back home in Leeds, limping, drained and stretched to the limit, unable to do anything but have a shower and sit on the floor collecting my strength. I never managed to study over the weekend, but I was always at lectures on Monday morning, bright and early. 'How did your weekend go?' fellow students would inquire. 'Very good. Spot of fell-walking in the Dales,' I would answer. No one but Anne knew my secret, and my double life added an extra element of excitement to it. Of course, I saw more danger than there actually was. There were plenty of Officers' Training Corps members on the campus who were technically in the same position as me. Nevertheless, I was very circumspect about whom I let into my house, checked my motorcycle carefully every day and tried to vary my routine as much as possible.

Over the moors and mountains at the weekends, I got to know my fellow recruits intimately. The man I respected most was the former Australian commando, John Leese. Naturally, he was known as 'Ozzie', but the nickname irked him. 'I was born in Manchester,' he would insist. 'I was only brought up in Australia. The fights I've had in Sydney over being called a Pom. Now I'm here in Blighty they call me an Ozzie! What the hell am I?' A further source of amusement to all of us was his occupation: he worked as an engineer in a sewage-farm. 'What kind of engineer are you, Ozzie?' they would tease him. 'I'm an engineer in a sewage-farm.' 'You mean you're a shit engineer?' 'That's right, I work with shit.' Shit engineer he might have been, but he was mustard as a soldier. As a commando in Australia, he had trained often with the Australian SAS, for whom he had an almost sacred regard. 'They were the best soldiers in Vietnam,' he told me. 'Made the Yanks' Green Berets look like amateurs. That "hearts and minds" stuff was a waste of time in Vietnam, because the people were on the Vietcong side from the beginning. The Ozzie SAS lived in the jungle for fourteen days at a time on their own supplies. They moved as quiet as leopards, and the VC were shit-scared of them. They'd hit 'em for close up and bug out like lightning. They were so efficient that they made 500 kills and lost only one man. That's what I call soldiers!'

Leese and the ex-REME mechanic Trevor Wyman were 'buddies' who usually walked together if we were set off in pairs. Wyman was a small, dark, noisy man, overactive and intelligent, full of jokes and energy. His civilian job was mechanic in an army base, and at the same time he held the rank of corporal in the REME Territorials. 'Bloody ridiculous!' he would say. 'I'm doing the same job as I used to do in the regular army for more pay and better conditions, and in my spare time I get paid for being a Territorial. It's like being paid twice for doing the same job!' He could hardly believe his good fortune, and he was amongst the most enthusiastic of the recruits. He and Leese were always first in at the final RV, and he was still chirping away happily on the drive back to Leeds.

Now the marches were longer and more exacting. Distances between RVs were extended, and the staff might drop an extra little task on you when you arrived: memorizing a 'shopping

list' to be carried to the next RV or even tipping out the
contents of your bergen and ordering you to carry them to the
next RV by hand. Finally, when the required distance had been
covered in groups and pairs, we were brought forward to the
'test weekend'. This consisted of a single, continuous long march
over the mountains, carrying a very weighty bergen. The big
difference between test weekend and the warm-up marches was
that this time you were completely alone.

All I remember about that test weekend is the start, the finish
and a few vague visions of the suffering in between. It was
winter. There was snow on the hills. I was turned out of the
Land Rover in the darkness of a freezing night and within
twenty yards had fallen into a fast-running river of melt-water.
The night was a moonless shroud where stars flashed angrily
like stifled braziers through a glacial mist. The icy water seemed
to freeze my muscles, as I clawed my way up the invisible rime-
covered bank. A great concave slope of a dale reared dimly
before me. The ground was hard but slippery. My boots squelched as I cut forward. I was so used to the weight of my bergen
that I could scarcely feel it. I squatted by a bush and got out my
pencil-torch, which illuminated my map with a reddish prick of
light. I checked my initial bearing with my Silva compass. I
picked out my direction and braced myself to start. I had paused
for no more than two minutes, yet already the cold was biting
into my flesh. I heard a slopping and sploshing of water behind
me and knew that the next contender had already been set off. I
didn't wait to find out who it was. I was off like a greyhound,
running across the turf. My compass was in my hand con-
tinually, and the wild, four o'clock images of monsters and
giants hovered on the edge of my vision: I was too intent on my
purpose to spare them a thought.

I remember dawn coming up that day: grey light and splodges
of thick, dirty cloud rising like smoke from the clefts in the
valleys, the bitter ache of the wind and the choking sting of cold
on the nasal membrane. I staggered into the first RV with
blisters already on my feet and my shoulders aching and sore
from the pack. I have a vague memory of sheltering behind a

rock later in the day and trying unsuccessfully to eat a sandwich Anne had made for me earlier. My mouth was so dry and empty of saliva that the thing was as inedible as cardboard. What my body craved was liquid and more liquid, and I learned on that march that tinned fruit and a flask of hot coffee were the ideal foods for the hills. I can recall nothing more till evening, coming down the last hill at a hobble, seeing the figures lurking in the mist, the heavenly shape of the motor-vehicle which spelt rest, Pete Green saying, 'Come on, Asher lad. You're last in!' I remember dropping my bergen and feeling light enough without it to take off. I had made it through the test weekend. Next stop was SAS selection.

We were waiting for transport to take us from Leeds to Brecon, to those familiar hills where Dave Walker had met his death. It was there that the selection course took place. Only minutes before the vehicle arrived, Trevor Wyman came up, clutching a letter. He was unusually quiet, and his face was a mask of tragedy.

'What is it, Trevor?' Leese asked him in surprise.

'They're throwing me out, Oz!'

'They can't do that! You've passed test weekend!'

'Yeah, I know, but they've done it!'

It was true. Wyman had been a soldier most of his life, yet he had failed his positive vetting for the SAS. We discovered later that he had a criminal record. He'd once stolen fifty pence from a one-armed bandit in the Naafi club. And Wyman was by no means the only recruit to fail the stringent SAS vetting procedure. One recruit had been thrown out because his grandmother was Ukranian. Failing out on the hills was one thing, but this digging up of secrets made us all shiver.

At Brecon we were housed in an ancient and very spartan camp, together with all the recruits from both 21 and 23 SAS who were trying for the selection. No matter what their previous rank, all recruits were considered equal. One of them was actually a lieutenant-colonel. In charge of the course was the RSM of 23 SAS, Paddy Moffatt, who was more than just another truculent Irishman. He was as fast and fearsome as a cobra. In his presence strong men quailed. Moffatt was one of the few men I have met in my life who could make people tremble just by being in the room. We were all scared stiff of him: he seemed the embodiment of the SAS.

In his opening address, Moffatt summed up the significance of the selection course. It was the core of SAS philosophy, and the thing which made the SAS the best unit of its kind in the world. 'When you have the right men, you can do any job required,' he said. 'The problem is getting the right men. The SAS learned its lesson in Malaya, when a lot of Malayan scouts, good soldiers in their own units, were useless in small groups, cut off from support. After a few days in the jungle, they'd had enough. The SAS realized that what it needed most was men who showed initiative, stamina, independence, patience and self-discipline, the resilience to work without support and to endure loneliness without deteriorating. There are other so-called special forces throughout the world who don't have such stringent standards, and who think that the very best technology is what counts. That is a serious mistake. Technology is only as good as the man who uses it. A pair of scissors can be as dangerous as a machine-gun in the hands of the right man.'

The selection course proper began quietly enough. We were dropped at preselected points in the Beacons and set off individually after being given the first reference. No one told us how far the march would be, but we knew the pattern. Each day the weight of our bergens would increase, and, as we grew more exhausted, the distance would be extended.

Now, I had to employ all the skills and craft I had learned in the build-up to final selection. I had to select a route which would allow me to preserve my energy: the shortest was not necessarily the quickest. The trick was to avoid obstacles such as cliffs, quarries and pot-holes, and to keep to the high ground, crossing re-entrants as near to the watershed as possible. You had to pace yourself, to get into a rhythm, marching uphill with your feet horizontal on the acute slopes, avoiding scree and bracken and keeping away from ice and snow and bogs. You had to make up time by running down the easy slopes and arrive at the RV looking alert and ready to take on the next leg.

The RVs were chosen so that the highest peaks of the Brecons were unavoidable, and the highest of all, Pen-y-fan, with its almost vertical cone-like summit, was crossed at least three times. There was snow and ice on the tops and blasting winds which sculptured the snow into odd-shaped, crispy drifts. The walkers spread out and were swallowed by mist. I had learned now all the tricks for surviving in such conditions. I had wrapped my toes individually in gauze to prevent them rubbing and had dosed them with mycota powder. I had covered the straps of my bergen with foam-rubber held in place with masking-tape. I no longer tried to sustain myself with inedible sandwiches. Instead I had brought with me a flask of hot coffee and tins of peaches in syrup, the only substance I would be able to get down after thirty miles in these hills. In addition to the 55-pound bergen, I now had to carry all the food and water I should consume on the way, plus an SLR rifle and 200 rounds of ammunition. The rifle had to be kept perfectly clean and operational at all times and carried at the ready no matter how exhausted I might be.

Each day we returned to base with aching feet and bodies: we dressed our blisters, treated our wounds and gathered our energy for an even more exhausting walk the next day. Each morning we hobbled on parade for the roll-call before dawn, and each morning our numbers were fewer. Only one in ten applicants passed the selection procedure from start to finish. Some failed on vetting; others fell out on the warm-up marches or on the preselection test; still others disappeared here at Brecon. The sub-zero temperatures, the long distances and the horrendous conditions took their toll. Men went down with exposure and had to be carried home on stretchers or casevacked out by chopper. One recruit had been found stuck to a tree he had sat down against, frozen solid. Another, several years previously, had sunk up to his neck in a bog and had waited two days until a farmer had come along to pull him out.

In between marches we were expected to be alert enough to take in lessons. When all we wanted to do was to collapse on our beds, the RSM's dog-shark face would be thrust in front of us in some smoky Nissen hut, explaining how to strip and assemble a Kalashnikov AK47 assault rifle, while our heads nodded and our eyes narrowed to bleary slits. 'And what is the first safety precaution with an AK47, ASHER?' The slim man's voice was hardly raised, yet it licked out with the lashing speed of a snake's tongue. At once I was fully awake. No one dared to sleep with the RSM. Jekyll may have been a bully, but we obeyed him because of the system. We obeyed Moffatt because to have defied him would have been unthinkable. He was more ferociously analytical than any officer, more perceptive than any psychologist: purely and simply the most terrifying man I have ever met.

During these interim periods we learned about the role of the SAS. It was a long-range reconnaissance unit, and its basic building-block was the four-man patrol. However, it was extremely flexible, and both smaller and larger patrols existed, depending on the job in hand. Stirling, the man who invented the SAS, had thought of the four-man patrol as ideal, since it would contain no leader in the sense that one man would do the thinking for the others. This meant that each member of the patrol had to be equally highly trained in the whole range of SAS skills, irrespective of his rank, and, in addition, each man had a specialist skill which made him an essential part of the unit. Stirling's idea had been a brilliant one with a special philosophy. The old concept of an elite unit was one officered by the aristocracy, but the SAS was a new type of crack force in which class was deliberately set aside. Stirling wrote: 'We believe, as did the ancient Greeks who originated the word "aristocracy", that every man with the right attitude and talents, regardless of birth and riches, has a capacity in his own lifetime of reaching that status in its true sense.' For me, this was a philosophy worth fighting for.

The final march of the selection was the dreaded 'Long Drag'. Fifty kilometres were to be covered in twenty hours over the wildest country. I remember being set off one morning up the steep side of a hill. I remember snatches of agony throughout the day. I remember sitting on a hillside above Tal-y-bont Reservoir and eating tinned peaches which tasted more wonderful than any other food had ever tasted. I recall nothing more till nightfall. I can try to replace myself on that last hill, already far beyond the normal bounds of exhaustion, still alone after trekking through snow and wind for almost a day. My feet are a raw and bubbling mass of blisters, especially where my pinched toes have rubbed together, despite the gauze inside my boots. I dare not stop to remove the boots, since I know that my tortured feet will instantly swell up like sausages and I will never be able to get them on again. If I sit down and rest, I may just fade off into unconsciousness and be found the next morning frozen to the ground. There are deep galls on my shoulder now and around the kidneys where the bergen has rubbed against the flesh like sandpaper. The sweat is cold under my shirt, but I dare not stop to put on my sweater. The heavy wool will draw more precious salt out of my pores and slow me down more rapidly. My feet, hands and face are raw with cold. I might be alone in this shapeless night. Perhaps everyone else has reached the RV hours ago. Time is running out. Perhaps my bearing is wrong. A wild blackness of hysteria and misery waits to engulf me.

I am climbing a snow-covered slope at a fifty-degree angle, leaning so low that my hand drags across the snow. Sometimes I use it to help me over a scree of rocks. The rocks feel like the inside of an ice-box. I place my tortured feet carefully, traversing the slope in a zigzag. I try to breathe rhythmically but sometimes sob instead. Each pace is like squatting in a fridge with a hundred-pound barbell on my back. For a second a vision of warmth floats before me: hot toast, melting butter, a blazing fire. I want to reach out to it, but instead I have to go on. It would be all right without the agony of these blisters. Every five or six paces I have to pause to ease the pressure, but only for a second. I will my body through a whirlpool of agony. My legs and feet are ordering me to stop, and I am talking to them as if they are something apart from me. 'You will go on! You will go on!' I can almost feel the reserves of fats and carbohydrates smouldering and melting into my bloodstream. The muscles arch and threaten to seize up like a motor-piston, then they ease up, hang loose, press on up that last hill, tense-relax, tense-relax, over and over and over. Walking is no longer an automatic reflex. It is an act of supreme will.

The peak of the hill is before me. The last few paces take a lifetime. My feet are one huge blister. It is like walking on hot coals. The night stretches out endlessly. Unless my map-reading is perfect, I will move straight past it. I start to run. It seems impossible that my body is capable of it with all the punishment it has taken. But here I am, running the last half kilometre, moaning silently as pain shoots through my body. Nothing is going to stop me, not my blistered feet, not my aching muscles. Running downhill is a different agony. Down through the night, down into the valley, out of the jaws of death. A faint yellow light in a hidden quarry. The ghostly square outline of a four-tonner truck. A scent of soup. A solid man with a buff-coloured beret is adding my name to the list. 'That's it, finished, lad!' he says. Other hands than mine remove the weight which seemed welded to my back. My body feels abnormally light without it. I have passed Long Drag, the hardest of all tests. I have walked right through the valley of darkness on nervous energy, and something is chanting inside me:

> If you can force your heart and nerve and sinew,
> To serve their turn long after they are gone,
> And carry on when there is nothing in you,
> Except the will, which says to you 'hold on',
> If you can fill the unforgiving minute,
> With sixty seconds' worth of distance run,
> Then yours is the earth and everything that's in it,
> And what is more, you'll be SAS, my son.

No, you can never quite recapture it in words. And to say you walked such and such a distance, carrying such and such a weight, conveys nothing. Whenever subsequently I have tried to explain in a few words the agony of SAS selection, and why these marches in the hills should be the basis for choosing members of the best unit of its kind in the world, my words have evoked responses like, 'That doesn't sound much!' This is the gap between words and feelings and experience. Baptism by fire, mastering kung fu, swimming through shark-infested waters – these seem to be more appropriate tests for SAS men. SAS selection is one of those things which 'doesn't sound much' until you try it. Like the SAS itself, it is simple, direct and deadly effective. But pain and agony fade quickly to become dim memories and pleasure alone remains. I can say only this: some of the strongest, most determined, most resilient men I have ever met were SAS, and I never found a single one amongst them who found the selection easy. For me, although the actual feel of the agony has gone, the selection remains a yardstick. I have crossed remote deserts and mountains on foot and under horrific conditions, yet I have never done anything quite so hard as the Long Drag.

I woke up the following morning with feet like footballs, and my first thought was to thank God that I'd never have to do anything that painful again. I didn't have long to wait for my next dose of agony, though. Within half an hour the medics came round with injections for our blisters. The substance they used was supposed to fill the blister cavity with a cushion more effective than nature's own lymphatic fluid. It was like trying to blow up a balloon that was already fully inflated. Men who had gone through the rest of the selection in silence were heard to moan in pain as the needle was applied. I almost hit the roof. I wondered if this was all part of the training.

Later, the survivors who could still walk hobbled to breakfast. A Green Jackets officer who happened to be passing stopped what he was doing and stood there laughing at us. 'Why on earth are you all limping?' he asked. 'Long exercise!' we answered, grimly. Later that day I marched into the CO's office and snapped to attention. As I did so, the largest of my blisters burst and filled my boot with liquid. I hoped my relief didn't show. The colonel had a friendly, foxy face. He had a reputation for being an eccentric, won for his action outside the British Embassy in Jakarta. The place had been stormed by an angry crowd, and he had patrolled the street outside, dressed in his clan tartan kilt and playing the bagpipes. The crowd withdrew in confusion. He had served in Malaya in the Int. Corps. He had been awarded the MC for his exploits in the Oman, where he was the first soldier over the summit of Jebel Akhdar.

The RSM, Paddy Moffatt, stood behind his desk, bristling at me with his lynx-like features. 'Asher,' he said. The colonel handed me a buff-coloured beret and a cloth badge. The badge was the Winged Dagger of the SAS regiment, with the legend beneath it, WHO DARES WINS. 'Welcome to the SAS family,' the colonel said. I thanked him, beaming, and saluted. That moment was an oasis, an island, a mountain, a peak of my life, a homely house from which to launch other adventures. I was to remember it time and time again during my own expeditions years later in the Sahara. Whenever the going got tough, whenever the side of me that I called 'the wimp' tried to persuade me to give up and lay down, I was able to say, 'You won't give up.' 'Why not?' 'Because you are SAS, my son.'

# 15

## *Combat Survival*

———

I was dropped from the Land Rover at night and sprinted away from the track and into the pine-forest. It was cold still, and I slipped my poncho over my head. I had no water and no means of making a fire. Before the exercise there had been a thorough body-search of all candidates to check that no one was carrying razor-blades, knives, Oxo cubes or other goodies hidden in their clothes or the orifices of their bodies. Some SAS men had been known to conceal the sulphurous heads of matches in their hair. Such things were always found, but no one knew if you got extra marks for trying.

In the forest it was very dark. Occasionally I heard the sound of far-away voices or the yapping of a dog. I knew the real danger would come at first light, and that by then I should have to find a secure place. Already I had fallen into the pattern of the escapee, moving at night and lying-up during the day. I tried to remember everything I'd been told about dog-evasion: 'Think dog!' the Veterinary Corps officer had instructed us. 'Dogs think in scent pictures, not in images.' As I walked, I automatically circled round in an attempt to lay a false trail. When I came to a narrow stream, I waded through it for half a mile before striking out into the forest again with frozen feet and squelching boots. The noise of my boots seemed thunderously loud. I stopped, sensing footfalls behind me. I listened with my mouth open, hearing only the shoosh of the breeze in the pines. The forest floor was soft and heavy with their needles.

Occasionally I squeezed into the shadows and the undergrowth and waited for five or ten minutes. I wasn't sure of the time, since I had no watch. Sometimes the shadows formed themselves into the distinct shapes of men, standing there silently and waiting to pounce on me as I squelched by. But they were no more than trees.

'Combat survival' was the second part of our selection course, and, although we had been presented with our berets, 'badged' as the SAS termed it, to fail this part meant the removal of our chances of serving with a sabre squadron. During the previous week we had been instructed by the staff of the SAS Survival School in techniques of 'living off the land'. They had brought with them a fat ewe, which one of them had slashed across the throat and hung in a tree without ceremony. 'The quicker you can butcher it, the better!' he told us. A good butcher could dismember the carcass of an entire cow in half an hour and carry off all the prime meat in two bergens. He showed us how to slit the skin and peel it off over the legs, removing the intestines, which were dropped into a specially dug pit. The technique came in very handy for me later during my journeys with nomads in the Sahara.

We were also instructed by characters with pepper-and-salt jackets and crusty faces who must have been game-keepers or poachers or both. They showed us how to set snares for rabbits, carefully disguising our scent with grass or earth, and how to rig up 'loop snares' on sticks to trap birds high in the branches of a tree. They demonstrated the use of the illegal 'gill net', which could be stretched across a stream to trap medium-sized fish by the gills, and how to gut the fish, skin the rabbits and pluck and draw the birds for the pot. They also passed on the secret properties of plants and fungi, noting those that could be eaten and those that could be used medicinally. They even told us how to catch insects and grubs, and how to smoke-dry meat under a tent to make 'biltong' or 'jerky'.

I could have done with some of that 'biltong' now, as I moved through the pine-forest. It was already getting lighter. Fool's dawn was followed by an eerie light of amber beyond the rim of the trees. Soon I was outside the pine-forest and into broken country with odd knots of deciduous shrubs and blackthorn bushes. I chose a dense thicket of low scrub, well away from the track, and, after checking the area, concealed myself in it. I laid my poncho over me and covered it with grass and twigs. I disguised my face, already blackened with mud, by covering it with my face-veil.

I must have dozed off, for I was woken by the sound of gutteral foreign voices, very near, and the bark of a dog. My heart burst into sudden percussion. I knew that this was only an exercise, but the adrenalin in my blood was real enough. So was the prickling of my scalp beneath the face-veil. I lay there stiffly, peering through the criss-cross pattern of my veil. Although the strange voices should have given me a clue, I was still unprepared for the squat soldiers with their big, bronze, oriental faces and slit eyes. I felt myself trembling. One of them held a black Alsatian on a leash. The men peered about, still muttering. The dog sniffed, but led them on past me. They must have walked within five yards of my place. As I watched them disappearing into the scrub, I couldn't believe that they hadn't found me. And their appearance had lent a new sense of reality to the exercise. Of course, I knew they were Gurkhas, but in my sensitized state, having seen no one else for hours, it almost seemed that I had really parachuted into another country.

'Escape and Evasion' was a skill developed by MI9 in the last war, the ancestor of my own unit, 23 SAS. E & E was an essential part of SAS training. Always we wore 'escape belts', which contained enough food and equipment to sustain us if we ever had to abandon our bergens. Our escape kit consisted of sugar, tea, rations such as Oxo cubes, chocolate and soup, blocks of Hexamine for fuel, fishing-line and hooks, snares, a small knife, a spoon, waterproofed matches, a mug, a torch, a button-compass and a small-scale map. Design of these escape kits was a personal matter, and the only instructions specified were that it must be small, compact, capable of being carried in a belt and provide sustenance for two days. After that, your combat survival skills came in.

I lay on the ground for another two hours, feeling decidedly hungry, and wishing we'd been allowed to carry our escape belts on this exercise. I had no idea how long I'd been out for. The object was to move towards a certain bridge on the opposite side of the wooded area, but since I had no map or compass, I doubted if I would ever make it there. During our training period we had been taught to navigate by the pole-star at night and the sun during the day. To prevent walking round in circles it was necessary to secure successive 'base' areas, moving forward from certain remembered land-marks step by step. Teams of trackers would be after us constantly, we had been told, but the longer we avoided them, the longer we would stay out of the 'pen'. That was where your interrogation started and where the second part of the exercise came into play: the so-called 'resistance to interrogation' phase.

I got up cautiously and began to move across country again, in the rough direction of the bridge. I was in no particular hurry to get there. I knew what would be waiting for me when I arrived. I felt hungrier than ever, and I stopped to pick some dandelion leaves, which could be eaten as salad. As soon as I had done so, I regretted it. A good searcher would see the broken-off stems and know at once that a fugitive had passed this way. I stuffed the leaves guiltily into my pocket and continued. Later, as I squatted warily in a thicket, I chewed them gratefully.

The morning passed slowly. The sun was nearing its zenith behind a bank of dirty clouds. Since the two Gurkhas had gone by much earlier, I had seen no one. I felt lonely and wondered if they'd forgotten about me. I imagined that all the other escapees had been caught and were even now in the interrogation-pen. Suddenly, I heard the growl of an engine. I dropped into the undergrowth and froze. Below the slope on which I was concealed a Land Rover was puttering very slowly across open land. I looped my face-veil over my head and sat stock-still. The Land Rover halted, and there were excited voices. As I watched, two men in combat uniform, but without berets or badges, dragged a third, poncho-clad man kicking and struggling out of the woods. The struggling man had a strong, square face, and I recognized him at once as the ex-commando John Leese. His hands had been tied behind his back, and he was blindfolded by what looked like one of his own puttees. Nevertheless, he was kicking out savagely at his captors, fighting with every ounce of strength. I saw one of his kicks connect heavily with his assailant's shin. The man danced around in pain. He shouted something at the other man, and they dragged Leese to the Land Rover and threw him in the dirt near its wheels. One of them bent down and forced the prisoner's head into the soft mud while the other calmly opened his flies. He urinated on Leese's back.

I waited until the vehicle had gone before making a move. I imagine that they had foreseen this. I had no sooner stepped out of my cover than a voice rasped, 'Hold it there!' A thick-set man in an old-fashioned SAS smock, carrying a rifle, came haring out of the bushes. I turned and ran. Vaguely I heard him yell something like 'everyone else is in the pen', but the word 'pen' added an extra boost to my flight. I have never been a fast runner, but I shot into the copse of trees like an Olympic sprinter. The man was too far behind me to catch up. In the heart of the wood I stopped and threw my face-veil over me. There was a movement on the edge of the thicket. The man was peering cautiously into the undergrowth with a wrinkled face. I hardly dared breathe. The light fell through the canopy of leaves in brindles, blending, I suppose, with the dappled patterns of my face-veil. The soldier advanced into the bushes, holding his rifle before him as if I were really a dangerous fugitive. He scooped past within two yards of me, but never even looked in my direction. I would never have dreamed that my camouflage was so effective.

He withdrew from the wood, and I stood there rooted, wondering what to do next. I couldn't stand there all day, but on the other hand, my hunter knew I was here somewhere and might be waiting for me. After about half an hour had passed, I decided to take the risk. I emerged carefully from the shadows. There was no one. I took two or three running steps towards the next cover, and then there was a snarl of triumph. A heavy figure threw himself on me, bringing me down in a rugby tackle. 'One move and you're dead!' he spat. His entire weight lay on my back, and in a second he had tied my hands behind me expertly. Then he ripped off one of my puttees and lashed it tightly over my eyes. The world went dim. The man shouted to someone else, and in a moment I heard the growl of an engine. He dragged me bodily down towards it. I didn't try to fight back as Leese had done. That was a waste of precious energy which I would need for the forthcoming interrogation. It was bad tactics to antagonize your captors needlessly. The engine stopped, and someone thrust me up against the tail-gate. 'What's your fucking squadron?' he demanded. I said nothing, clamping my lips. Rough hands seized me and threw me into the back of the vehicle on top of a pile of sweating bodies, already trussed up like chickens. As the engine started again, someone asked, 'Who's that?' It sounded temptingly like Leese's voice, but something prevented me from answering. In this exercise a single word meant pass or fail. The 'enemy' might easily use a stool-pigeon to extract information.

The first thing I heard when the vehicle stopped was someone screaming. I was thrown into a muddy puddle and left there face down. I could make out only vague shadows through my blindfold. I half sensed movement around me. The screaming went on. There were shouts and terrible curses and the sound of heavy blows followed by someone crying. A dog barked savagely quite near me. Two pairs of hands suddenly dragged me out of the mud and through what I perceived under my blindfold as a cathedral-like entrance. It seemed dark inside. Someone untied my hands and pulled a sack over my head. 'Against the wall!' a disembodied voice ordered me. 'On your toes and fingertips!' It was the spread-eagle search position familiar to me from Northern Ireland. All the weight of the body rested on the finger-tips and toes, and in a very short time the hands and feet lost all feeling. It was agonizing to hold the position for a long period: it came out of the same textbook of tortures as Jekyll's 'Torture Position Number One'.

Dislocated noises continued. Shouts, thumps and a sudden wail of real pain which made me jump so much that I forgot my position. The instant I moved, someone kicked viciously at my feet. 'Clever sod, eh!' a voice said, and suddenly a dog roared right next to me. I froze. The dog barked threateningly again, and I dearly hoped it wasn't loose. It sounded like a monster. Then two pairs of arms clamped round me, and I was marched forcibly into another room and made to stand against a wall.

There was silence. It was impossible to tell whether or not I was alone. The puttee, still tied tightly around my face, restricted my breathing and bubbles of mucus ran down my cheeks. Very quickly my fingertips and toes went dead. Grey hours passed, a swirling, pulsing, dancing parade of words and images. Time was punctuated only by inevitable bouts of thumping and kicking as my position flagged. Gradually, though, the constant beating dislodged the puttee, and through the thin substance of the sack I was able to see other shadowy forms also standing against the wall. I was thirsty and incredibly hungry. Suddenly there was the sound of a door opening and someone asked, 'Wanna beer, John?' 'Cheers!' another self-satisfied voice answered. There was a click and a rush of air as a can was opened, followed by the delicious malt smell of beer. There were sucking and gurgling sounds. 'Aaah! I really needed that!' the voice said. 'It's good stuff!' 'Wanna banjo?' the first man asked. 'What sort is it?' 'Bacon and fried eggs.' And the room was filled with the savoury smell of egg and bacon. It reminded me of egg-and-bacon breakfasts at home as a child and almost made me cry. 'Bloody good, these eggs!' a voice said.

Silence again. Terrible, aching emptiness of hours. Hands around me and suddenly I was being marched out again, so quickly that the sudden surge of movement almost made me faint. I stumbled and my head was rammed against a wooden door. I felt cool outside air, and I was thrust into what must have been a hedge. Finally I was dragged into another room, forced down on to a stool, and sack and puttee were whipped off my head.

*

I was in a dimly lit office which might have been underground, for there were no windows. The place was lit by a smoky oil-lamp, and the wall was partly covered by old tattered paper sacks with foreign lettering on them. There was a broken-down table in front of me and behind it sat a man in a foreign uniform. He had a broad, smooth shiny face, jet-black curly hair and a Stalin moustache. He looked almost doll-like and unreal.

'What is your name?' he asked me in a lisping voice.

'Private 24246810 Asher,' I told him, slumping forward passively in the chair. It was unbelievably delicious to sit and be spoken to as if I were a human being. Yet I remembered the lessons of my 'resistance to interrogation' instruction: always appear more tired than you are: no interrogator wants an unconscious prisoner.

'Date of birth?' he asked.

I told him.

'Where were you born?'

A warning-bell tinged in my mind. Under the Geneva Convention I was obliged to give my name, rank, number and date of birth. If I divulged one scrap more of information, I would fail the test. 'Sorry, I can't answer that question, sir,' I said, reciting the learned phrase like a robot. Always be polite. Never antagonize the interrogator. But give away nothing.

'You told me *when* you were born, so why not *where* you were born?'

'I'm sorry, I can't answer that question, sir.'

'What's your rank?'

'Private 24246810, Asher.'

'Private or trooper?'

'I'm sorry, I can't answer that question, sir.'

'You've just told me you're a private, now you can't tell me if you're a private or a trooper! That's stupid, isn't it?'

'I'm sorry, I can't answer that question, sir.'

And so it went on and on and on. Date of birth, rank, number, name. Name, rank, number, date of birth, over and over like a record. I knew that the interrogator was trying to trick me into saying anything – anything at all, even the words 'yes' or 'no' would be a triumph for him. In Korea, where these sensory-deprivation techniques had been learned, Western soldiers and airmen had been tricked into saying 'yes' or 'no' to innocuous questions, and had later found themselves admitting responsibility for war crimes and massacres in which they had played no part. Their answers had been tape-recorded and added to a different question. 'Is it true that your platoon massacred a thousand women and children?' 'Yes.' 'And you felt no regret for having done so?' 'No.' The original question had probably been as innocent as 'Do you smoke?'

My interrogator, like all the others on this course, was an expert. He was a member of the Joint Services Interrogation wing, a group of linguists and psychologists drawn from the army, navy and airforce. He knew that any scrap of information, no matter how trivial, could be pieced together with others to form a detailed picture. The first objective of the interrogator was to make the prisoner talk.

'Would you like a cigarette?' he asked me, holding up a packet of Benson & Hedges.

'I'm sorry, I can't answer that question, sir.'

'Suit yourself. I'm only trying to look after your comfort. It makes no difference to me whether you stay here for two days or three! What kind of work do you do, anyway?'

'I'm sorry, I can't answer that question, sir.'

'Are you sure you wouldn't like a cigarette?'

'I'm sorry, I can't answer that question, sir.' I was suddenly reminded of the old TV quiz game, where the quiz-master interviewed contestants and tried to trick them into saying 'yes' or 'no'. Another man stood behind the contestants with a giant dinner-gong, which he beat as soon as they spoke the forbidden word. I enjoyed the thought, but I was careful to keep the smile off my face. I slumped forward more convincingly, wondering how much longer I'd be allowed to sit there. That was the problem. It was a lot nicer sitting here facing the interrogator than it was standing against a wall on the numb ends of your finger-tips with a sack over your head. It was nicer, and the interrogator knew it was nicer. That was how the sensory-deprivation method worked.

The gong never went. The officer made a sign to the guards standing behind me, the sack was slapped back over my head, and I was rushed out again. Once more against the wooden door, once more into the hedge, once more the disorientation walkabout. Once more against the wall on finger-tips and toes. There began the same numb and swirling limbo, the same parade of empty, meaningless thoughts, the same agony of aching muscles. I had no idea how much time passed. I might have been there a full day already. Occasionally I could hear other prisoners being marched in and out. As hours passed, I began to feel neglected. Why weren't they bothering with me? Wasn't I important enough? Once I was distracted by what sounded like a fight. 'You think you can get clever with us, do you?' a savage voice demanded. 'Break the bugger!' someone else jeered. 'I'll break the bastard's nose!' the first voice said, and there followed the crash of fist against flesh, and a snap and groan that sounded very real. I learned later that one of the prisoners, the same lieutenant-colonel who had been with me on the selection course, in fact, had been given a broken nose.

But that was the only distraction. Otherwise time was a meaningless void without beginning or end. Time was an empty night filled with numbness in the arms and legs and an ache like a festering wound. I prayed that someone would take me back to the interrogator. He had seemed a nice, cultured man. I longed to be sitting in that cosy room again, talking, talking. But there lay the danger. Talking was exactly what I must not do. If I said the forbidden words, there would be more than a gong and the forfeit of five pounds. It would mean failure after all those weeks of agony. I wasn't going to fail now.

I had no idea how much time had passed before the guards seized me again. When the sack was removed this time, I found myself in a much larger office, where three men in combat gear sat behind tables. They wore white arm-bands, I noticed. This was supposed to mean that they were neutral.

'I'm the medical officer,' one of them said. 'Have you got any complaints about the way you've been treated?'

I looked at him incredulously. He had a narrow, rat-like face.

Surely he didn't think I would fall for this 'medical officer' routine? 'I'm sorry, I can't answer that question, sir.'

He immediately started to laugh. 'You don't understand,' he protested, touching the precious white arm-band. 'Weren't you told that the white arm-band means neutrality?'

The gong was waiting over my head. 'I'm sorry, I can't answer that question, sir.'

'All I want to know is if you have any injuries!' the man said, seeming frustrated. 'Have you?'

'I'm sorry, I can't answer that question, sir.'

He ordered me to remove my clothes, and I peeled them off until I stood naked before him. 'Bend over!' he told me. Feeling very humiliated, I did so. This must be part of the 'softening up', I realized. The man wrote something on a sheet of paper. 'I want you to sign this to say that you've not been injured,' he said, proffering the biro. I made no move to take it. 'Sign nothing!' my instructors had told me.

'I'm sorry, I can't answer that question, sir,' I said, knowing that it wasn't a question but wanting to fill the vacuum somehow.

'Stupid!' the soldier commented. 'Very well. Get your clothes back on and get back to the pen!'

Back against the wall with a sack over my head. Monotonous time passed like sludge. No indication of day or night. Tired, hungry, thirsty. Suddenly, a guard forced me down to my knees. It was an awkward enough position, but after the spread-eagle it was deliciously comfortable. An unseen hand thrust something rough into my mouth. I recognized it at once as half a cake of Weetabix. I chewed it viciously and swallowed at once. An often-applied trick, they had told me, was to offer food or drink to a prisoner, then remove it again before he'd had a chance to enjoy it. My mouth was so dry that the cake gave me no pleasure. It was difficult even to swallow it. A long time afterwards, it seemed, someone held a mug to my lips, and I was able to get a single swallow of water. Then it was back against the wall.

Hands seized me and after a moment I was back in the

interrogator's office. A different officer clad in some foreign uniform addressed me. 'Name?' he snapped.

I told him.

'Rank, number, date of birth?'

I told him.

'Hm, Asher,' he said. 'We've information that you've been seen stealing ammunition from the armoury. Trooper Leese saw you, so don't try to deny it!'

Leese! What had that sod been saying about me?

'I'm sorry, I can't answer that question, sir.'

'Leese says you're not only a thief, you're a queer. Queer as a concrete parachute, Leese said. Is that true?'

'Sorry, I can't answer that question, sir.'

'What's your date of birth?'

I told him.

'The same day as the Queen's, isn't it?'

'I'm sorry, I can't answer that question, sir.'

'That's a coincidence, isn't it, since you are a bloody queen?'

I had visions of strangling Trooper Leese if ever I got out of this.

Back against the wall, and after more interminable hours I was seized for a fourth time. This time, when the guards removed my sack I was sitting in front of two officers who wore combats with white arm-bands and black berets with the badge of the Int. Corps. 'The exercise is over for you, Trooper Asher,' one of them said. 'You've passed. Well done. Now, how did you find it?'

Tricks within tricks, I thought. 'I'm sorry, I can't answer that question, sir.'

The officer grinned. 'No, no!' he said. 'It's really over. Don't you see the white arm-bands?'

'I'm sorry, I can't answer that question, sir.'

'Look, Asher, you can't go on saying that for ever. You'll have to trust us this time.'

I looked at their Int. Corps badges, their white arm-bands and their apparently genuine expressions of exasperation. I had to make a leap of faith. 'Very good, sir,' I said.

'That's better! You've no idea how difficult it is to convince some of you SAS lads that the game's over. It really is. You've done all right. But you could have signed the doctor's paper. That was genuine.'

'I was so geared up, sir,' I said. 'No one warned me about the doctor.'

'You weren't the only one!' the officer said, smirking. 'What time do you think it is?'

'About 9 a.m., sir.'

'It's actually eleven. Two hours out, but not bad over a long period. You see the body has a kind of in-built clock, doesn't it?'

I nodded dumbly, not yet able to believe it was really finished. The Int. officers told me to go and get a well-deserved cup of tea, and I went through a door into a featureless courtyard of grey, windowless walls. The courtyard was empty, and at one end was a red and white striped barrier. There were no guards. I insinuated my way across the open-ground, still believing that they would pounce on me before I made it. But there was no other movement. I reached the barrier and ducked beneath it, stepping back into the realm of reality, the sleeper emerging from the dream. Further down the track was a Nissen hut where I found Leese sitting by an urn of coffee. 'Now what the hell have you been saying about me?' I asked him, grinning.

'I'm sorry, I can't answer that question, sir,' he said.

# 16

## *A Warrior Elite*

———

During the week I was back at my tutorials learning the principles of semantic shift, the grammar of Chaucerian English and theories of linguistic behaviourism, and at weekends I was in a different classroom, imbibing the principles of telegraph, ground-waves, sky-waves and skip distances. Signals were vital to an SAS patrol, and a good signaller was worth his weight in gold. The SAS used Morse code, far more efficient over long distances and very effective in their deep-penetration role.

We had to be able to send and receive Morse at high speed. I took home a special practice-buzzer, and for hours every day Anne would hear the mysterious dah-dah-dit-dit of Morse trickling out of my top-storey room. It was like learning a language, I discovered. All the symbols were combinations of dots and dashes, but to be a real operator you had to recognize the symbol in its entirety, like a word of a foreign tongue. I made more progress with Morse than I did with Chaucer's Middle English. I came to see how vital the radio-link was to a force which operated in a hostile country in such tiny numbers. The four-man patrol was a unit small enough to disappear into the landscape, yet skilled enough to sting the enemy like a hornet. While each patrol member was a specialist – a radio-op, a demolitions-man, a linguist or a medic – he was also cross-trained at a basic level in each of the other skills in case of casualties. The signals skill was the most important. One of the dangers a patrol ran in Europe was that of being 'Direction

Found', or 'Dee-effed', by sensitive Soviet tracking equipment, which could detect the exact source of a radio emission. Like the hero of John le Carré's realistic spy novel *The Looking-glass War*, the patrol could then be picked up or its position shelled.

In my lecture room at Leeds University I was studying the effects of the Norman Conquest on the development of Middle English, but in my spare time I was living and breathing Soviet forces. 'Know your enemy' was an adage that the SAS took very seriously, and every member of the sabre squadron had to be expert in recognition. Within a few weeks we could tell at a glance which Soviet unit a soldier belonged to by his shoulder flashes, and could recognize each piece of Warsaw Pact equipment, armoured-cars, tanks and aircraft immediately. The Warsaw Pact forces were really the 'big battalions', with overwhelming numbers of men and tanks and aircraft. If a Soviet invasion of western Europe came, we learned, it was likely to be in the autumn when Soviet conscripts were called up. By retaining the previous year's national servicemen, the Russians could double their forces in a single sweep, having a fully trained corps ready for action and another of equal size in reserve. But victory does not necessarily go to the 'big battalions'. The SAS was a uniquely flexible unit, capable of operating a guerrilla war independently and living off the land for months, blending in with the civilian population if necessary and emerging to deliver blows far out of proportion to its size.

By the time we had completed our recognition course, we knew our Warsaw Pact counterparts so well that we could say what type of bed Ivan slept in and what he ate for breakfast. We learned that Soviet troops were efficient and disciplined, but also politically indoctrinated. In the SAS even a trooper could take vital operational decisions, but the Russian army was rigidly structured. NCOs and junior officers were unable to make use of their initiative on the battle-field and had to refer decisions up a strict chain of command.

In my tutorials I was translating the *Battle of Maldon* and learning how the Saxon Byrhtnoth was struck down by a Viking blade amongst his hearth-companions. In my other classroom I was being taught how to treat gunshot wounds from high-velocity missiles, which caused four-fifths of the casualties in battle. Every SAS trooper had to have a grasp of basic first-aid, since deep in enemy territory the SAS patrol would be beyond the reach of field hospitals. 'We have worked out for you that a ton of elephant charging you at $7\frac{1}{2}$ miles an hour equals almost exactly the energy expended by a half-ounce grenade fragment travelling at 4,000 feet per second,' the medical manual told us. 'In simple language, to be hit by a grenade fragment is comparable to being hit by an angry elephant.' If death didn't happen at once, we were instructed, then prompt action from the patrol could almost certainly save the casualty's life. Most deaths from gunshot wounds were caused by blood loss or secondary shock. Blood loss could easily be staunched by simply applying a finger to the wound, but shock was less easily dealt with. High-speed missiles caused a condition the medics called 'cavitation': they ripped through the muscles and sucked in dirt, germs and clothing. A high-velocity missile wound was simply a wound caused by a very small object travelling at a very high speed. 'It may be argued that large objects travelling at high speed produce similar effects,' our manual added. 'But such wounds are dealt with by the Almighty, not by humble SAS patrol medics!' Sometimes I longed for the days of Byrhtnoth, when high velocity meant a bow and arrow.

In the library I was studying the evolution of Indo-European languages from something like Sanskrit, and in the demolition ranges I was learning how to set up claymore mines to cripple advancing enemy patrols. 'It's better to cripple an enemy than to kill him,' our demolitions instructor said, 'because a wounded man has to be looked after and even evacuated, so it ties up a whole team of soldiers. A dead man is no problem. They can just leave him where he is.'

The claymore was designed admirably for crippling. It shot out about 700 particles of steel like ball-bearings, each one of which could zap a man within hundreds of metres in a certain direction. I doubt if I should really have made a demolitions expert. It required a truly Machiavellian frame of mind. You had to be able to create nasty little booby-traps and anti-handling devices. When abandoning camp, you booby-trapped tempting items like maps and documents. You inserted mercury-tremblers on door-frames and contact-switches under toilet seats. Nowhere was safe from the efficient booby-trapper. We were taught how to disrupt railways in true Lawrence of Arabia fashion, derailing trains carrying men and supplies, destroying marshalling yards, running-sheds and tunnels. We learned how to make charges of different shapes and sizes, detonating them electronically or by acid time-pencils. An efficient demolitions man could cause small acts of sabotage the repercussions of which were far greater than the effort required to perform them.

My lecturer in philology was explaining that the invention of the printing-press was the true beginning of civilization, and my instructor in nuclear, biological and chemical warfare was explaining how an SAS patrol could survive if that civilization should be destroyed in one gigantic mushroom cloud. The chances of surviving a nuke increased dramatically if your body was even a few inches below ground. Eighteen inches of good earth between you and the surface meant staying alive during a nuclear explosion only miles away. 'Dig for life!' they ordered us. We had the best NBC experts from Porton Down advising us on 'nuclear survival', which soon became another essential ingredient of our training course. Surviving the blast was one thing: living through the fall-out phase was another. We were issued with charcoal-lined 'monkey-suits' designed to suck up noxious gases and liquids like blotting-paper. The suits were worn with a respirator, rubber gloves and overboots. We had to be able to move silently and shoot straight in this get-up, looking like gigantic two-legged insects. Part of the NBC course consisted of 'surviving' in a gas-chamber with concentrated CS gas floating about. In this atmosphere we had to be able to eat and drink wearing our respirators. We carried auto-inject phials against certain nerve gases and tablets called Oxemes against others. Yet NBC training was a skill no one relished. There was a general feeling that if things got that bad, there wouldn't be much point in carrying on. With customary patience the SAS coached us out of that attitude. Nuclear war was not the end. Someone would survive to carry on, and that someone was likely to be the SAS.

The men of my squadron were miners, teachers, factory-workers and plumbers, ex-craphats, ex-Paras, ex-mercenaries. We had a single staff sergeant attached to us from 22 SAS who acted as a permanent instructor. When I first joined the squadron, the staff sergeant was a Welshman, Taff Barnes. Lean, shrewd, efficient, Taff was respected by everyone as a 'warrior'. He had fought with the SAS in Borneo in the sixties. More recently he had been in Oman, training Baluchi soldiers and leading teams of them against communist insurgents. The accolade 'warrior' was high praise amongst the SAS. Apart from soldiering, what Taff did best was organizing wild mess nights. 23 SAS was probably unique amongst British army units in not having separate messes for officers, NCOs and other ranks. We all mucked in together. After the eating and the boozing came games of strength: arm-wrestling, walking across the floor on bottles, lifting beer kegs. An old piano which hadn't been played for years stood in a corner of the mess. The ideal end to a perfect evening, according to Taff, was to have the entire squadron line up and attempt to dive through it. No one ever succeeded, although there were a great many sore heads. Taff was determined that he would get through it one day. It was mind over matter, he said.

Taff's replacement was Don Hoburn. Don came straight to us from the SAS Counter-Revolutionary Warfare wing, which half a decade later would become for the public synonymous with the SAS. The CRW arose surreptitiously in the late sixties during a 'quiet period' for the regular regiment. It was used to train SAS men in the techniques of close-quarter battle (CQB), mainly for use as bodyguards. By 1975 the CRW was a permanent cell, manned by teams drawn from the permanent SAS sabre squadrons on a rota basis.

In the January of that year a civil airline was hijacked at Manchester airport by an Iranian student. The Iranian demanded to be flown to Paris. His knowledge of geography was slight, so he was fooled into believing that Stansted Airport, Essex, was Charles de Gaulle. At Stansted, Don Hoburn and the SAS team were waiting for him. They stormed aboard, only to find that the pistol carried by the Iranian was a replica. One soldier was bitten by a police-dog as he left the aircraft. The CRW team was used a second time in the December of that year. The Provisional IRA cell which had been responsible for the recent spate of bombings was cornered in a flat in Balcombe Street, London. They surrendered after a six-day siege on hearing that the SAS were on hand.

Under Don's supervision a team of men was chosen from our squadron to be trained in the techniques of close-quarter battle in the so-called 'killing house' at Hereford. We learned how to react to ambush in civilian cars, and how to take out terrorists in a crowded room, rolling and firing double-taps from our Browning pistols. We learned to shoot the terrorist and spare the hostage, to shoot in the dark and to clear stoppages. Although 23 SAS had no role in anti-terrorist fighting, as did 22 SAS, you never knew when such skills might come in handy.

By now I was a fully trained SAS soldier. On a Friday evening I put away my notes and books, and by midnight I might be patrolling the plains of Denmark, trying desperately to evade the Jaegerkorps. The exercise might involve being picked up by Danish naval vessels or dropped by helicopter. On other occasions I might 'disappear' from my lectures for a fortnight and return exhausted and pounds lighter, having spent the time living in a hole in the ground in the Black Forest or being chased by the elite West German Border Guards. Only Anne knew the real secret of my 'disappearances'.

Second year turned into final year. Anne applied for graduate entry in the police, failed, and was accepted as an ordinary PC in the West Yorkshire Metropolitan Force. I toyed with the idea of joining the Royal Hong Kong Police, but by the time graduation day came I was still undecided. As we gathered on the campus to receive our degrees, I felt both lost and empty. I had the overwhelming sensation that by joining the SAS I had somehow wasted a great many opportunities that would never come again.

Anne was away all week training with the boys in blue. I enrolled as a post-graduate teacher at Carnegie College, one of the most famous Physical Education colleges in Britain. In a sense it was like joining the army again: spotless whites for gymnastics, blues for athletics, track suit and tennis-shirt for teaching and blazer with silver discobolus for the staff-room. We learned to teach everything from rugby to roller-hockey, but I was hopeless at team games. Luckily, I was able to specialize in the things I enjoyed most: mountaineering, canoeing, sailing, walking and orienteering. I kept up my weight-training, jogging and fencing, and by the end of the year I was as fit as a professional sportsman.

At the same time, I passed the SAS junior NCOs' course at Hereford, and was posted to the Recruit wing to help train new recruits up to selection. I still took part in exercises in my spare time, but my new masters at Carnegie were surprisingly un-sympathetic. 'The Territorial army is just an excuse to have a good time and get drunk at the country's expense!' my course tutor said. How little he knew about the Territorial army. They were the most enthusiastic soldiers in the country.

As months passed Anne slipped further and further away from me. Ironically, she now began to develop that same 'worldly wise' attitude which had so often kept me aloof from other undergraduates. The words 'commies', 'coons' and 'pinkos' started creeping into her vocabulary, I noticed. She was taking steps into the 'outside world', whilst I remained a despised student. Her job brought her into the company of eligible men with good looks, money and charm. To be fair, it wasn't all her doing. The police like to keep their own to themselves, and tend to disapprove of exterior relationships. When we moved to a new flat in Leeds, I had to suffer the indignity of staying out one night while her sergeant came to inspect it. 'He has to make sure it's up to the required standard!' Anne said. Every police-constable had to serve a two-year probation period, and if you completed that successfully, they reckoned they'd got you. By the end of two years you had been drawn into the new society and lost almost all previous associations.

I watched Anne slowly swelling with importance like a ripen-
ing fruit. I had never thought of the police as an elite, but now I
realized that they were. They had powers not possessed by the
ordinary individual and so belonged to a kind of state within a
state. Their care in looking after their own came home to me
one day when two detectives stopped me near our flat and
asked me what I was doing there. When that was cleared up,
Anne invited me to a celebration night at her new station. In
the lavatories later, someone asked me which station I belonged
to. 'I'm not a policeman!' I said. No one spoke to me again all
evening. Perhaps they didn't quite know what to say.

# PART THREE

*The SPG*

# 17

## *Green Hills of Ulster*

One evening before Anne went on night duty, she told me, 'If the phone rings, don't answer it. There's some chap I met on a course who's been pestering me!' 'OK,' I said, but I felt miserable. Some weeks before, rummaging through a drawer in search of a pencil, I had come across a postcard on which was written, 'Looking forward to seeing you when I come up. Love, Ted.' This might, of course, have added up to pestering. I wanted to believe so. But the day I returned from a week in Paris to discover the dustbin packed with empty beer-cans made me wonder. After all, Anne never drank beer. The girlfriend she said she had partied with didn't either. And I happened to know that they weren't on speaking terms.

I settled down to watch TV with a can of lager and a packet of cigarettes. They were showing a cartoon called 'The Lonely Giant', I remember. It was the story of a fierce giant who frightened all the children away except for one blind little boy. The story made me feel even more miserable. I had just lit a cigarette when the phone rang. I won't answer it, I told myself. I promised Anne. I took another puff of the cigarette, expecting the phone to ring off, but on it went. I tried to ignore it but the buzzing seemed to grow louder and more insistent, like the drone of a cornered bee. It'll ring off in a minute, I said to myself. Has to. But the ringing went on and on. It clanged on until it seemed to fill the empty room, rattling the windows and the doors. I finished the cigarette. 'BURR-BURR' went the

phone. I began to feel uneasy. Normally, I reasoned, people stop
after ten rings. But the phone had been going now for a good
ten minutes. There was only one explanation: whoever was
ringing must *know* I was here. Since the only person who knew
I was here was Anne, it must be her. Simple. I got up and lifted
the receiver.

'Hello,' I said.

'Is Anne there?' a man's voice asked me.

'I'm afraid not,' I said. 'She's working nights.'

'Who is that, then?'

'This is Mike.'

'Oh, I see.' Pause. 'Well, could you tell her that Ted rang?'

'Yes.'

The phone went dead. The first feeling that hit me was guilt
at having broken my word to Anne. The second was a sense of
sadness long staved off. I had the awkward, heavy suspicion
that I had really known who it would be all along.

'Did the phone ring?' Anne asked casually when she arrived in
the morning.

'Yes, it was someone called Ted . . .'

Her face contorted, but it was rage not guilt. 'You absolute
bastard!' she said.

And that was the end between Anne and me. Ted was a
detective-constable. I suppose that, as well as the necessity of
finding a job when my PE course ended, was the reason I joined
the Royal Ulster Constabulary as a Special Patrol Group officer,
and made the worst mistake of my life. I had to escape to some
dangerous place, where I would be reminded every day that my
life had a vestige of value left. If I was unlucky, then at least I
should have achieved an honourable death. Of course, I'd never
really been interested in a policeman's lot. Booking people for
illegal parking or drunken driving wasn't my idea of a satisfying
career. At heart I was still a soldier, but it seemed a waste of my
years at university to rejoin the regular army, even the SAS. I
had heard through contacts that a new Special Branch unit was
being formed in Northern Ireland. It would be an undercover
anti-terrorist squad trained in close-quarter battle by the SAS.

The name of this unit was E4A. If I had any ambition, it was to become a member of that. Naturally, I would have to complete my two years' probation first. But in the RUC, probationers didn't necessarily have to pound the beat for two years. They could join either the Traffic Branch or the Special Patrol Group. I had never been interested in cars or driving, but the SPG, a military-style anti-terrorist unit, was just my cup of tea.

I resigned from my SAS squadron, and in October 1978 left for Northern Ireland. In the RUC training centre at Enniskillen, County Fermanagh, I underwent twelve weeks of intensive training. As well as drill, hard PT, swimming and life-saving, we were instructed in law and police procedures. Part of the course consisted of memorizing vast quotes from the manual, known as 'definitions'. The only one I still remember is the first, 'courtesy': 'courtesy is an essential quality and one which will smooth many a path. The public have a right to expect it, and with it its complementary quality, good temper. It should be remembered that an angry man is quite incapable of exercising the judgement so often needed in the performance of police work ...' It was definitions like this, I understood later, which had led to the training centre being referred to as the 'Dream Factory' on the streets.

The RUC had been reorganized in 1971 after the great blow to morale it had received at the beginning of the Troubles. The paramilitary formations had been scrapped, and a bottle-green uniform had replaced the old SS-style black one. Apart from reflecting a homely Irish colour, the uniform was supposed to rid the force of the epithet 'black bastards' which followed them everywhere. By pure Irish logic, it didn't. RUC men were known more politely as 'Peelers', and referred to themselves collectively as 'Robert', both in deference to Sir Robert Peel. They were proud of saying that Peel had founded their parent unit, the Constabulary of Ireland, in 1822, *before* the famous Bow Street Runners.

'Criminalization' was the key word for what had happened in Ulster since I had been there with the Paras. Giving the IRA political status as prisoners had been a costly blunder. Now, a terrorist was to be treated as a common criminal, and the force responsible for bringing him to justice would be the police, not the army. The new chief constable, Sir Kenneth Newman, launched a recruitment drive, hoping to expand the force to a strength of 6,000. The army began to disappear from the streets.

My fellow trainees were mostly Protestants from Belfast and rural areas of the province. A few were Englishmen or Scotsmen married to Irishwomen. There was a smattering of Catholics, who remained in the training centre at weekends, unable to return home for fear of their lives. The weekends were endlessly lonely for the handful of us alone in the vast halls of the old building. According to a skeleton diary I kept at the time, my weekend would go like this:

*Friday, 15 December*
Thought I'd have a quiet weekend. At 7 p.m. Gerry arrived with James. Had a few drinks in the Harp and Crown. Went to the Killyhelvin Hotel, where they searched us before entering. Had a few more drinks and ended up back at the TC with a bottle of Black Bushmills.

*Saturday, 16 December*
Got up late. Gerry and James decided to go through to the Republic, and asked me to join them. James is a Southerner who has been in the British CID. He says that if anyone at home knew where he was during the week, they'd murder him. We were inspected by a fierce-looking Gardai at Belcoo, who noted the Southern number-plate. Drove past Yeats's grave and up the west coast, past Earl Mountbatten's house on Donegal Bay. Sea wild and deep Prussian-blue. Stopped in Donegal for a few drinks. It felt far more peaceful than the North. Then drove back to Enniskillen for some drinks in the Harp and Crown.

*Sunday, 17 December*
Ulster is dead as a doornail on a Sunday. I woke with a terrible hangover, and tried desperately to cram the definitions for tomorrow's exam. Gave up when John and Gerry arrived. Went with them for a few drinks in the Manor House Hotel.

One Saturday afternoon, towards the end of my training, I was walking through Enniskillen. My way led past the town library: it was closed, but, having nothing to do, I spent a few minutes peering sullenly through its plate-glass windows at the books. I meandered back to the training centre and was no sooner through the barrier than there was a tremendous explosion. Several of the windows near by shattered, and I saw lumps of debris flying into the air high over the roofs of the houses. The reserve-constable on the gate phoned through to the guardroom immediately. 'Sure it's the town library, so it is!' he said. 'It's lying all over the High Street!' In later years both the training centre and the Harp and Crown pub opposite were the targets of IRA attacks.

The following week the commandant called me into his office and read me my assessment: 'This man is a native of England and has a university degree,' it ran. 'He has military experience, works well under proper motivation and is recommended for early promotion.' The commandant asked where I should like to be posted, and I requested the Special Patrol Group. A few days later our postings were announced. I had been posted to the SPG, Belfast.


When my weapon-training was completed, they issued me with a Walther PP pistol and sent me to join my SPG section in Tennent Street. It was in the very heart of the Loyalist ghetto of Shankill, like a medieval keep in a rambling peasant village. There were the inevitable forty-foot-high mortar fence and thick steel gates guarded by a concrete bunker. A prune-faced reserve-constable frowned down on me from an arrow-slit in its battlements. The portcullis slid smoothly open. The minibus passed through a wide archway cut into the fortress wall, and I alighted in the courtyard behind.

The duty-constable showed me to my third-floor room, which smelt of dust and vomit. 'Sorry about the smell,' he said. 'This is where they come to sleep off a drunk!' 'What, the prisoners?' 'No, the Peelers.' He pointed to a concertina of thick metal plates balanced on rusty rollers by the window-frame. 'Armour-plated shutters,' he explained. 'The Peelers don't bother with them when they've taken drink, but my advice is to shut them after dark. We're not safe from attack here. The Provies have shot us up once this year already. They drove up from Agnes Street as cool as cucumbers and opened fire with an Armalite. If you lean out of the windows, you can still see the bullet-holes!'

My new section was sprawled out across comfy chairs in their section-hut, in every stage of undress. Carbines and sub-machine-guns were propped against the walls. Walther pistols lay inside upturned caps. Bullet-proof vests with half-inch steel plates stood up on their own like suits of black armour. The TV was on, and the announcer was saying, 'A spokesman for the Civil Rights Association said today that Republican prisoners in the Maze Prison would continue their so-called "blanket" campaign until they are accorded the political status which was taken away from them in 1976. There are now believed to be between 250 and –' The rest was drowned in a hearty jeer from the SPG.

The inspector was a kindly man called Ian McStorr. He had once been a platoon commander in the B-specials. 'Our job is anti-terrorist patrols,' he said. 'Which is probably why you're here, with your military experience. We work in uniform or in civvies, according to the job. All the boys are trained in special firearms, and we also support the undercover squad, the Bronze section. Bronze collects information, and we act on it. We don't have any prejudice in the SPG. A terrorist is a terrorist, whether he's Catholic or Protestant. There are no Catholic or Protestant policemen, and there's no "English" policemen either. There's just policemen. We have a good team spirit in the SPG. I think you'll enjoy working with us.'

He introduced me to the section: a station-sergeant, four sergeants and twenty-odd men. As he did so, a squat and unkempt constable called Keating shouted, 'Not another Brit! We've got one in the section already!' I couldn't tell whether or not he was joking.

That night, after the rest of the SPG men had gone home, I

went back to my room. There was a party next door and I stuck my nose in to introduce myself. I was quietly sipping beer from a paper-cup, when a constable in half-dress staggered up to me.

'You the new SPG man?' he demanded.

'Yes.'

'You English?'

'Yes.'

'Then get back to your own country, fucking Brit!'

'Wait a minute,' I said. 'This is Britain, isn't it?'

Before I could dodge, he emptied the contents of his cup into my face. 'This is Northern Ireland, you fucking Brit bastard!' he swore. Several of his colleagues dragged him away, and while I was wiping the beer out of my eyes a sour-faced woman police-sergeant came up. 'I think you'd better leave,' she said. I squinted at her, in disbelief, to make sure she was talking to me. As I walked out, someone said, 'Don't be too hard on him. His wife's just gone off with a Brit!'

I lay on my dusty, vomit-smelling bunk, listening to the burble of chatter from next door. Somewhere across the city I thought I heard a machine-gun stutter. Then I realized it was a car starting. I was about to drift off to sleep when I remembered something. I got up and heaved the armour-plated shutters into place.


The following day I was assigned to mobile-patrol in a scarred and battle-fatigued Makralon Land Rover. Its fibreglass skin was marked by the impact of thousands of stones and bottles. There were two neat bullet-holes on one side.

'Isn't it a bit vulnerable?' I asked Keating. 'If anyone lobs a petrol-bomb in the back door, we'll be roasted!'

'It's either this or the Hotspur – the armour-plated version,' he said. 'And that's a sweat-box, so it is. In the Makralon ye can see the world going by.'

'He means the honeys in the city-centre,' said a tall, ectomorphic constable called Spencer, grinning and climbing into the driving-seat. A hawk-faced sergeant called Ross got in beside him, leaving Keating and I to take up the rear. Keating, bulky in his full-metal jacket, settled himself on the right. He cradled an M1 carbine like a toy in his massive hands. I took the place opposite him reluctantly.

'Look,' I said. 'I should sit there.' Keating looked at me as if I'd made a rude noise.

'Why?' he demanded.

'I've got the Stirling, and it can't be fired left-handed. The hot cases would fly into my face. If we get bumped, I won't be able to open fire.'

'This is the way we do it,' Keating replied tersely. 'You clever Brits know everything!'

Sergeant Ross turned slowly in his seat and regarded me with steady eyes. 'You may be right,' he said. 'But we have our own ways of doing things. If you have a complaint, put it in writing to the commander!'

It was, I thought, a bad omen for my career in the SPG.

We drove down the Shankill. I tried to pick out the places I had known on my 1972 tour, now seven years behind me. It was like reliving a nightmare. The area looked even more derelict than it had done then. Where the cosy red-brick streets had been was a blitz site of broken beams, twisted tin and shattered masonry. A new development had risen out of the rubble, a massive modern block which no one had ever lived in. Every single window had been smashed by vandals. Its walls were smeared with mostly incoherent graffiti like the entrails from tribal sacrifices. The only sentence among them which made sense ran: WE NEED REDEVELOPMENT LIKE A HOLE IN THE HEAD.

'Used to be a marvellous area, this,' Sergeant Ross said, as if moved to apologize for it. 'The houses so neat and clean. Why, every twelfth of July the place was decked out with streamers and flags and bunting, red, white and blue. Every house had its own flag-pole and flew the Union Jack. There was a special archway built at the entrance to each street and the Lodges used to march through with the fifes playing and the Lambeg drum beating. 'Twas grand, so it was!'

'Then the Troubles started,' Keating said. 'Now look at it!'

We drove past the end of the Shankill, past the place where our OP had stood on Unity Corner. We turned down Millfield, where we had stood-to for the Tartan gangs, and across the end of Divis Street. The high-rise monstrosities of Divis Flats towered above us. In those flats lived 6,000 Catholics, almost half of them unemployed.

'Did you ever go in that place?' Keating asked me. 'Disgusting, so it is. They've got rats in there. The Taigs are filthy swine. You could give 'em a mansion and it'd be filthy tomorrow. They all sleep together in the same bed and piss on the floor and throw their rubbish out of the windows! Filthy swine!'

'Isn't it just the design of the place?' I asked him.

'Ach, you don't understand because you're a Brit,' Keating said.

'Ye'll never understand, ye weren't brought up here,' Spencer added. 'These people are stinkers, so they are!'

As we turned off towards the city-centre, a red Cortina pulled in behind us. An almost idiotic grin spread across Keating's face. 'That's yer mon Patrick Brady,' he said. 'Provisional who runs an illegal taxi-service. The Provies scare the official taxi-drivers off and run their own service. The money goes to the IRA. Shall we stop him, skipper?'

'Wave him in,' Ross said.

The Rover creaked to a standstill, and Keating jumped out. I leapt into a doorway and covered the others, while Keating and Ross sauntered to the car's unwound window.

'What about ye, Pat?' Keating said, beaming.

Brady smiled back. 'What about ye, Constable Keating?' he replied, handing over his tattered blue licence.

'Who're the passengers?' asked Keating, gesturing to the man and two women sitting in the back. 'Or should I say clients?'

'Och, just friends, ye know, like.'

'OK, Pat,' Keating said, producing a collating form. 'What's your address?'

'Sure ye know that! It's on the licence, anyways.'

'Tell me again, I've forgotten.'

'29 Estroil Gardens.'

'And what's your occupation, Pat?'

'You're not supposed to ask that!'

'You telling me my job? What do you do?'

Pat began to look angry. He was evidently fed up with this game. 'Look, ye're not pissin' me off with this harassment, ye know!' he burst out. 'I dunno why ye do it! Only wastin' yer own taym!'

'Look, Pat,' Keating said, grinning with pleasure. *You* know ye're a taxi. Ye're passengers know ye're a taxi. *We* know ye're a taxi, but we can't prove it. We know yer profit goes to the Organization, but we can't prove that either. That's why I'm going to stop ye every time I see ye. Just to let ye know we haven't forgotten.'

Pat went red and looked as if his head would explode. But he evidently thought better of saying something indiscreet.

I was expecting someone to take a pot-shot at us or at least lob a brick. It never happened. The most dangerous thing that happened was a fight between two prostitutes and two Pakistani sailors. It happened at the Chinese take-away, down by Donegal Quay. When we arrived, the sailors were evidently getting the worst of it. A crowd of matelots and tramps of all nationalities was cheering them on, swaying drunkenly. The Chinese cooks were jabbering in Cantonese and laying bets on the outcome. We arrested the sailors, sallow underfed men, for their own safety, and put them in the back of the Land Rover. The two prostitutes tried to get at them where they sat, cursing with voices like the fog-horn of the Ulster ferry. A one-legged man stumped in and alleged that a prostitute had snatched his crutch in the kerfuffle. She had hit him over the head with it, he claimed. We laughed all the way back to the station.

Bill Mulligan was the inspector in charge of the Bronze section. His men, specially selected, were meant to dress like ordinary citizens. Mulligan learned through an informant that the Provies were about to attack Bangor. Scores of police families lived in the quiet seaside town. For a fortnight we patrolled Bangor in plain clothes, looking out for suspicious characters.

We followed a car carrying two unkempt, bearded men for most of the morning. It wasn't until the car stopped and the two men got out that we started to laugh. They looked exactly like policemen trying to look like ordinary citizens. Bill Mulligan was furious.

I decided to explore the Shankill and visit the city-centre on foot. There were still a few neatly kept houses along the street. But the nearer you got to the city-centre, the more they took on the look of an artillery range. Almost every window not boarded up was barred. Concrete bollards blocked every space where a car might be left near a building. Some of the small shops flourished obstinately. Others were bricked up and derelict like rotten molars in a once-perfect set. The old pubs had closed down after persistent fire-bombings and shootings. Those that were left had been rebuilt over and over again. I walked past the Berlin Arms, the Brown Bear and the Royal Bar. Each one was guarded by a contingent of 'look-outs'. They were crop-haired youths who stood with their hands in their pockets. They stood with their legs slightly apart, fixing passers-by with a hostile stare. A stranger going into one of these pubs took his life in his hands. Many a terror shooting had started here.

I was glad of the Walther pistol in its shoulder-holster. Stories of humiliations and beatings were too persistent to ignore. There was a sergeant at Tennent Street whose hands had a permanent tremor, dating back to the time he'd been kidnapped by look-outs. They had forced him to drink his own urine and played Russian roulette on him with his own pistol. I had my Walther cocked with the safety-catch on. No one would be playing Russian roulette on me, whichever flag they saluted.

I crossed the road to avoid walking past the look-outs on the Royal Bar. As I passed, a tall, skinhead youth with an earring peeled off. A few minutes later he crossed the road and followed me, twenty yards behind. I hoped it was just coincidence. He was still behind me when I reached the 'segments': the barriers which prevented vehicles from entering the precinct. To get through them you had to submit to a body-search by the Civilian Search Unit. Not until I was wedged in the queue did I realize the danger I was in. The searcher would discover my pistol and demand an explanation. Then I would have to show him my warrant-card. Everyone in the queue would at once know my identity, including the youth with the earring hustling up behind.

The searcher frisked the man in front of me. I put my hand in my pocket and removed my warrant-card from its case. My turn came. The searcher felt around my shoulders, armpits and waist. His hands felt the hard lump under my arm and stopped moving. I brought my card out of my pocket and uncurled my fingers just wide enough for him to see my card. For a second I was afraid he would nod in relief. But the man was a true professional. He let me pass without a sign of recognition.

But the same was not true of the searcher in Woolworth's. She was one of the crew employed for insurance purposes, just as a formality. In my case, the formality was a dangerous one. I was already inside the shop before I understood the trap I was in. The woman was buzzing the queue with a metal-detector: a steel ring on the end of a stick. No sooner had she waved it in my direction than the bell dinged and a red light flashed. The woman looked at me in terror. Several shop assistants stopped what they were doing and stared my way. People in the queue were craning and jostling to see what the delay was. Finally, I had to produce my warrant-card. The woman nodded. I rushed by, angry, embarrassed and scared. I left the store by the nearest exit.

I doubled back to the segments and paused in a doorway to check if the skinheaded youth was still following. It was a habit that became second nature in Ulster. There was no one in sight, so I hurried on up North Street. Two Peelers in bottle-green were walking sedately past the shops. I was glad to see them, and stepped off the pavement to cross the road in their direction. As I did so, a car swerved past me, hooting madly. I jumped out of the way and my Walther pistol dropped out of its shoulder-holster and clattered into the road. I pounced on it, expecting to find two weapons pointing in my direction. No one seemed to have noticed. The Peelers were still pacing unhurriedly down the street.

Not ten minutes later another car passed me and hooted. At once I had my hand on my pistol. Then I recognized the driver as my sergeant, John Ross. 'Hop in!' he said. On the way up the Shankhill, he told me to get ready for another Bronze operation. 'Another fucking Bronze operation!' was the way he had said it.

A Provie called Liam Rafferty was supposed to be holing up in a house in Steam Mill Lane, by the docks. Bill Mulligan had learned this through an informant: 'a solid-gold source' he said. We were briefed at five thirty in the morning at North Queen Street station. I was appointed arresting officer. 'Be careful with this one,' Bill Mulligan advised me. 'Don't take any chances. He's dangerous!'

The army back-up and search team arrived, and we drove through morning dampness to Donegal Quay. The street we halted in happened to be called Tomb Street. I hoped it wasn't a bad omen for the operation. The army back-up boys fanned out along Steam Mill Lane. They propped themselves up in nooks and crannies with their flak jackets and SLRs. The search team poised themselves for action with their drills and jemmies and black bags of burglar tools, their mirrors and snakes and ladders. The Special Patrol Group took up a commanding position in front of the house with their carbines and machine-guns. 'Keep your Walther somewhere you can get at it easy,' Ross said. 'I'll be there with you, don't worry.' We slapped the velcro tabs over our full-metal jackets. I checked that I had a round in the chamber of my Walther. I checked that my baton was still secure in its secret pocket in my trouser-leg. There was an expectant silence.

Ross and I marched steadily, not too fast, not too slow, up to the door. The house looked ramshackle and on the edge of dereliction. If there was going to be any shooting, I thought, it would be very soon now. I rapped on the door. Nothing stirred. I rapped again. Still nothing. Sergeant Ross looked around uneasily, aware of all those high-powered weapons trained on our backs. There was a sudden scrabbling behind the door. I took a single step backwards to clear my way for a shot. The door creaked inwards. A tiny, frail, much wizened old head poked out. It opened a little wider, and I saw that the frail

coconut of a head belonged to a stooped little woman, at least
eighty years old.

'We have reason to believe that Liam Rafferty lives here!' I
said. My voice sounded to me like the bully-voice of a storm-
trooper. 'And we have a warrant to search this house.' The old
lady looked bewildered. Then she looked terrified as the army
search team barged in with their exotic equipment. The house
was narrow, dirty and smelly. The old lady slept in a sleeping-
bag on a sofa on the ground floor. Evidently she was unable to
climb the stairs. Christmas decorations still hung on the walls
from God knew how many Christmases past. There was a
tangle of mildewed tinsel and stars which had lost their shine.
In the middle of them was a faded photo of John F. Kennedy.
There was no trace of anyone else in the house. We decided to
abandon the operation. The old lady cried as we tramped out.
Ross spoke to her kindly, but at that moment I knew I shouldn't
be there. I had no right to bring misery to an old lady like this.
My lust for adventure, my loathing of humdrum experience, my
search for an honourable death, had all led me here: the tears of
an old woman who should have been allowed to live out her
last years in comfort and peace.

As we climbed back into the Land Rover, Ross said, 'The
Bronze are useless cowboys. All this shit, and what do we
achieve? Scaring the hell out of a poor old lady.'

'Precisely.'

Every time you switched on your radio, you would hear an
advertisement for Ormo bread: JUDGE: 'Harry McMurdo, you
have been found guilty of a serious crime. You are sentenced to
ten years in prison on a diet of bread and water. Have you any
questions?' MCMURDO: 'Yes, m'lud. Will the bread be Ormo?' Bill
Mulligan brought the section to Castlereagh for another briefing.
He was a short, slight man with long dark hair and the
regulation Bronze section beard. The Bronze section thought
that beards made them look more like ordinary citizens. 'Thank
you for coming so early,' Mulligan said. 'We didn't have any
option,' said Keating. 'That's right, you didn't,' Mulligan
snapped. 'Now keep quiet!' He had learned from an informant

that the Provies would be moving explosives that morning from the Falls Road to the Wedge. The informant said that the bomb would be in a bread-van. 'Any questions?' Mulligan asked. 'Yes, sir,' said Keating. 'Will the bread be Ormo?' That morning we drove around Belfast, frantically stopping bread-vans. All we found was bread.

Mulligan's informant must have continued to convince him, for the operation in the Wedge went on for weeks. After a fortnight we knew every bread-van in the area. One morning Sergeant Connor and Constable Powers were searching a van in Castle Street, when a sniper opened up on them. The shots missed, but Powers found two rubber gloves by an open window. When we arrived on the scene moments later, an ugly crowd had gathered. Castle Street was the most dangerous street in the city-centre. The people there seemed disappointed no Peelers had been shot.

Wilfred Powers was an ex-navy chief petty officer who wore his uniform with the flare of a guardsman. His accent betrayed his English minor public school origin. He had drifted into the SPG via the Republic. 'I'm only here as a mercenary!' he would say. One afternoon his patrol came under fire from the Ardoyne shop-fronts. Wilfred spotted the flash and got a bead on the gunmen. He cocked his SLR and squeezed the trigger, but at that moment the driver panicked. He slammed down on the accelerator, jerking the whole vehicle forward. Wilfred's shots went wide and hit a little girl.

Luckily the little girl did not die. Wilfred went to visit her in hospital, but the father told him to get lost. It was RUC policy to move officers after a shooting. Wilfred, his wife and six-month-old son were moved to a house in Newtonards. It was a Loyalist estate, but the local yobs soon found out he was a policeman. They took to gathering outside his house and jeering 'black bastard', sometimes when he was away at work. Naturally, the threat to his wife and baby made him furious.

Wilfred and I became natural allies as the only two 'Brits' in the section. They were rude to us in a way they could never be openly rude to the two Catholics. They were rude enough about

them behind their backs. 'Ye can never trust a Taig!' Keating
often told me. 'Not even one in a green uniform! They're a
different race. They even smell different. You wouldn't understand because you weren't born here!' Sergeant Connor was a
Catholic from Banbridge, and the youngest sergeant in the
section. He had had the benefit of accelerated promotion: it was
RUC policy to promote Catholics fast. This only increased the
sense of grievance from the Protestant Peelers. Connor had had
to move flat several times in the past year because of anonymous
telephone calls. 'Ye black bastard!' a voice would say. 'Ye
traitor! We're going to finish ye, so we are!' Connor would
arrive in the section-hut looking worried, and we would go out
for a drink to help him forget.

Almost every evening we were not working was spent in an
alcoholic haze. It was the only way of easing the pressure on us.
Some Peelers, such as Keating, drank half a litre of rum a day.
We never went out without our pistols, though. One night
Connor and I were drinking beer in the Botanic pub, when a
thin, balding man came in.

'Ye know who that is?' Connor asked. 'That's Liam Rafferty!'

I looked at the weedy man as he was served with his pint at
the bar.

'Shouldn't we lift him?' I asked.

'He's not wanted any more,' Connor told me. 'That was last
month's news.'

Later I went to relieve myself in the gents, and Rafferty came
in after me. He took up the stall next to mine, though all the
others were empty.

'What about ye?' I said, affecting a Belfast accent.

'What about ye, constable?' he replied.

We moved on hurriedly to the Wellington Park Hotel, next
door. Two attractive dark-haired girls were sitting on their own.
We asked permission and sat down next to them. They were
exceptionally sweet and pleasant. 'Where do you come from?' I
asked one of them. 'The Falls Road,' she replied. We finished
our drinks and moved on somewhere else.

This kind of pressure could reach boiling point. A Special

Branch man I knew was enjoying a quiet drink in the Abercorn when a Provie walked down the street outside. The SB man just happened to be brooding on his brother, killed in a Provisional bombing. The face of the Provie, who was known but not wanted, made him lose all reason. He charged out of the bar, gun in hand and chased the Provie the length of the street. He cornered him at the segments and pounced on him, forcing his Walther into his ear. 'I'll kill you, Taig bastard!' he was still shouting when a police patrol pulled him off.

On any excuse – the birth of a child, or someone's birthday – we would celebrate on epic proportions. The celebration would take place at our own hut, safely guarded in the bowels of the fortress. 'Another wee one!' Keating would cry, and soon the entire section would be rocking and reeling to the sound of 'The Sash' and 'Old Derry's Walls'. The drink coaxed out the hidden loyalties. 'Ye fucking Brit bastard!' was an epithet I got used to hearing when the section was drunk. 'You're a Brit, but ye don't respect the Union Jack or the Queen like we do!' Keating told me. 'Why, when I was at a cinema in England half the folks didn't even stand up for the Queen!'

'You need the Queen,' I said. 'Without the Queen and the flag you're just a smear of orange on an island of green. Without the Queen you lot have no identity.'

'You fucking Brit bastard!' they would say. 'Fuck off back to your own country!'

'If you think the Queen gives a damn about you, you're mistaken!' I would goad them.

'Listen!' Keating once said. 'One day we'll march down the Falls Road with the Union Jack flying and the Red Hand flying and the band playing "The Sash", and we'll mow the Taigs down with machine-guns, so we will!' No Catholic policemen and no Protestant policemen. The Dream Factory, I thought.

After one such epic celebration, six or seven of us moved on to the Abercorn night-club in town. Perhaps our rowdy jokes attracted attention. When Keating and another constable went outside to the lavatories, a bunch of Provies was waiting for them. Keating drew his Walther. 'If you don't fuck off, I'll blow yer brains out!' he said. This was what they were waiting for. A moment later the Provies were on the phone to the local police-station. 'Some thugs are in here threatening us!' they said. Another SPG patrol arrived and called us outside to search us. By this time Keating and the other constables had managed to conceal their weapons in their cars and down the backs of chairs. The only policemen still carrying weapons were Sergeant Connor and Constable McCall, both of them Catholics. They were arrested for threatening behaviour and detained at Castlereagh.

Easter Saturday was celebrated by a football match. The match was, as usual, Orange versus Green. The Orangemen lost and came out of the stadium looking for blood. They stood in front of us, waving their Tartan scarves and singing, 'Spot, spot, spot the loony!' We escorted them down the Crumlin Road towards the city-centre, chanting, whistling and waving their flags.

Someone had planted a tricolour on the roof of Unity Flats. 'I'd like to get that down and wipe my arse with it!' Keating said. The flag also infuriated the Tartan marchers. They jeered and heckled as they tramped by. This brought the Catholics on to their balconies. They had little cairns of broken paving-stone prepared for such events. As the Protestants passed beneath, chanting and making rude gestures, the Catholics pelted them with stones. The crowd dispersed into the city-centre, but the Catholics stayed on their walkways, hurling stones at passing cars.

Inspector McStorr appeared in a Makralon Land Rover, driving in with the battle-screen up, through a welcome of bricks and bottles. 'Get yer helmets on, boys!' he ordered. We assembled on the opposite side of Upper Library Street, just out of range.

'Where are the shields?' Sergeant Ross asked.

'There are no shields!' Keating said.

'Fuck the shields!' McStorr said. 'Get at 'em before the army take over!'

Sergeant Ross drew his baton as if it were a sabre. He pulled his visor down. 'CHARGE!' he yelled. We ran across the road in a ragged dog-leg. Wilfred went down with a lump of concrete on the shoulder. Bottles and stones whistled past my ear and bounced across the asphalt. 'Black bastards!' someone yelled. We reached the haven of the walkways and sheltered beneath them. An army snatch-squad in olive-green helmets came sprinting across behind us and halted in the open. The cow-faced corporal in charge grinned at us. 'What the 'ell are you 'idin' there for?' he crowed. What appeared to be half a neatly bisected kitchen sink suddenly dropped down from on high and clunked against his helmet. A look of complete bemusement came into his eyes. Instead of timbering over as I expected, he dashed into cover with the rest of us.

Easter was a time of incidents, and gave us all the jitters. It was the time the Republicans celebrated the Easter Rising of 1916. Then we drove around with our weapons cocked and waited for someone to shoot. One evening, after we had driven round on tenterhooks all day, we pulled into Tennent Street with sighs of relief. Just before Spencer cut the engine, a voice came over the radio: 'CONTACT! CONTACT! WE ARE UNDER FIRE IN CROMAC STREET!' The SPG patrol which had taken over from us had been ambushed. A sniper had fired twelve rounds from a Kalashnikov which had sliced through the Makralon skin. A Peeler had been injured in the arms and legs. Two bullets were found lodged in his bullet-proof jacket. We listened to the contact report, then opened our bar and poured ourselves a 'wee one'. We had driven down Cromac Street three times that day. Only God and the sniper knew how near we'd come to being hit.

We had no time to enjoy our drinks. Minutes later the radio went wild with reports of bombs. Ross came running in and ordered us to get togged up. We raced through the night to Atlantic Avenue. A bank was blazing in pink and orange flames. It had exploded only minutes before, and two children passing had been injured by flying bricks. An ambulance was already carrying them off to the hospital. We sealed off the roads and escorted the fire-engine in. Then, always aware of our vulnerability in the middle of the flame-lit street, we withdrew into the nooks and crannies. That night twenty-nine bombs exploded in the province.

Easter Sunday was bright and sunny. We patrolled in armour-plated Hotspurs because of the increased risk. 'Let's visit the Ardoyne,' Ross suggested. 'To pay our respects.' Inside the narrow wedge of streets the windows were festooned with tricolours and starry-ploughs. We drove past the notorious IRA 'war memorial', with its neat marble plaques and its list of volunteers killed in the struggle. Two well-known IRA men, Martin Meehan and Ian Gilmore, were chatting by the memorial. They didn't even glance at the Hotspur as we passed by. We drove out of the Ardoyne, down through Woodvale and into the Shankhill. The tricolour was still flying on Unity Flats. 'I'd like to spit on that in front of them, so I would!' Keating said. We drove past a derelict gable-end on which was scrawled: WE SHALL NOT DESERT THE BLUE SKIES OF ULSTER FOR THE GREY MISTS OF AN IRISH REPUBLIC! Everyone except me cheered.

On Easter Monday a prison officer called Michael Cassidy was shot dead in the village of Clogher, as he came out of the church during his sister's wedding. A soldier was shot dead in the Grosvenor Road. Sergeant Connor received another threat on the telephone, and said he was thinking of moving flat. At the end of the afternoon Keating came in, very excited, with the tricolour from Unity Flats. 'I told you I'd get it down!' he said proudly. He pinned it on the wall and wrote on it with an ink marker: CAPTURED BY THE AGENTS OF BRITISH IMPERIALISM. FOR GOD AND ULSTER!

Bill Mulligan briefed us for a special Bronze operation. This time the 'target' was a Protestant terrorist, William Carson. An informant had told Mulligan that Carson was about to murder a Catholic lawyer called Sean McVay. We spent a whole day crawling around the New Lodge near the lawyer's flat. Then it occurred to one of the Bronze section's bearded men to check if he was in. In not more than half an hour we were called back to the station.

'What's up?' Keating asked Bill Mulligan. 'Isn't he in?'

'No, he isn't,' came the still, small voice. 'McVay has emigrated to Canada!'

# 18

## *High-risk Profile*

---

The Operational Training Unit had recently been formed to train us in counter-insurgency drills. We learned how to engage close targets with pistols and sub-machine-guns, how to react to snipers and ambushes. 'This course will teach you how easy it is to be hit!' our instructor said.

Keating looked at him incredulously. 'Sure we know *that* right enough,' he said. 'It's how to avoid being hit that we want to know!'

The OTU had gloomy news for us. 'The terrorists have the advantage,' they said. 'They have good local knowledge, and surprise is always on their side. All we can do is show you how to react.'

'At least we have bullet-proof vests!' said Keating.

While we were practising close-quarter shooting, another soldier was killed in Belfast. A corporal in the Blues and Royals was blown to bits investigating a bomb scare. He didn't have a chance to react.

The next day the news was worse. Brigadier Glover's report on future terrorist trends had fallen into Provie hands. It revealed the army's fears that the IRA could not be defeated in the foreseeable future. They had been reorganized. The traditional military structure of battalions and brigades had gone, and in its place were Trotskyist-type cells containing three or four men. Only the cell commander had access to the hierarchy, so that the wider structure could not be known or penetrated.

There were supposed to be specialized cells dealing with assassin-ations, snipes and bombings. 'Lot of crap, so it is!' was Keating's view. 'Can ye see the gougers in the Ardoyne operating in "cells"? Sweet Jesus, the only cells they know are the ones at Castlereagh!'

'Don't be so sure,' Ross answered. 'The Provies aren't stupid. They've had a lot of high-calibre recruits lately.'

'The Provies *can* be defeated,' Keating said. 'We should declare war on them. We know who they are. We could stiff the clatter of them tomorrow, if we were given a free hand!'

Hard-liners like Keating believed that 'declaring war' on the IRA was the real solution. We should stake them out and bump them off, just as if this were a 'real' war, they said. More thoughtful men like Ross knew that this 'gut reaction' was the reason for all Ulster's ills. Once we declared a 'shoot to kill' policy, the IRA would look like bonafide soldiers in the eyes of the world. Their adversity would give them new shape and identity. That is the problem with adversity. A 'shoot to kill' policy would have been a victory for the IRA.

We spent a whole day learning anti-ambush drills. 'This is no use!' Keating said. '*We* should be doing the ambushes!'

'Like the SAS at Ballysillan Post-Office,' Wilfred said.

'What happened?' I inquired.

'We got a tip-off from Bronze about a very active Provie bombing unit,' he told me. 'They were going to plant a device at the Ballysillan Post-Office centre. It was a good tip, so they tasked an SAS team. We were there as back-up. Well, just before midnight, four Provies appeared with their bomb. The SAS were hidden in the hedge. They zapped three of them and one got away.'

'It was good work,' Keating said. 'That's what I call good shoot-ing.'

'Except for Hanna,' Ross said. 'Don't forget the other casualty. He was a Prod, just walking home from the pub. He ran into an SAS bullet, poor bugger!'

Ross was the officer who had found Hanna's body in the hedge.

We drove home from the OTU course by Strangford Lough. The sunshine pelted down, turning the water to blue onyx. The meadows were green and slashed with yellow gorse. There were pebble-dash cottages and gardens filled with daffodils. In Portaferry people were jaunting along the promenade, eating ice-cream and devouring chips out of paper-bags. 'Don't they know there's a war on?' Keating said. The Troubles seemed a million miles away. We arrived back in Belfast just in time to be called to the Lord Mayor's parade. A police-constable had been machine-gunned in both legs from a passing car.

James Taggarty was walking coolly along North Queen Street when Keating spotted him. Keating drank a lot, but he was good on faces. In a second he was out of the Land Rover and pounding along the kerb. Taggarty didn't try to escape.

'You're arrested!' Keating told him. 'Section twelve.'

'What the hell is section twelve?' Taggarty demanded.

'Prevention of Terrorism,' Keating said. 'Perhaps you tell Special Branch about a certain constable being shot in the legs. Get in the bloody mobile!'

Taggarty was lank-haired and mouse-faced. He looked half starved. 'So this is an example of the fine new quality of recruit they've got in the Provies!' Spencer jeered at him.

'Don't talk to the bastard!' Keating said. 'Sure he'd stick a knife in ye!' He cradled his little carbine and squared his chin at Taggarty. 'Know where you're going?' he asked him. 'You're going to Castlereagh. They've got a new tracker there who'd love to speak to ye. His brother was killed in the Bessbrook explosion last week, so he was. You know, the one that stiffed four Peelers. They say he's very cut up about it. Very close they were. Just crying out to get revenge on them that done it.'

Taggarty blanched when Castlereagh was mentioned. It had a grim reputation. Suspects there were held in windowless cubes for up to a week. They might be denied sleep, stripped, beaten or humiliated. No one wanted to be taken to Castlereagh.

After we had handed Taggarty over to the Special Branch at Castlereagh, we drove back towards the Shankill. 'He'll get what's coming to him!' Keating said.

'He's innocent till proven guilty,' Ross insisted.

'We're fighting a war, skipper,' Keating said. 'Sure we're doing him a favour. Imagine what would have happened if the Shankill Butchers had got hold of him!'

Only a few weeks previously the Shankill Butchers had been given a total of forty-two life sentences. They were a Protestant terror gang from the Shankill, and had murdered nineteen Catholics in horrific circumstances. They had trussed one man up in a dentist's chair and beaten him repeatedly about the head with a stick pierced by nails. Afterwards they slit his throat with a razor. The Butchers had operated with impunity for several years, despite the fact that they met together regularly in well-known Shankill pubs. The police didn't suspect them. They stayed aloof from the paramilitaries. Their leader, 'Basher' Bates, was a member of the Ulster Defence Regiment. Some people called them the assassination squad of the UDR.

Sergeant Ross was a man I respected: he was polished, educated and clever. 'The only solution to the Troubles I can see is a united Ireland,' he once told me calmly. 'You're a Brit, but I'm Irish. I may be a Prod, but then so was Wolfe Tone. I'm proud to be an Ulsterman, but I'm not British.'

'They'll unite Ireland over my dead body,' Keating said. 'If they tried it, I'd become a terrorist, so I would.' I looked at his eyes and saw that he was deadly serious.

'You're a gouger in uniform already,' Wilfred told him. 'You wear police uniform so that you can get at the Taigs legally!'

'You're a Brit bastard!' Keating said. But I knew Wilfred was right. Some policemen and a lot of UDR men wore the queen's uniform to legalize their crusade against the IRA.

'What did you expect?' Wilfred asked me. 'You may be here for adventure, but they're fighting for wives and families. It's all right for you and me to look at it impartially, but it's hard to be impartial when you're fighting for survival. No wonder they're biased. The amazing thing is that they're not *more* biased!'

One morning I came on duty to find Ross gone. 'Transferred to Bronze section,' someone said. Keating and I had been transferred to Sergeant Malone's crew. I soon realized how lucky I had been with Ross. Malone was squat, powerful and aggressive. You could easily imagine him hooded in a balaclava and carrying a pick-helve. On my first patrol with Malone, we drove to the RUC base at Sprucefield, and on the way we called at a local bar. The bar was ancient, with flagstone floors and wood panelling. The ferret-faced barman welcomed us. 'What'll it be, boys?' he asked. 'It's all on the house to youse!' Behind the bar was an Orange Lodge banner embroidered with a picture of a B-special constable. 'Those were really the good old days!' the barman said.

'Aye,' said Malone. 'They should never have got rid of the Bs. They had the local knowledge. They knew everything that was going on!'

'But didn't they just knock seven bells out of the Catholics?' I asked him. 'I heard that the only things the Bs knew how to do was march and shoot!'

Three pairs of eyes regarded me as a priest might regard a blasphemer. 'The Bs knew how to tell a Taig bastard!' Malone said. For the rest of the time Malone and Keating drank pints of Guinness and ignored me. I felt uneasy. We were on duty, and all this was highly irregular. I remembered the outing with Spider White in my Para days guiltily. When we finally tumbled out into the street, Malone was 'blootered', as he put it. It was all the others could do to prevent him singing 'The Sash' at the top of his voice.

'This isn't police work,' I muttered as we climbed into the vehicle. 'We should be out fighting terrorists!'

'Aye,' Malone said. 'Fighting them is right. That's exactly what we should do! Have you ever thought of going offensive?'

'What do you mean?'

'I mean staking the gougers out and zapping them! That's the only way to win this war, so it is!'

I looked at him carefully: he was 'blootered', but I had a feeling that he was perfectly serious. To be honest, I had to admit that I had considered it. Almost every RUC man, especially those who were ex-soldiers, must have considered it at some time. It seemed logical: fighting the IRA was like fighting with one hand tied behind your back. What tied you was the law. You were allowed to use minimum force to apprehend a suspect and nothing more. But the IRA weren't bound by that law. Naturally, none of us wanted to be a sitting target. But neither did we want to end up on a murder charge.

The following day was miserably cold. We were tasked to cover an Orange march through the Catholic section of the Ormeau Road. We stood shivering in doorways for what seemed like hours, until the band came into view. The bandsmen wore purple livery, blowing with bloated red cheeks into their fifes. The drummers beat a rapid tattoo on their side-drums, and the marchers marched to the boom of the great Lambeg drum. The 'music', bounding and reverberating savagely off the walls, was an unmistakable message of hate. The Lodge members followed on, bowler-hatted and umbrella'd, with their orange collarettes. As they passed the enemy streets, they pulled themselves up, standing tall and erect. A great, double-poled banner flew above them, depicting King William of Orange on a white charger. The fifes blew more furiously and the Lambeg drum beat louder, as they strutted past the Catholic enclave. When the band passed us, Malone and Keating seemed to grow in stature like the marchers. They lifted their heads and swayed almost imperceptibly to the bounding beat. 'It's glorious, isn't it?' Malone asked me. I looked at the marchers and at the little knots of 'enemy' that had gathered: a few wild-eyed toddlers and half a dozen mildly interested adults. Further along the road was a section of soldiers, crouching in doorways with their rifles at the ready, wondering what it was all about. 'It's pathetic!' I said.

Malone's face darkened suddenly and he scowled. 'It's glorious, so it is!' he said. 'You Brits don't understand. Sixty thousand of us gave our lives for your country on the Somme! And still you don't understand. This is *our* celebration. I don't care what anyone says! This is *us*!'

That day drove a wedge between Malone and me. We hardly spoke after that. When I rode with his crew, I had to endure endless hours of abuse. Now I was the one on the defensive. I was the only member of the section truly alone, without wife or family, without a strong root in that society. I came to see more clearly the huge mistake I had made. The conflict here was a tribal thing: either you belonged to one side or the other. Most RUC men were scrupulously honest. They were the bravest men I ever met. But most of them had been reared in that strong Loyalist culture which had also bred the paramilitaries like the UDA and the UVF. Sometimes they were required to go against 'their own people', but they could never forget where they had come from. It was that sense of identity which sustained them: even other 'Brits' like Wilfred had been drawn into the culture through marriage. I was the only odd-man out. I had no reason to be here, I soon realized: this was not my war. In the end, what I was doing was immoral for me, whereas it may not have been for my colleagues. Throughout evolution and history there has been but one law which has ultimately determined man's path: survival. A man must look after his own.

'You're the kind of person nobody wants!' Keating told me on one occasion. Sometimes, returning alone to my stinking cell-room, I plumbed the depths of despondency. Even here there was no respite. It was supposed to be shared between myself and another constable, but at least half a dozen others kept their equipment there. The lockers were crammed with mouldy bits of uniforms, patched overcoats, cracked riot-helmets, worn-down boots and unwashed socks needing darning. There were dirty beer-glasses from some late-night revel, greasy cups, plates and saucers. There seemed a never-ending flow of people in and out. Often a constable would stagger in, full of liquor, 'blootered', 'blitzed' or 'steamboats', and collapse on the other bed. A moment later I might hear him puking copiously on to the floor, and in the morning the smell of fresh vomit added a new dimension to the savoury atmosphere. The room was meant to be cleaned by an old man called Billie the Brush. He was a bent and tubercular old fellow with a purple face, and he rarely managed to clean the room. He spent most of the day shuffling up and down the corridor, trailing a brush, a cigarette hanging out of his mouth, coughing. The other half he spent 'resting':

sitting on the stairs on a folded newspaper, a cigarette in his mouth, coughing. Whenever I entered the washroom in the morning and prepared to freshen up with a shave, he would invariably shuffle in behind me with a cigarette in his mouth, and cough. I began to wonder if he was a spy for the UDA.

I felt trapped. If I entered a butcher's shop or a baker's, the fish-and-chip shop down the street, or even the public library on the Shankill, I felt threatened. My English accent made people suspicious. I became frightened to open my mouth. Often I just pointed to what I wanted, as if I were a complete foreigner. The worst of it was that people naturally assumed I was a squaddie in plain clothes, which made me even more of a target. In any shop or public building I developed the habit of standing with my back to the wall and watching the door every time it opened. I suppose this made me look doubly suspicious. If anyone spoke to me in the street, I regarded him automatically as an enemy. Once, when a young man asked me for a light in Atlantic Avenue, I almost shot him. Only the tightest of control prevented me from pulling my pistol out. When I passed the UDA look-outs by Shankill pubs, I felt their eyes following me and measuring my every step. I knew that I was becoming paranoid, but I was unable to prevent it. The very streets, the derelict houses, the shop-signs and the graffiti breathed a foetid breath of hostility. The city was literally alive with hatred. When I walked through the streets, I felt like the victim in a Disney movie, where the houses developed fanged mouths and demon eyes and watched me gloatingly, waiting to pounce.

Once I went to get a haircut at the local barber. The face I saw in the mirror was no longer my own. It was the face of a savage animal, a raw, red, primitive face, an ugly, hunted face. I saw the demon, Sweeney Todd eyes of the barber leering at me in the mirror. 'How'd ye want it, surrr?' he asked me suggestively. I saw the razor glinting in his hand, a faint spangle of light reflected on its stainless-steel blade. 'I've changed my mind!' I told him. 'I haven't got time for a haircut!'

Every time I entered a shop or a pub, the searcher would find my pistol. I would wait for his muscles to tense, then produce my warrant-card. I knew that there was always a chance of being 'fingered'. Sometimes barmen or waiters would begin asking pointed questions. If that happened, I would finish my drink and leave. I soon realized that carrying a pistol could be a nightmare. I noticed that searchers rarely felt around the ankles, so I bought myself a diamond-shaped throwing-knife which I strapped around my calf. I practised throwing the thing against the straw mats in our section gym, but I was never very successful. I carried the knife on several outings, and it was never discovered, but I quickly understood that it would be useless if I were really attacked.

Wherever I went, I felt that I was being followed. I would hear footsteps behind me, but when I looked there was no one. I saw shadows flitting about on the periphery of my vision. I got into the habit of stopping to look behind every few minutes, stepping suddenly into entrances or changing direction abruptly. One evening as I walked to the library, I passed a man polishing a motorcycle. He grinned at me as I walked by. 'I see they've let you out, then!' he said cheerily. I was so shocked that I hurried into the library and took up a defensive position in front of the door. If people were beginning to recognize me, I thought, then I was really in trouble. I tried to vary my route and my ports of call. But habit is the structure on which life is based: the process of building on familiar and secure bases. It was difficult not to use the same shops, and if I avoided walking down the Shankill to the city-centre, I had to go through the back-streets. The twisting labyrinth of the ghetto could be even more dangerous. It was inhabited by known UDA murderers and killers of the Shankill Butcher stamp. They were not above machine-gunning two plain clothes detectives who were walking there one night. Once I almost bumped into Jim Craig, the local leader of the UDA. He was a big, broad-shouldered man with a bull-neck. 'Good evening, constable,' he wished me as I passed.

I had no car and was unable to get out of the city without a friend. And I had hardly any friends. Many of my colleagues had adopted the attitude that if I was not for them, I must be against them. You had to be on one side or the other. I couldn't hold a proper conversation with any civilian now: he or she might be an enemy. I couldn't even talk to my colleagues. I couldn't understand what they were talking about. They spoke in whispers, about people and places I didn't know: they used a patois that I couldn't quite grasp. Was it my imagination that the conversation stopped when I went to join them in the section-hut? I started to take driving-lessons from a school on the Shankill. The woman in the office was aggressive and highly strung. She asked too many questions about my job. The fact that I had to make fixed appointments made me vulnerable for a stake-out, I thought. I missed one lesson deliberately for this reason, and the woman got very excited. 'I'll make sure you don't get lessons anywhere else in the city!' she told me. Her nervousness made me more suspicious. I never went back again.

I suffered from nightmares, and the slightest sound woke me up. In order to get to sleep, I drank large quantities of beer. There was nothing unusual about this in the RUC. But it didn't help. It made me aggressive, argumentative and abusive. Often the night would end in a fight between myself and one of the others. One of us would generally finish with a broken head or a bloody nose. When they called me a 'Brit bastard', I screamed back that I would return as a sniper for the Provies and wipe them out. 'That's going straight to Special Branch!' Keating said. I would wake up with a guilty conscience and a terrible hangover. It wasn't only the headache that affected me. I felt vacant and completely desolate. My life was devoid of meaning. I was a worthless individual, wasting my life and my talents here in this hateful place. And the misery was of my own making. That was the worst of it. I had spent eight years of my life pursuing this. The Paras, the SAS and now the SPG: all a blind alley leading nowhere, leading me here. I had worshipped at the high altar of violence. This was the pay-off.

Wilfred was one of the few people who remained a friend. He had a sense of loyalty to me because I was a 'Brit' like him. But Wilfred was soon in trouble again. A group of youths gathered outside his house one night and pelted his windows with stones.

One stone smashed the bathroom window, the glass narrowly missing his little boy. Wilfred's wife looked through the jagged window at the youths below. 'One of them's got a gun, Wilfred!' she shrieked. That was the last straw for Wilfred. He charged out, Walther in hand, and the thugs turned and ran. He shot one of them and the bullet penetrated the youth's shoulder. Wilfred told me that the lout just stood there with the bullet in him, not moving. When Wilfred ran up to him, there was no blood and the boy said nothing. It wasn't until later that Wilfred realized he had actually shot the boy.

Wilfred and his family were whisked away from their home on the same day. They were installed temporarily in the police-station at Portaferry. In keeping with its sleepy surroundings, the station was an ordinary detached house with a tiny office built on the side and a giant mortar fence around it. It happened to be vacant when Wilfred and his family moved in. Not long afterwards he invited me to stay with him. His wife Linda was a Protestant from Monaghan, a slim, bewitching girl with jet-black hair. In the pub across the road we sank several pints of beer. With every pint Linda looked more bewitching. We carried on drinking back at the house. 'You know, I'm not happy!' Linda told me with unexpected intimacy.

'Really?' I said.

'You shit!' Wilfred bawled at me. 'Are you trying to get off with my wife!' He showed me to a bed out in the corridor where I was meant to sleep, and I collapsed on it in a stupor. In the middle of the night I woke up bursting for a pee. I groped groggily for the light-switch and found a button on the wall, which I pressed. Immediately the walls started to shake. There was the sound of thunder clanging along the passage. The whole house seemed to come alive with the ringing. I had to hold my hands over my ears. The noise must have carried right across the town. In the morning Wilfred shook me awake roughly. 'Bloody idiot!' he said. 'You rang the station alarm!'

We arrived back in Belfast to find that a bomb had ripped through the bus depot outside the Ardoyne. When we got there, the shell of the building was still burning, and two or three single-deckers were on fire. An angry crowd had already gathered. 'Bastards!' they shouted as we debussed and made ready to charge.

'Hold on!' Malone said. 'These are Prods, so they are! They're shouting at the Taigs, not at us!'

'Bring back the B-specials!' the crowd was chanting. It must have been music to Malone's ears. Still under the influence of last night's high jinks, Wilfred said, 'I'm going into that place on foot! Anybody coming?'

'I will,' I said, not wanting to be outdone. It was terrible bravado to push into the Republican ghetto on foot after a bombing. There might easily have been snipers already in place. At that time I thought Wilfred had challenged me into it in order to get his own back for the previous night. I followed him because I didn't really care if I was shot. Looking back, I don't think Wilfred did either. His days on the RUC were already numbered. After the inquiry into the shooting of the youth, he was forced to resign.

The following day we were sent to the Maze Prison. We had to escort a couple of Provies from there to Castlereagh. I found the bleak walls of corrugated iron chilling. It seemed as impersonal and antiseptic as a hospital. But inside the H-blocks prisoners were 'on the blanket'. They lived in cells smeared with excrement and running with urine. They slept on lice-ridden mattresses and piles of rotten, maggot-infested food. The Maze was the physical embodiment of the government's 'criminalization' policy. Convicted terrorists were now regarded as common criminals, not political offenders. The British had made a serious blunder when they accorded prisoners 'political' status. It gave them a high profile in the world's press, because it seemed that they had been gaoled only for disagreeing with the government. Actually, most of them had been gaoled for murdering, robbing, torturing, maiming and possessing firearms. The prisoners hated the Maze, despite the fact that it was the most modern prison in Europe. They had loved the old Long Kesh, with its barbed wire fences and Nissen-hut compounds. In Long Kesh it was like being Steve McQueen in *The Great Escape*. The Maze was less romantic.

More than 200 prisoners in the Maze were refusing to wear prison uniform. To have accepted it would have been to accept that they were ordinary criminals. The prison governor decreed that they should be given blankets to cover themselves with when exercising. In April 1978 one of the Republican prisoners went berserk and attacked a warder. The other warders dragged him off to a solitary-confinement cell and thrashed him senseless. The prisoners went wild and started to smash their cell furniture. Riot squads had to go in and rescue what was left. The prisoners, reduced to only their blankets, refused to leave their cells. They began to use the floor as a latrine. When piles of stinking excreta mounted, they slapped it on the walls with their hands. The only way the warders could cleanse the cells was by smashing the windows and hosing in disinfectant. Riot squads would frog-march the prisoners out, and the warders would burst in with pressure-hoses and obliterate the filth. The prisoners would march back in and the process would begin again.

We had breakfast in the prison canteen. It was bacon, egg and soda-bread served by grim-faced trustees in grey uniforms. Having the prisoners serve my food gave me a sense of disquiet. Malone must have noticed it. 'That's nothing!' he joked. 'The cooks are on the blanket!'

The Provies we had to escort were wearing more than blankets. They had agreed to wear prison uniforms for this outing. They were carried in a prison van known as a cellular. It was divided into separate cubby-holes, each just large enough for a man to sit in. Malone gave me the unenviable task of sitting in the cellular with the prisoners. 'Look out for Donnelly!' he said. 'That one took a pistol off a prison officer and shot him with it!' Donnelly was a tall youth with shoulder-length brown hair.

As soon as the van started off, he began to shout to the other prisoner across the partition. I rapped on the door. 'Shut up!' I said. Donnelly turned and looked at me. No other word was spoken between us, but that look said it all. In those dark eyes I saw reflected a picture of myself, sitting here in the uniform of an oppressor. I had never sought to be an oppressor of others. I had left school at eighteen, fired with a lust for adventure. That lust had become perverted over the years: there was no adventure to be found here.

I saw something else too: this Donnelly was like me. He came from a long line of Republicans, stretching back generations. As a youth he had probably been brimming with idealism, proudly marching off on the Glory Road. But there was no glory: the quest had soured into murder and atrocity, it had led him here. If I had been here to protect my wife and family, I might have felt differently. But I was here from choice. This was not my war, as those wars in far-off places had been my father's and my grandfather's. I knew suddenly and certainly that I could no longer be a fighter in someone else's war. I no longer believed in the system.

The following week we were back on 'bomb watching' operations. Bill Mulligan and his bearded men received yet another tip-off from a solid-gold source. There was a cache of explosives and weapons buried on a plot of land in Little America, the source said. We went in at first light and probed the waste land from top to bottom. It was a dangerous job, for the bomb cache could have been booby-trapped. It could even have been a deliberate lure. After two hours of patient probing, all we brought to light were some used contraceptives and a dead cat. Mulligan wasn't deterred. He wanted to tighten up on explosives being brought from the Falls Road into the Short Strand. He posted us to the Republican districts of west Belfast, where the army had previously patrolled. Now the army were being phased out: the police were being ushered into what the bureaucrats called a 'high-risk profile'.

One afternoon we were making a vehicle check in Divis Street.

'I hate this crap!' Keating said. 'This is a sure way to get recognized!'

'This used to be a good city once,' Malone said. 'I used to drink in a bar in the Falls Road, so I did. They all knew I was a Prod, but they didn't care. I worked for McCauley's, see, in the bar trade. They wouldn't employ Catholics at McCauley's. One day I met another Prod in the bar. "What's a good McCauley's man like you doing in a rebel hole like this?" he said. I told him to shut up, but he kept on with the crack. I had to leave: I never went back.'

Just then there was a muffled shot. A man came racing around the corner from Castle Street, yelling, 'Someone's been shot!' We ran into Castle Street to find a crowd gathered outside a butcher's shop. On the floor inside a man in a butcher's apron was bleeding to death. Before we could fight our way to him, men poured out of the local bars and blocked our way. They looked very ugly, spitting at us and trying to push us back. Someone snatched my carbine, and I gave him a crack on the head with the muzzle. We were hemmed in now by bobbing heads with red eyes and beer-breathing mouths. Hate was written large on every one of them. For a moment I thought they would tear us to pieces. 'MOVE BACK!' Malone told them, baring his teeth.

'Knock his cunt in!' someone shouted.

'Kill the black bastards!' shouted another.

'MOVE BACK!' Malone shouted again. We were standing shoulder to shoulder with the crowd around us. My knuckles on the stock of my rifle turned white. I was determined not to be afraid. It was us or them, and a man was dying. We all stood there for a moment, two tribes poised on an instant of history. Then an ambulance bell rang. A white ambulance screeched to a halt, and two medics charged out with a stretcher. It was like the last-minute arrival of the cavalry. The crowd wavered and retreated a few steps. The medics dived into the shop and returned a few minutes later with the dying man on the stretcher. He was as white as a ghost and bleeding from the nose. He didn't make it to the hospital.

The Lower Falls was all Provie country, and the butcher was a member of the Official IRA, the Stickies. It was the Stickies, not the Provies, who had planted the bomb in the Aldershot Barracks back in 1972, though since then they had given up attacks on the security forces. The Stickies were left-wing

Republicans who believed that no proper solution to the question of Northern Ireland could be achieved until the working-class Protestants and Catholics joined forces. Theoretically they were right: no war of popular revolution against a strong state can succeed without the support of the majority. In Northern Ireland the Protestants are the majority. They had not, however, declared a truce with their offshoot, the Provisionals, and feuds constantly flared up between them. In 1975 one such feud resulted in eleven dead and fifty injured and continued until two Catholic priests managed to patch things up. The butcher's death may have been the result of such a feud; it may also have been no more than the settlement of an old score. In this city, old scores could be settled for about the price of a bottle of Guinness.

On the surface it seemed impossible that Loyalists and Republicans could ever join forces on anything, let alone for the sake of a united socialist Ireland. There were, on the contrary, certain things they would collude over. For many years both the IRA and the UDA had been funding their activities by protection rackets. They started by collecting 10p a week from each householder, 'to make sure teenage thugs didn't break their windows'. The rackets had developed into multi-million pound, Mafia-style organizations, with a vested interest in continuing the Troubles. The organizations had steadily moved into the building trade, setting up as employment agencies. They would extract an agency fee from the prospective employee, and then force the employer to use him with the threat of sabotage. There was strong evidence dating back several years that the IRA and the UDA had held secret meetings in Europe and agreed to carve up parts of Belfast between them, like old-style American gangsters. The more I discovered about the complexity of the situation in Northern Ireland, the more it sickened me: Provies, Stickies, Taigs, Prods and Brits; INLA, UDA, UVF and UFF; SDLP, Unionists, Loyalists and Peace People; Orange Orders, Black Orders and UDR men who murdered Catholics; and Protestants who called themselves Irish. It was too much for me: all I saw here was a confusing mass of tribes and clans struggling for power in a land that was too small for them. I had given everything I had to throw myself into this cesspool. I had come here trying to find a 'tribe' to belong to, and instead I had found only enemies. I had to escape: I had to be free.

One morning, while we were on plain clothes duty in the city-centre, I strolled over to a news-stand in North Street. The newsagent had a copy of the *Guardian*. It reached Belfast only rarely and was often a day late. I had been an occasional *Guardian* reader in my student days, and seeing it brought the memory of those times back with a sudden gulp. I bought it and sat back with it in the car. It was the day of 'Education Guardian', and I thumbed through the advertisements for teaching jobs. One stood out from the rest:

> Teachers wanted for the Sudan. The Sudan is a developing country and cannot afford ex-patriate salaries. Enthusiasm more important than experience. Climate harsh but people friendly.

'People friendly' was the part that impressed me. I knew nothing at all about the Sudan. I even had to look for it in the atlas to ascertain where it was. I had seen Charlton Heston in *Gordon of Khartoum*, I remembered. I had never met anyone who had been there. But no special qualifications were required other than basic teaching certificate, which I possessed. What better place to escape to than somewhere I'd hardly even heard of? A few moments later the radio crackled. We were called to an incident in Castle Street. I put the paper down and instantly forgot about it.

On the way home the next day we passed some drunken louts brawling outside the Brown Bear pub in the Shankill. We stopped the vehicle and tried to break it up. 'Come on, boys, now!' Malone told them. 'Sure you're not wise! There's no need for this, so there's not!' I seized one of the louts by the arm, and just as I did so an angry crowd came surging out of the pub. 'Kill the Peelers!' they croaked. Three or four skinheads tried to grab me. I thought they would tear me to pieces. Visions of the horrible scene in Castle Street reared up before me. I looked around to see why the others hadn't helped me,

and found with a shock that I was alone. They had all run off
back to the vehicle, which was even now revving up ready to
pull away. For a terrifying moment it looked as if I were going
to be left completely alone with a drunken crowd. I groped
desperately for the handle of my baton. One of the skinheads
caught my arm and for a second I wrestled with him. Then the
heavy wooden stick leapt into my hand as if it had a life of its
own. A new confidence flowed through me. I pushed the skinheads back and grasped the nearest one by the throat. Just then
a stocky figure came running from the revving police vehicle,
and a massive arm hauled me out of the fray. It was Wilfred.
'Come on!' he yelled. 'Get out of it!' We sprinted for the vehicle
and just managed to get in before it lurched off.

'You lot of bastards!' I said, looking at Malone and Keating.

'You bloody ijit!' Malone said. 'Don't ye know those were
Loyalists? Don't ever get involved in trouble in your own back-
yard!'

That night I sat on my stinking bed in my stinking room with
my Walther in my hand. I was twenty-six years old, and I had
squandered the best years of my life on this. I had lost everything, even my self-respect. I clicked back the safety-catch of my
pistol. The click seemed to echo in the room. I held the pistol up
and lodged its warm muzzle squarely against my temple. It
would have been so easy. Death lay a hair's breadth away: the
end of all my struggling. I had fought myself into a trap, and
now I was finished. I had spent my life reaching for something
that was beyond me: adventure, glory, power, the urge to
belong. Anything would be better than this.

But I never had the courage to pull the trigger. Or perhaps,
even then, I saw the possibility of light at the end of the tunnel,
the possibility of change. A new chance. A new life. A world
without guns and badges. I clicked the safety-catch back on and
unloaded the pistol. As I put it away in the drawer of my table, I
saw a scrunched-up copy of the *Guardian* lying there. I remembered the advertisement for teachers. Later I wrote a letter
of application to the Sudanese Embassy in London. I posted the
letter the following day.

# *Epilogue*

---

Sitting in a mud-walled house on the edge of the Great Sahara, with a seething coriolis wind clawing at the doors, I tuned in to the BBC World Service. The drawl of the broadcaster came from a long way off broken up by static ... 'This is John Tidmarsh ... with *Outlook*.' The words 'Northern Ireland' formed an instant image in my mind. It was only a matter of weeks since I had left there, but already I had become another person. Here on the banks of the Nile, in the vast Sudan where there was room to lose half the world, the eternal battles of that tiny island far away seemed as pointless and insignificant as those of termites.

'Eighteen soldiers have been killed by a series of bombs near Warrenpoint in County Armagh,' he was saying. 'It is believed that most of them belonged to the Second Battalion of the Parachute Regiment.' I sat up. For a moment the mud walls faded. I was no longer in the Sudan. I was no longer in the Sahara. I was back on those bleak streets, wearing a maroon-red beret. I was back with Cooper, Robbins, Hensby and the rest. There was an unexpected heaviness in my stomach. Despite everything, bonds had been forged which were still in me: bonds I could not forget.

An army truck had been carrying a platoon of Paras along the Warrenpoint Road, when a bomb concealed in a haycart had exploded. The truck had been pulped, the soldiers shattered and flung across the road. Small-arms fire had opened up from across the lake, from within the Republic, and reinforcements dropped by chopper had dashed for the shelter of an old lodge-gate. It was there that the second bomb had taken them.

So the Provos got their revenge on Bloody Sunday, I thought, remembering the cheers, thirteen bodies lying dead on the streets of Derry, Gurung's steel-black eyes, the rubble of the officers' mess in Aldershot. Wedged in my memory: part of me that wanted to be closed off but could not be.

'What's up?' my colleague asked. 'Look as if you've seen a ghost!' Not one ghost but many. Ghosts marshalled in squads, sections, platoons and companies, in patrols and troops and squadrons. Ghosts with beige-coloured berets and winged daggers, maroon stable-belts and bottle-green forage caps.

'The troops should get out of Ireland,' my friend said. 'Fascists, that's what they are. Lot of psychopaths!'

'Amazing when you think of it,' someone else said. 'I mean, doesn't it make you cringe to think of all those uniformed psychopaths walking about Britain?'

I had kept quiet about my background, but still it amazed me that intelligent, sophisticated and well-educated people could be so ignorant. I should not have been surprised. They were exactly what I would have been had I not embarked on my long journey through violence. At first, mixing with these intellectuals, I had felt ashamed of my past. But I came to see that I had learned something valuable that most of my peers had not. I had explored the darkness which is half of every human existence. Shun it as one might, it still remains. In trying to distance themselves from violence, my new colleagues were performing that peculiarly human act of dehumanization which made all the bloodshed possible in the first place. For all their liberal ideals, they were no different. None of us is any different. We are all killers, more or less.

Three years later I gave up teaching to take on a test as demanding as SAS selection. I went to live with a nomadic tribe on the edge of the Sahara. This tribe valued nothing so much as courage and endurance: they were a stern, rugged people who had survived for centuries where survival was only just possible.

These nomads lived by a code as strict as anything I had known in the SAS: a man must defend his travelling companions until death; he must offer hospitality to complete strangers and guard them with his life while they dwelt in his tent; he must share every last drop of water and every last piece of food; he must take upon himself the sacred duty of revenge, especially for an affront to the honour of his tribe. These people had no outlets for their violence as we had had in the army, I realized. There were no fist-fights to determine pecking order, no milling. Fist-fights are, after all, a kind of game played to a set of conventions. These nomads did not know how to make a fist: they carried daggers and were not slow to use them. Every fight was a fight to the death.

To them, war was a limited affair: a skirmish in which one or two people were killed and honour was satisfied: a fight to defend your life and wife, your land or livestock. These were things a man could fight for, I thought. There was no shame in being a warrior. It had been an honourable profession since the dawn of time. But our society had become so huge and complex that you were fighting not for things that really mattered but for an abstract concept, or merely a 'police action'. It was then that I learned my final lesson: fight, but do not fight another man's war.

These nomads had few of the illusions of so-called civilization. They did not, as Carl Gustav Jung said, 'believe in the welfare state, in universal peace, in the equality of man, in his eternal human rights, in justice, truth or the Kingdom of God on earth'. Their struggle for existence over the millennia had taught them the sad truth. 'Man's life consists of a complex of inexorable opposites – day and night, birth and death, happiness and misery, good and evil. We are not sure even that one will prevail against the other, that good will avenge evil or joy defeat pain. Life is a battleground. It always has been and it always will be. If it were not so, existence would come to an end.'

I switch off the radio. My mind wanders back in time to not much more than a month previously, to the streets of Belfast,

festooned once again with Union Jacks and bunting as the
'Twelfth Day' dawns. At every street corner children are building
alps of ancient furniture and old tyres: bonfires to exorcize the
spirit of popery from the land. In City Square the first Orange
Lodge marches past the cenotaph. In the leading party are
Grand Masters from all over the world, including Africa, togged
up in their shiny bowlers and Orange collarettes with hierogly-
phics. The music starts, harsh, gutteral, militant. Fifes and
drums harking back to the Golden Era of the Boyne. The Lodges
come on, Lodge after Lodge: bowlers, sabres, drums and marching men. From Shankill and Sandy Row, from Sydenham and
the Village, from Glasgow and Edinburgh, Argyll and Perth,
Portsmouth and Ontario. Orange, blue and silver. Banners flying
heavy against the ropes, rows of Union Jacks, Scots lions, St
Andrew's crosses, Six-counties flags, Red Hands, the purple-
star-on-orange-field flag of the Grand Orange Order itself. Lodge
banners woven of many colours and swelling with names:
'Rising Sons of India', 'Shankill Road Defenders', 'Tiger Bay
Volunteers' and 'Ulster Specials'. On and on they come, tramping
to the familiar stirring thump of the Lambeg drum, as the fifes
stutter out 'The Sash', 'Old Derry's Walls' and the 'Green Beret'.
The pipes and fifes and drums rattle and clash, the banners
shake and scintillate, the bandsmen march on in Jacobean cos-
tumes, girl accordion-players in mini-tartans, boys in chequered
glengarries, ultramarine-striped pantaloons, Prussian and Yankee
outfits, light blue, maroon, black and scarlet: the colour-guards
with their drawn swords and ceremonial spears, the Lambeg
drummers welting away at their skins and prancing in ecstasy.
Here, I see, is Ulster's heritage. Nothing says more about the
state than this parade. The ecstatic faces, the tramping feet, the
thrumping drums, the display of colour. The more a culture is
pressed into a corner, the more violently colourful it will become.
Adversity defines us.

I take my eyes away from the marching lines to look at my
colleagues. For a moment I am shocked. They are standing in a
line, chests out, heads up, as I have never seen them, and each
one has removed his jacket to reveal a black collarette beneath

The Royal Black Order. The elite of the Orangemen. They wear their true uniform at last. One of them sees me staring and grins. 'Now do ye understand it?' he asks. 'It's not somethin' ye read in books! It gets into ye blood, so it does!' That says it all. It is beyond the rational. It is the exposition of all that is dear to Protestant Ulster. In a single day, Orange solidarity reaffirms its faith in its own invincibility. It is a tribal thing. I cannot share it, for I am not of their tribe. I have not been raised in their mythology. Under duress they might be, but this march says, 'Look at me! This is who I am!'

Two days later I stand on the deck of the *Ulster Queen* as she pulls out of Belfast Lough. County Down lies off to the south, deceptively green and tranquil. Flakes of mist veil its thickly wooded beaches. There is a fog over the broken city, but to the north I glimpse the peaks of the Antrim Hills. The steamer rattles on through still, Prussian-blue waters. A flurry of seagulls plays in the ship's wake with perfect grace. Leaving Ulster is not just leaving a job, it is leaving a life. Eight years along a blind alley, a journey across a man's greatest waste land, a journey through violence. Now I am gripped with both fear and excitement. I am cast adrift in the sea of time. The self that has been me for eight years or more has begun to dissolve. Now I am on a voyage to become my opposite, and later perhaps to veer back and become something in between. Has it been eight years wasted? All experiences change you and the degree of change is directly related to the intensity of the experience.

Belfast is fading off the bows. Soon it will be a lost city, blanketed in the mist. I turn my back on what has been and look east. A new horizon in a universe constantly expanding. Room to move and grow. My journey through the dark side is over. For everything there is a season. And a time for every purpose under heaven.